MW00762556

Adding Value to Libraries, Archives, and Museums

Adding Value to Libraries, Archives, and Museums

Harnessing the Force That Drives Your Organization's Future

Joseph R. Matthews

LIBRARIES
UNLIMITED ™

An Imprint of ABC-CLIO, LLC

Santa Barbara, California • Denver, Colorado

Copyright © 2016 by Joseph R. Matthews

All rights reserved. No part of this publication may be reproduced, stored
in a retrieval system, or transmitted, in any form or by any means, electronic,
mechanical, photocopying, recording, or otherwise, except for the inclusion of
brief quotations in a review, without prior permission in writing from the publisher.

Library of Congress Cataloging-in-Publication Data

Names: Matthews, Joseph R., author.
Title: Adding value to libraries, archives, and museums : harnessing the force that
    drives your organization's future / Joseph R. Matthews.
Description: Santa Barbara, CA : Libraries Unlimited, [2016] | Includes
    bibliographical references and index.
Identifiers: LCCN 2015037584 | ISBN 9781440842887 (paperback) |
    ISBN 9781440842894 (ebook)
Subjects: LCSH: Library administration. | Library planning. |
    Libraries and community. | Libraries—Technological innovations. |
    Value added. | BISAC: LANGUAGE ARTS & DISCIPLINES / Library &
    Information Science / Archives & Special Libraries. | LANGUAGE ARTS &
    DISCIPLINES / Library & Information Science / Collection Development.
Classification: LCC Z678 .M365 2016 | DDC 025.1—dc23
LC record available at http://lccn.loc.gov/2015037584

ISBN: 978-1-4408-4288-7
EISBN: 978-1-4408-4289-4

20 19 18 17 16   1 2 3 4 5

This book is also available on the World Wide Web as an eBook.
Visit www.abc-clio.com for details.

Libraries Unlimited
An Imprint of ABC-CLIO, LLC

ABC-CLIO, LLC
130 Cremona Drive, P.O. Box 1911
Santa Barbara, California 93116-1911

This book is printed on acid-free paper ∞

Manufactured in the United States of America

Google and the Google logo are registered trademarks of Google Inc., used with permission

This book is dedicated to:

Paul and Lisa Matthews
James and Erin Melcher

Who add value in the lives of their children
Every day and in every way

Contents

Acknowledgments

This book has been an interesting journey of exploration around a critical topic that does not get much attention in the specialized journals of librarians, archivists, and museum professionals—namely, how to add value. As I have considered this important topic, my views have been shaped by numerous conversations and email exchanges with a number of colleagues from the United States, Canada, Australia, Singapore, and Great Britain.

The book has been much improved by conversations from several colleagues including Stephen Abram, Robert Dugan, Ken Haycock, Peter Hernon, Margie Jantti, Rebecca Jones, Brian Mathews, Danuta Nitecki, Megan Oakleaf, and Carol Tenopir. I would like to especially acknowledge the thoughtful comments from Carl Grant, who carefully reviewed the entire manuscript. In addition, Robert Boyd, Anthony Bernier, Peter Hernon, Stephen Matthews, and Ian Fitzpatrick provided thoughtful comments on drafts of various chapters for which I am indebted.

Once again, the dynamic interlibrary loan team at the California State University San Marcos Library—Debbie Blair and Teri Roundenbush—were able to track down a wide variety of articles and other resources that were of great assistance in completing this book. Thanks much!

Thanks also to Emma Bailey and Barbara Ittner of Libraries Unlimited for their patience and understanding in making this book a reality. Gordon Hammy Matchado provided able editing assistance that improved the readability of the text. And finally, thanks to Kathryn Suarez, the publisher of Libraries Unlimited, for agreeing to produce a book with some color figures in order to "add value" to the reader's experience. Ta!

Introduction

Imagine a world where everyone was constantly learning,
a world where what you wondered
was more interesting than what you knew,
and curiosity counted for more than certain knowledge.

Imagine a world where what you gave away
was more valuable than what you held back,
where joy was not a dirty word,
where play was not forbidden after your eleventh birthday.

Christopher Locke, Rick Levine,
Doc Searls, and David Weinberger[1]

The premise of this book is really quite simple. *First,* the concept of adding value is bandied about in the management, marketing, and strategic planning literature but is rarely broken down and discussed so that anyone can really understand the concept and, more importantly, learn how they can add value in the work that they do. *Second,* change is all around us and affects us as individuals mightily and our libraries, museum, galleries, and archives in some pretty significant ways. In addition, many observers believe that the rate of change is accelerating, which is also a cause for concern. So perhaps it would be prudent to explore what forces in our society, and in the field of information technology specifically, are affecting our lives and our treasured institutions of libraries, museums, galleries, and archives, and discover how organizations need to change in order to add value for their customers.

Third, libraries and other cultural institutions have a long history of adding value when access to books and other physical objects was limited by the cost of acquiring them. These organizations developed ways of organizing their physical collections and providing intellectual access by developing catalogs (and rules to guide the creation of metadata for the catalog). The many ways libraries added value to the traditional library were identified and discussed by Robert Taylor in his classic 1986 book *Value-Added Processes in Information Systems.*

Fourth, given the significant amount of change we are all experiencing in our lives and our increasing dependence on the Internet, people are no longer required to visit the library and other cultural organizations to gain access to this content. Thus, these organizations need to figure out how to add new value to their collections and services as the perceived value of the library and other cultural institutions is rapidly diminishing.

Fifth, the power of the individual has increased greatly. Whether the individual is called a user, consumer, or customer, each of us has become empowered as we have moved from the isolated to connected, from information shortage to a surplus of information, from unaware to informed, from passive to active.

And *sixth*, sometimes small incremental improvements are not enough. Faced with the reality of the frenetic pace of change we experience today, organizations must take a step back and assess how it is they connect with their customers. They should be asking themselves: are we still providing a deep level of value to our customers or is the value proposition waning? Rather than considering evolutionary change, perhaps it is time for us to consider the unthinkable—let's embrace radical thinking and reinvent our organizations so that value abounds.

After exploring the literature devoted to ways to add value and having numerous conversations with colleagues from several disciplines over the past few years, I have come to the conclusion that there are five ways that cultural institutions can add value now and into the future. I call these five ways the 5Cs Diamond—content, context, connection, collaboration, and community. Each of these methods is explored in much greater detail in subsequent chapters of the book.

Organization of the Book

This book explores the concept of how organizations add value to the products and services that they produce and/or provide. To assist in the process of exploring the concept of adding value, the use of a business model is introduced as well as the broader topic of strategic planning (Chapter 1). Over the course of the last 100 years of so, libraries and cultural institutions have developed a wide range of methods to add value in an environment of information scarcity. These methods for adding value in libraries have been best articulated by Robert Taylor in a wonderful book written in 1968 (Chapter 2). Others have extended Taylor's work, but as we have moved to a world of an information-rich environment that is accessible 24/7, the perception of the value of the library and the local collection is being diminished rapidly (Chapter 3).

The five ways that libraries, archives, and museums can add more value in the lives of their customers now and into the future are introduced (Chapter 4), and the continuing importance of providing access to content—both physical and digital content—is explored in some detail (Chapter 5). Libraries and other cultural institutions have historically understood the value of adding context to the content found in their collections, but today, these cultural organizations must find ways to add even more context. The available tools that provide context are explored in considerable detail (Chapter 6).

Creating and building connections with people in our local (and worldwide) communities is yet another way organizations can add value in the lives of their customers.

Moving out of the library and interacting with users in their daily lives and seeing the tools that they currently use to access, organize, synthesize, and reuse information will assist any library in better understanding the needs of actual and potential users of library services (Chapter 7). And a really exciting opportunity for libraries, archives, and museums to engage with users around the world is to begin developing collaborative relationships. This group of people, sometimes called the crowd, can be engaged, and they can contribute to cultural organizations in many exciting ways (Chapter 8). Some of the ways in which cultural institutions have been collaborating with a much broader audience is explored in further detail (Chapter 9).

The concept and importance of platform and especially of a library as platform is elaborated in some detail. The concept of platform can also be extended to the library as physical space, sometimes referred to as a third place. The end result of this activity is that it helps to build community by providing a range of tools and resources with which to discover and create new knowledge (Chapter 10).

The end result is that library leaders must step up to the challenge to reinvent the library but aligning itself with broader organizational goals and objectives. This book argues that libraries need to embrace innovation that is disruptive rather than the slower evolutionary (small changes) approach to making libraries relevant in today's society (Chapter 11). And finally, each individual librarian and professional working in libraries, archives, and museums must recognize that they need to change so that they too understand the importance of adding value in the lives of their customers (Chapter 12).

Note

1. Christopher Locke, Rick Levine, Doc Searls, and David Weinberger. *The Cluetrain Manifesto: The End of Business as Usual.* New York: Basic books, 2001, 183.

1

Adding Value

Librarians, whose lives and remarkable expertise
have been focused on the collection and care of these things,
these books and other materials, feel this challenge even more than I.
They struggle to justify their existence, purpose, and value
in an amorphous, digitized, and universally accessible world.

John Lombardi,[1] former chancellor,
University of Massachusetts

The notion of "adding value" is at once intuitively appealing and intellectually challenging. How does any organization add value? Why should information professionals be concerned about adding value? For whom does the added value serve? The literature on defining value is disjointed, and few authors distinguish between "value" and "added value." While the majority of the literature pertaining to adding value relates to the for-profit sector, a careful analysis of this literature suggests that any organization must provide value to its members or customers in order to continue to exist. What do we mean when we say something is "valuable"? Does the concept of adding value apply to both products and services? Thus, it is sensible, if not essential, to explore in greater detail the concept of "adding value."

The word "value" comes from the old French *valoir*, meaning "to be worth." And worth, aside from its obvious link to the concept of wealth, is concerned about what people think will enrich their lives. And every product or service has value in the lives of the individual—both recognized and unknown.

Adding value is accomplished by using the talents, skills, and expertise of staff members in a set of processes to produce a product or service. Note that technology may not be a necessary ingredient in the process of adding value. In the profit-making sector, almost all effort is devoted to adding value that will maximize the gap between the revenue generated by sales and the costs to produce the product or service. Determining how value is added from the work of library and information professionals is a bit more multifaceted, as library-related products and services are rarely sold (even if it was possible to establish a price that would yield a profit). In the end, value is created by meeting customer needs by clearly understanding how a customer benefits from the use of library services.

The fairly complex issues surrounding the phrases "the value of information," "valuing information service," and "valuing a library" have been explored in some detail, and I suggested that outcomes-based approaches that are aligned with organizational goals and objectives resonate better with external stakeholders.[2]

Adam Smith developed one of the foundational notions of economics when he asserted that it was important to distinguish between "value-in-exchange" and "value-in-use." The "value-in-use" or "utility theory" approach recognizes that the customer generates value through use (and the library, archive, or museum *facilitates* value creation by providing access to its collections, services, and tools). Ultimately, value creation is, or should be, the fundamental basis for any cultural organization. *Facilitates* implies, to some degree, cocreation of value as the customer gains access to collections, services, and tools—using a set of resources (physical or virtual) selected and provided by a cultural organization for another's benefit.

Every business or not-for-profit organization is facing direct or indirect competition from other organizations, and these other organizations will likely use many of the same processes and activities that add value. The key for long-term success is to identify one or more processes that are unique and that differentiate the organization from its competitors. One of the key concepts of the management and marketing literature is that every successful organization has found a way to create value for customers that its competitors have not been able to. Yet, for the past 50 or more years, managers have been focused on managing activity rather than value. Most people when they go to work don't even consider the possibility of identifying ways in which they can add more value to their organization or in the lives of their customers.

Value is at the core of organizational purpose. Process or activities performed by employees are how value is created. This notion of creating or adding value has been called a "value proposition," a "customer value proposition," a "unique value proposition," a "sustainable competitive advantage," or a "sustainable value proposition." One useful way to think about a value proposition is that it is a positioning statement that describes for a specific customer segment (market segment or subgroup) what the library does uniquely well. The value proposition should state clearly how the library eliminates (or reduces) a specific "pain" experienced by a customer segment as well as identifying how the library creates "gain" for the customer.

A value proposition is a clear statement that:

- Is a promise of value delivered to the customer.
- Explains how the service solves customers' problems.
- Delivers specific benefits.
- Explains why the customer should use the library and not the competition (differentiation).

If you can't explain it simply,
you don't understand it well enough.

Albert Einstein

If you need to read a lot of text that attempts to explain your value proposition, you have it wrong. If after reading your cultural organization's value proposition your customers start to ask questions, then you have it wrong. Oftentimes, managers will list benefits and equate this list with the customer's value proposition. These perceived benefits may, in fact, offer the customer no real value or be equivalent to other options and thus provide no real differentiation of the cultural organization's service offerings. Thus, a value proposition is not about a cultural organization's offerings or its collections but rather about what the customer experiences in terms of meeting an information need at a moment in time. A good value proposition will be something the customer can visualize and get excited about. In short, add WOW and eliminate "ouch."

Michael Treacy and Fred Wiersema identified three value disciplines or approaches to creating value:[3]

1. *Operational excellence*—focuses on price leadership by providing convenient, low-cost solutions (think of Costco or WalMart). Companies seek to minimize overhead and transaction costs.
2. *Customer intimacy*—focuses on customer needs—not price (think of Nordstrom's, Four Seasons Hotels). This means segmenting and targeting markets and tailoring offerings to precisely meet the needs of each segment.
3. *Product leadership*—focuses on innovation and being responsive to customer needs (think of Procter & Gamble, Nike, Google, FedEx). The organization focuses on creativity and flexibility.

Very few organizations can focus on more than one of the value disciplines at the same time, and thus as part of the strategic planning process, an organization must choose what to focus on. Strategic planning is discussed in more detail later in Chapter 4.

Only the customer can identify (and in many ways estimate) the value that is created by the investment of monies (to build and equip buildings) and human capital. Customers subjectively and objectively define the value of the cultural organization's collections and services by voting with their feet and their fingers—in our growing virtual world (use of services). If customers are choosing other options, then they have made a value choice and decided to ignore the cultural organization. The customer defines value, and each customer will define it somewhat differently, depending upon his or her needs. In most cases, value is based on a combination of factors—convenience, time and effort to use the cultural organization, and so forth. If you want to add value, you need to know where it starts.

Logic Model

If we are going to explore how an organization adds value in the life of a customer, it is important to consider the outcomes that will likely arise from using the cultural organization's collections and services. Some organizations have been focusing on the total customer experience as they provide different types of experiences (visual, auditory, and collaborative pathways) so that individuals can develop critical thinking skills and knowledge creation.

Stephen Covey in his books and workshops urges us to "start with the end in mind." Thus, it is recommended that a cultural organization should use a logic model for designing service interactions. In basic terms, a logic model is an "if . . . then" model that predicts a cause-and-effect relationship as shown in Figure 1-1. A logic model makes a specific statement of the activities that will produce the change and results you expect to see for a particular group of customers. A logic model can also

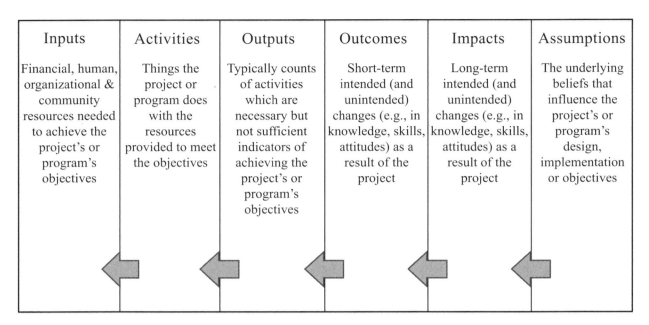

Inputs	Activities	Outputs	Outcomes	Impacts	Assumptions
Financial, human, organizational & community resources needed to achieve the project's or program's objectives	Things the project or program does with the resources provided to meet the objectives	Typically counts of activities which are necessary but not sufficient indicators of achieving the project's or program's objectives	Short-term intended (and unintended) changes (e.g., in knowledge, skills, attitudes) as a result of the project	Long-term intended (and unintended) changes (e.g., in knowledge, skills, attitudes) as a result of the project	The underlying beliefs that influence the project's or program's design, implementation or objectives

Figure 1-1 Logic Model.

be thought of as a conceptual map, a blueprint, a road map, a framework for action, or a mental model. The use of the word "logic" refers to the logic of how things work (or how we think things work) rather the logic encompassed by the fields of philosophy, mathematics, or computer programming. Logic models were popularized in the non-profit sector, for example, United Way, and are being increasingly used by cultural organizations.

Starting on the right-hand side of the logic model, there are the beliefs (or hope) that if a project or program is provided, it will lead to the desired impacts. The impacts are the changes that result in an individual as the result of a program or project participation. For example, the desired impacts for a public library's summer reading program might be that each participating child spend more time reading with his or her parents or an adult each day as well as maintain or improve reading skills over the course of a summer based on standardized reading tests (perhaps administered by the local schools). These two impacts could be measured based on a report by the adult at the conclusion of the summer about the time spent reading with each child and the local schools reporting reading test results.

Moving to the left or Outcome section of the model, the library could keep track of the confidence in reading the child feels, the improved vocabulary for each child, and so forth. Moving further to the left, the Output portion of the logic model would track the amount of use of library collections and services for each child—the books read by each child, time spent reading alone and with his or her parents, number of pages read, and so forth.

And the Input portion of the logic model identifies what resources are needed to offer the summer reading program. These resources might include staff time, facilities, technology (if an online summer reading program is offered), incentives provided to the children for continued participation, marketing and so forth.

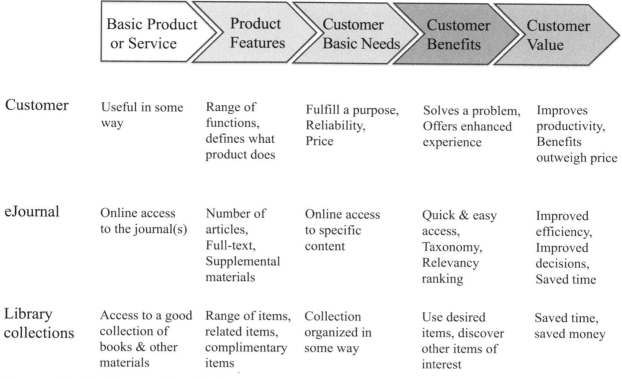

	Basic Product or Service	Product Features	Customer Basic Needs	Customer Benefits	Customer Value
Customer	Useful in some way	Range of functions, defines what product does	Fulfill a purpose, Reliability, Price	Solves a problem, Offers enhanced experience	Improves productivity, Benefits outweigh price
eJournal	Online access to the journal(s)	Number of articles, Full-text, Supplemental materials	Online access to specific content	Quick & easy access, Taxonomy, Relevancy ranking	Improved efficiency, Improved decisions, Saved time
Library collections	Access to a good collection of books & other materials	Range of items, related items, complimentary items	Collection organized in some way	Use desired items, discover other items of interest	Saved time, saved money

Figure 1-2 Understanding Value.

The value of the logic model is that it encourages people to imagine a future that the cultural organization can influence. And the way organizations go about their imagining really influences the effectiveness of their organization. It is important to take the time to imagine what success will look like in the lives of the cultural organization's customers. Figure 1-2 illustrates the steps in the process to move from a product or feature to understanding the benefits and value from the customer's perspective.

The future success of libraries will be measured by the variety of business models that they are able to devise and implement.

Brian Mathews[4]

Business Model

An organizational value model, oftentimes called a business model, describes the basis of how an organization creates, delivers, and captures economic, social, and/or other forms of value.[5] The whole idea is to break the activities of a "business" down into a manageable number of building blocks. This process of using building blocks allows you to clearly see how all the pieces of an organization fit together. The use of the business model should also help clarify and reveal how value is created and delivered to the customer. Regardless of the model that is chosen, and there are several models from which to choose, a business model should be able to answer three fundamental questions—as seen in Figure 1-3:

- **Who's** your customer? What portion of the community is the cultural organization currently serving? Are you planning to target a specific geographic population or a demographic population (sometimes called a market segment)? What are needs of each market segment? What market segments are you only marginally reaching or not reaching at all? Why are some market segments not using the cultural organization at all? Who are your most important customers? How satisfied are your customers? How frequently are your customers using the library, archive, gallery or museum?

- **What** is your value proposition? What need is being fulfilled or what problem is being solved? How does the customer benefit from using the cultural organization? What does the customer gain, and how is a customer pain eliminated or moderated? What is unique about the cultural organization service? In order to better understand the cultural organization's value proposition, the organizaiton must consider all of the services and information resources that people actually use (rather than simply adopting a cultural organization perspective).

- **How** are you providing value? What key activities does the cultural organization perform to deliver value to the customer? What are your key resources and assets? How do you reach the customer (physically and virtually)? If the cultural organization collaborates with a partner, can it deliver even more value to the customer?

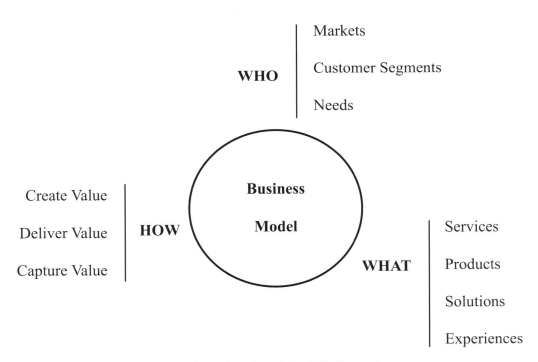

Figure 1-3 Important Organizational Value Model Questions.

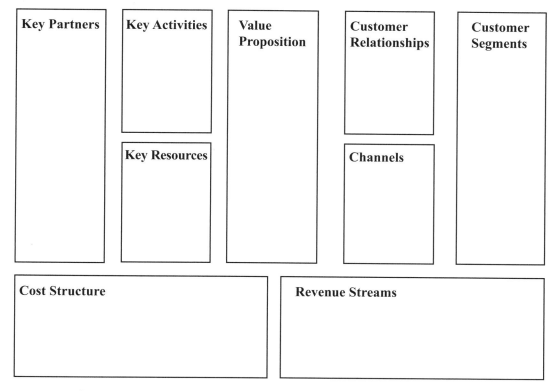

Figure 1-4 Business Model Canvas. Copyright and Creative Commons License 2014, Strategyzer .com.

Organizations are facing an increasing amount of competition. Often, this increased competition is the result of a new disruptive entry that is changing the way value is being created, delivered, and captured. The end result is that people are finding options of more value than provided by the traditional library or cultural organization.

The business model canvas, developed by Alexander Osterwalder and Yves Pigneur, which has been applied and tested in a wide variety of organizations located around the world may be seen in figure 1-4.[6]

The business model canvas is similar to a strategic blueprint that can be implemented through organizational structures, processes, and systems. Business models emphasize a holistic approach to how an organization does its thing as well as seeks to explain how value is created. The nine building blocks in the business model canvas include:

- *Customer segments.* An organization serves one or more segments of the target population. The organization needs to ask itself: for whom are we creating value (and what value is the customer expecting)? To better satisfy customers, an organization may wish to group customers into distinct segments with common needs, behaviors, and other attributes. One important question is how does the library create value for each different customer segment?

- *Value propositions.* The value proposition is the bundle of services that attract specific customer segments to the organization rather than using another option (of which there are likely many). The value proposition satisfies a specific customer need or solves a customer's problem. Most importantly, the value proposition communicates what is unique about an organization's service offerings compared with the competitors. In short, the value proposition is the promise an organization makes that differentiates itself in the marketplace.

- *Channels*. This building block describes how the organization shares with each customer segment the value proposition message. Is the organization able to deliver value using social media channels? Do customers find the cultural organization as they use the network-level tools and apps they routinely use in their daily lives?
- *Customer relationships*. What are the types of relationship that each customer segment expects the organization to establish and maintain with them? In addition to providing self-service to many customers, an organization may also provide personal assistance and automated services, engage with a user community, and cocreate value with its customers. Are cultural organization workflows set up to maximize the value delivered to the customer or to maximize internal operations?
- *Revenue streams*. Any organization needs to generate sufficient revenue to sustain its services and grow. For-profit companies need to generate sufficient cash from each customer segment that their operating costs are covered plus generate additional revenues to represent profit (some or all of which is set aside to help generate growth by investing in additional staff, equipment, and so forth). Not-for-profit organizations need to generate funds from donations (or grants), or the cultural organization must provide justification to a parent organization to maintain or increase its budget. What services provide sufficient value that customers are willing to pay? How are customers currently paying (how would they like to pay)?
- *Key resources*. This building block identifies the assets needed to make the business model work. These key resources might be financial, physical, intellectual, or human (staff).
- *Key activities*. Key activities identify the important things an organization must accomplish to operate successfully. Key activities can be grouped into three categories: production or services processes, problem solving, and the platform/network.
- *Key partnerships*. This building block describes the network of suppliers and other partners that make the business model work well. A partnership may be needed to reduce risk and uncertainty, acquire particular resources and activities, and optimize the allocation of resources and activities.
- *Cost structures*. This building block identifies what are the costs incurred to operate the business model. Costs have the following characteristics: some are fixed costs while some are variable costs. And economies of scale and economies of scope may play an important role. It is also clear that for almost every cultural institution that value creation is subsidized—funds are provided by a parent organization rather than total revenues being generated by the gallery, archive, library or museum itself.

Perhaps the most important aspect of the business model is the value proposition since it identifies the value the customer receives. Value is created for each customer segment through a different mix of elements satisfying each segment's needs. Among the many elements that may contribute to customer value are:

- *Performance.* Improving service performance has been a traditional and successful way to create value; yet, this approach can reach saturation limits. For example, the personal computer industry relied on this approach for many years but has now fallen on hard times as smaller and more convenient devices such as laptops, tablets, and smartphones provide equivalent performance.

- *Cost reduction.* Assisting customers in reducing their costs is clearly an important way to create value. Rather than incurring the expenses associated with having to buy, install, and maintain software themselves, a customer can choose a lower-cost hosted software solution (Software as a Service or SaaS).

- *Accessibility.* Making services and products available to customers who previously were unable to access them is another way to provide value. The development of mutual funds allowed many people of modest means to build a diversified investment portfolio.

- *Price.* Providing a similar service at a lower price is a fairly typical way to satisfy price-sensitive customer segments. But it is not possible to compete solely on price without also significantly changing the other building blocks. Southwest, the low-cost airline, has designed a unique business model to enable low-cost air travel with the result that many people who could not afford air travel now routinely travel on Southwest.

- *Experience.* The total customer experience of visiting a store such as Apple, a museum, an amusement park such as Disneyland can provide real value to the visitor. Visiting a "Build-a-Bear" store provides a unique customer experience that is valued by many (even if the price is high to create a bear). The authors of the *Experience Economy* suggest that there are significant benefits that arise when a great customer experience is provided.[7] It is important to understand how operating policies, procedures, and processes add value, by eliminating any frustrations that the customer may experience, so that the total customer experience is awesome.

- *Brand.* Choosing a specific brand will, for many, deliver value regardless of the cost. At the high end of the market, consider Nike shoes, a Rolex watch, a Mercedes Benz automobile, a Gucci handbag, among a host of options to reflect wealth or status. At the other end of the spectrum, "underground" brands such as that for skateboarders or surfers demonstrate those that are "in."

- *Convenience.* Making things more convenient or easier to use can also create value. Apple offers customer convenience when searching, downloading, and listening to digital music using an iPod and their iTunes store. And clearly, Google provides real value through its fast and convenient search engine.

- *Newness.* In some cases, value is created for a customer by providing a product or service that is entirely new. The development of the iPhone (and now all of the competitive smartphones) integrated several technologies in a new and easy-to-use manner that created real value for the customer.

- *Customization.* Tailoring products and services to specific customer segments creates value. Many companies and organizations offer ways for a customer to obtain a unique customized product or service.
- *Customer incentive program.* An organization may use a customer incentive program by offering coupons, sales, giveaways, promotions, and so forth to build customer loyalty.
- *Service quality.* The service quality that an organization delivers to its customers can add real value. Among the factors of service quality that are important are: reliability (do you do what you have promised in a consistent manner?), courtesy, competency, and responsiveness.

While it can take some sustained thinking, it is possible to create one or more value propositions by completing the two sentences as shown in Figure 1-5. The goal of this exercise is to get you to create a first draft and then revise, revise, and revise until anyone whom you show the value proposition sentences to immediately "get it."

Among the many advantages of using a business model is that it shows in a visual way how all the pieces need to work together to create value; it can assist in translating business plans into business processes, provide a common language to talk about the goals and opportunities of the organization, and act as a reality check to ensure that all the bases are covered.

The business model describes the rationale of how any organization creates and delivers value for its customers. The business model allows anyone to better understand

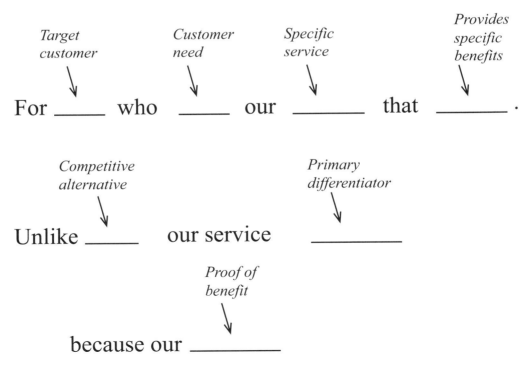

Figure 1-5 Value Proposition Sentences.

the ways in which strategy can be implemented through organizational structures, processes, and systems. Notice that the cost-related components are on the left-hand side of the model, while the value-related building blocks are on the right.

As an illustration, in times past, library collections were created as resources were scarce and expensive. Services such as the catalog and reference were developed to provide improved access to these collections. Controlled vocabularies were used to improve the accuracy and consistency in the library catalog. Everything had its place due to physical limitations (an item could not be in two places at once).[8] The end result, at least from the customer's perspective, are some fairly complex systems (lots of people just don't get that Dewey thing). This, in turn, has led to a collective wealth that has been held hostage by redundant operations and collections. In effect, the library, archive, or museum was the center of the universe (the hub of the wagon wheel) rather than interrelating with other nodes in a large and complex network.

The business model template can be used to describe the logic of the value-added processes in an existing organization such as the traditional warehouse library as shown in Figure 1-6.

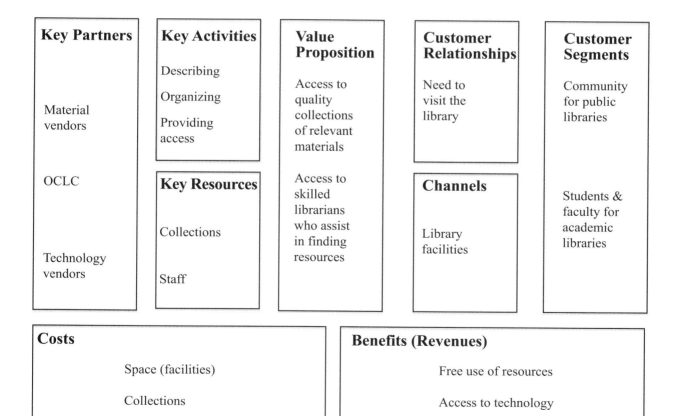

Figure 1-6 Business Model of the Traditional "Warehouse" Library.

As a library moves from the traditional "print or physical materials" library to the digital library, or from providing access to atoms to providing access to bits and bytes, the way in which it interacts with and provides value to its customers must also change. The nature of information is changing from constrained access to ubiquity; from expensive to fairly low cost or free; shaped by professionals to be shared by everyone; from mass consumption to broad-scale participation and sharing; from often waiting to always immediately accessible using our mobile devices; and from stand-alone silos to being embedded in a networked world that is always on.

Lorcan Dempsey has suggested that our users are operating at the network level, while libraries, archives, and museums continue to operate at the institutional level.[9] Organizations continue to manage local infrastructure that creates little distinctive value. Cultural organizations must build their value proposition around the user's workflow given the increasing amount of time people are connected to the Internet. Thus, it is possible to begin to better understand what the digital library of the future will look like by using the business model canvas as shown in Figure 1-7.

Clearly, the digital library offers the prospect that new value propositions will emerge—new customer groups (market segments) are being reached by digitizing collections and engaging customers in new and creative ways. If digital materials are offered without copyright restrictions (some have called this "copyleft"—offering the

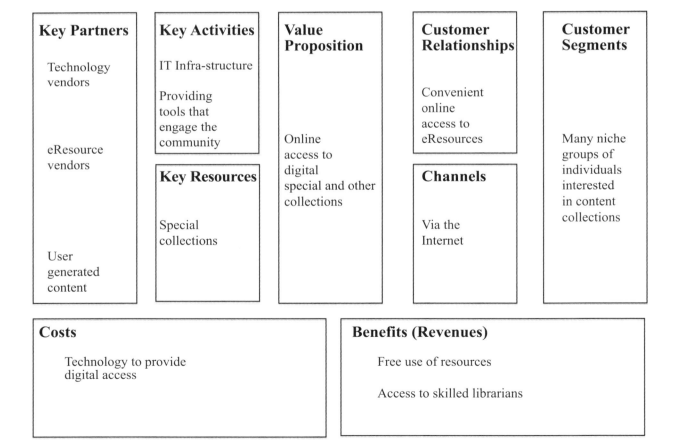

Figure 1-7 Digital Library of the Future Business Model.

right to distribute copies and modified versions of a work and requiring all modified versions to be free also), then users can reuse, sample, tag, enjoy, and repurpose the content in new and interesting ways. The end result is a larger, less academic audience who is reached (who may be very knowledgeable about a specific topic) than the number of users who currently use the physical library.

Value Proposition

The whole notion of adding value is so important that one of the important tools to assist any organization in developing a better understanding of how a customer benefits from a product or service is to develop a value proposition that clearly conveys the ways in which value is transmitted. One really useful tool is to develop a value proposition map, as shown in Figure 1-8, by identifying pain relievers, gain creators, and customer jobs.[10]

The components of the value proposition map include:

- *Customer jobs.* The things your customers are trying to get done in their work or in their lives. These might be functional jobs, social jobs, and/or personal jobs.
- *Customer pains.* Customers experience frustrations and annoyances in attempting to complete a task or trying to get a job done. Customer pains might include undesired outcomes, problems, and characteristics; obstacles; and risks of undesired outcomes.

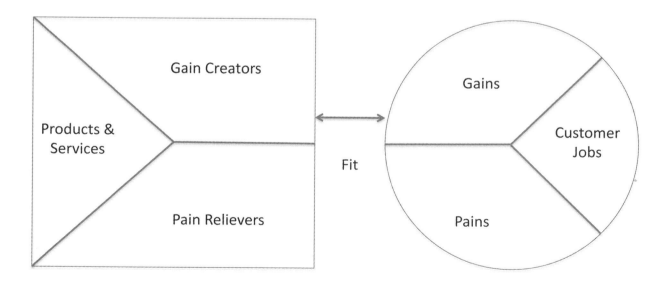

Figure 1-8 Value Proposition Map. Adapted from The Value Proposition Canvas, Strategyzer. Creative Commons 2014.

- *Customer gains.* What are the customer benefits and outcomes that are required, expected, or desired? What would make your customers more productive and happier?
- *Products and services.* The bundle of products and services offered by your organization. Your products and services will likely be physical (tangible), intangible, and digital.
- *Pain relievers.* The ways in which your products and services reduce or eliminate the things that annoy your customers as they attempt to complete a job.
- *Gain creators.* Describe how your products and services create customer gains in the form of benefits and positive outcomes.

Intangible Value

The term "intangible value" is also known as "intangible asset" or "intellectual capital." An intangible asset is not physical in nature and is capable of producing future benefits. In a review of the literature, Petros Kostagiolas and Stefanos Asonitis suggest that there are three types of intangible assets: relational capital, organizational capital, and human capital.[11] Stephen Town, the thoughtful University Librarian at the University of York, and Martha Kyrillidou formerly of the Association of Research Libraries have expanded upon the notion of intangible assets and developed a value scorecard for academic libraries that has four dimensions:[12]

1. *Relational capital.* This dimension has two components: competitive position capital (reputation and reach) and relational capital (external and internal relationship development).
2. *Library capital.* This dimension also has two elements: tangible capital (collections, environments, and services) and intangible capital (intangible assets, organizational capital, and human capital).
3. *Library virtue.* Library virtue is composed of the social capital beyond the library (contributions to research, learning, employability, professional intent, and other common goods).
4. *Library momentum.* This dimension focuses on the capital gained or saved by the library's services and collections.

The employees and processes of an organization are responsible for value creation. Some employee and process characteristics are positive in nature (let's call these drivers), and some are negative (let's call these barriers). Figure 1-9 lists some of these characteristics.

Guillaume Van Moorsel has advocated for the use of a client value model that helps to establish a common definition of value elements (a value vocabulary) for libraries and their clients.[13] The client value model is particularly helpful for fine-tuning existing services.

Drivers	*Barriers*
Employee Dimensions • Unique skills • Training • Experience • Team work • Satisfaction	*Employee Dimensions* • Lack of skills • Shortage of experience • Insufficient rewards • Distrustful culture • Heavy workloads
Process Dimensions • Innovation is encouraged • Knowledge assets • Future focus • Trusting environment • Core competence	*Process Dimensions* • Lacking knowledge of customer segments • Distrust of co-workers • Old technology • Relucatance to embrace change

Figure 1-9 Factors of Value Creation.

Summary

In this time of rapid change, it is time to "deconstruct the library" (as well as all other cultural institutions) as suggested by Sarah Pritchard.[14] The process of deconstruction can assist us in gaining a better understanding of how all types of libraries add value for their customers.

It is particularly important to acknowledge that every cultural organization exists to facilitate value creation in the lives of its customers. And customers create value through the use of cultural organization services and collections. Value creation results from an interactive process through which the customer is benefited.

Regardless of the method chosen to explore ways to add value (sometimes this process is called strategic planning), any cultural organization must be able to answer three important questions:

Question 1: Who do we serve? Which customer segments does the cultural organization currently serve? What different customer segments does the cultural organization distinguish?

Question 2: What do we offer? What "unique value proposition" does the cultural organization offer to each customer segment? What are the benefits that a customer segment gains by using the cultural organization's offerings?

Question 3: How do we do that? What is the business model that assists the cultural organization in delivering value to the customer?

Checklist for Adding Value

	Yes	No

What

	Yes	No
What are the limitations of the cultural organization's service/product?	☐	☐
What is the competition doing that isn't necessary?	☐	☐
What resources do I have that I can leverage to enhance the cultural organization's service offering?	☐	☐
What are the cultural organization's competitive advantages?	☐	☐
How well is the cultural organization's value creation process understood?	☐	☐
This cultural organization understands what processes add the most value for each customer segment?	☐	☐
Does the cultural organization offer solutions and experiences?	☐	☐
Are complementary services and experiences offered?	☐	☐
selectively eliminate or reduce a service as well as create and introduce a new service?	☐	☐
Does the organization look at the customer experience?	☐	☐

Who

	Yes	No
Does the organization select a competitor and identify the market segment it is serving	☐	☐
What market segments does your cultural organization serve?	☐	☐
What are the core needs of each customer segment?	☐	☐
What are the customer segmentation criteria?	☐	☐
Do you segment according to work to be done or task to be completed?	☐	☐

How

	Yes	No
What new technologies could the cultural organization use to eliminate the need for certain offerings?	☐	☐
How can I completely eliminate an existing service (while creating a new service) that will add value to the customer?	☐	☐
Have you looked at reinventing the way you deliver services?	☐	☐
Do you use data to consistently improve your cultural organization's website?	☐	☐
Have you developed new partnerships to extend the reach of the cultural organization?	☐	☐

If you answered "no" to one or more of the questions in the checklist, then your cultural organization is not doing all it could to add value.

Main idea:	Understanding how a cultural organization adds value
Opposing view:	The same ol', same ol'—maintaining the status quo, assuming traditional services are good
Key terms:	Adding value, business model canvas, value proposition, unique value proposition
What has changed?:	The competitive environment
Catalyst:	The Internet
Open debate:	How does a cultural organization add value? What other ways can be used by a cultural organization to add even more value?

Notes

1. John Lombardi. On the Research Library: A Comment. A Presentation at the Library Assessment Conference: Building Effective, Sustainable, Practical Assessment, September 25–27, 2006, in Charlottesville, Virginia. Available at http://libraryassessment.org/archive/2006.shtml

2. Joseph R. Matthews. "Valuing Information, Information Services, and the Library: Possibilities and Realities." *portal: Libraries and the Academy*, 13 (1), 2013, 91–112.

3. Michael Treacy and Fred Wiersema. "Customer Intimacy and Other Value Disciplines." *Harvard Business Review*, 71, 1993, 84–94.

4. Brian Mathews. "Flip the Model: Strategies for Creating and Delivering Value." *The Ubiquitous Librarian* blog. October 28, 2013. Available at http://chronicle.com/blognetwork/theubiquitouslibrarian/2013/10/28/flip-the-model-a-pre-print/

5. I trust that librarians and other cultural organization professionals will not object too strenuously to the use of the term "business model." Talking about and understanding an organization's business model is obviously very important in the for-profit sector and increasingly in the nonprofit sector as well.

6. Alexander Osterwalder and Yves Pigneur. *Business Model Generation: A Handbook for Visionaries, Game Changers, and Challengers*. New York: John Wiley & Sons, 2010.

7. Joseph Pine and James Gilmore. *The Experience Economy: Work Is Theater & Every Business a Stage*. Cambridge, MA: Harvard Business School Press, 1999.

8. David Weinberger. *Everything Is Miscellaneous: The Power of the New Digital Disorder*. New York: Holt, 2008.

9. Lorcan Dempsey. "Reconfiguring the Library Systems Environment." *portal: Libraries and the Academy*, 8 (2), April 2008, 111–120.

10. Alexander Osterwalder, Yves Pigneur, Greg Bernarda, and Alan Smith. *Value Proposition Design*. New York: Wiley, 2014.

11. Petros Kostagiolas and Stefanos Asonitis. "Intangible Assets for Academic Libraries: Definitions, Categorization and an Exploration of Management Issues." *Library Management*, 30 (6/7), 2009, 419–429.

12. J. Stephen Town and Martha Kyrillidou. "Developing a Values Scorecard." *Performance Measurement and Metrics*, 14 (1), 2013, 7–16.

13. Guillaume Van Moorsel. "Client Value Models Provide a Framework for Rational Library Planning (or, Phrasing the Answer in the Form of a Question)." *Medical Reference Services Quarterly*, 24 (2), Summer 2005, 25–40.

14. Sarah Pritchard. "Deconstructing the Library: Reconceptualizing Collections, Spaces and Services." *The Journal of Library Administration*, 48 (2), 2008, 219–233.

2

How Libraries Have Traditionally Added Value

Intertwingularity is not generally acknowledged—
people keep pretending they can make things deeply
hierarchical, categorizable, and sequential when they can't.
Everything is deeply intertwingled.

Ted Nelson[1]

Shiyali Ranganathan, the founder of modern library science, proposed his *Five Laws of Library Science* at a time when information scarcity was the norm and protecting the library's collection was a professional priority.

1. Books are for use.
2. Every reader their book.
3. Every book its reader.
4. Save the time of the reader.
5. A library is a growing organism.

His five laws have influenced every generation of librarians since they were published in 1931.[2] Rather than attempting to update them with more modern and inclusive terminology, it is perhaps more interesting to observe that implicit in embracing these laws is the reality that the laws form the foundation upon which libraries are organized to add value in the life of the reader.

The *First Law* emphasizes use and access (at least in my view) rather than the type of material in a library's collection. The question that should arise is to determine whether the library provides collections and services that promote and invite the use of resources?

The *Second Law* focuses on the library's collections and services meeting the needs of a community of users. Are the library's collections adequate to fulfill the expectations of its community of users (or potential users)?

The *Third Law* revolves around the issue of access. Are materials in a library easy to find and use? Libraries developed classification systems so that materials of a similar topic would be physically located near one another.

The *Fourth Law* emphasizes efficiency—the user's efficiency. The goal of course is to minimize the barriers to access and use. So topics such as hours of operation, wayfinding and signage, staffing at service desks, reducing the time spent waiting for an item (or service) are all important and have a real impact in the life of the customer.

The *Fifth Law* is about flexibility and change. The library must both adopt and adapt to new technologies and the new ways users are using recent cutting-edge technologies. Rather than expecting our users to visit the library (physically or virtually) we now must be "in the flow" of where our users are. The objective of the fifth law is to ensure that the library changes and is able to add value as the lives of the library's customer's change—often in very dramatic ways.

Lynn Silipigni Connaway and Ixchel Faniel have prepared an insightful report using Ranganathan's five laws as a framework to synthesize available research about user behavior as a way to demonstrate ways libraries can add value today.[3] Connaway and Faniel's interpretation and reordering of the five laws are shown in Figure 2-1.

Robert Taylor, an influential library school dean, wrote *Value-Added Processes in Information Systems* in 1986.[4] This book became one of the most highly cited[5] and influential works in the field of library and information science. Taylor's insight was to focus on the *user* and the *information use environment* in an attempt to better understand how librarians and libraries add value.

Ranganathan's Original Five Laws	*Connaway and Faniel's Reordering*
Save the time of the reader	Embed library systems and services into users' existing workflows
Every person their book	Know your community segments and their needs
Books are for use	Provide the necessary infrastructure to deliver physical and digital materials
Every book its reader	Improve the discoverability, access and use of resources within users' existing workflows
A library is a growing organism	

Figure 2-1 A Reordering of Ranganathan's Five Laws. Lynn Silipigni Connaway and Ixchel Faniel. *Reordering Ranganathan: Shifting User Behaviors, Shifting Priorities*. Dublin, OH: OCLC Research, 2014.

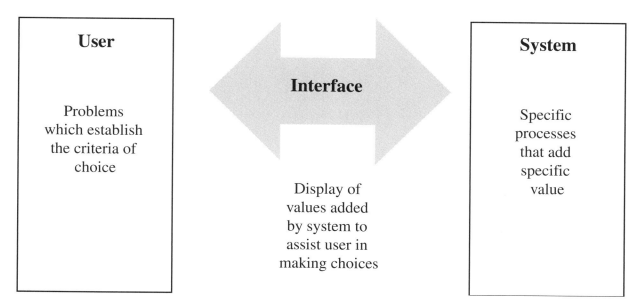

Figure 2-2 Taylor's Information Use Environment. Robert Taylor, *Value-Added Processes in Information Systems*. Norwood, NJ: Ablex, 1986. p. 49, figure 4.1.

Taylor's Value-Added Model

Taylor's value-added model is based on the basis that people interact with systems within a context called the *information use environment or IUE* as shown in Figure 2-2.

The information use environment focuses on the study of information in its contexts, and the user is placed at the center of this conceptual framework. There are four parts of the *information use environment*:

- The *user* (client or customer) is an individual who actively seeks (or receives) information from a formal information system in order to achieve some objective, either personal or work related.
- The *problem*—The user's primary criterion for judging the value of the system will vary depending upon need.
- The *interface* between the system and the customer (or the "negotiating space")—After interacting with the system, the user is able to determine the likely value or utility of the information given his or her particular information need.
- The *system* (a series of value-added processes).

Another way of viewing the information use environment, shown in Figure 2-3, illustrates that the user is actually interacting with both the system and content when he or she is searching or browsing for information.[6]

Taylor asserts that each interaction with the information use environment changes each time it is used. Problem dimensions have certain characteristics, which establish the criteria for judging relevance of information to a specific problem or a class of problems.[7] Susan MacMullin and Robert Taylor identified a total of 22 unique types of problem dimensions as shown in Figure 2-4. It should be noted that these dimensions are not independent of each other and they may not be applicable in all situations.

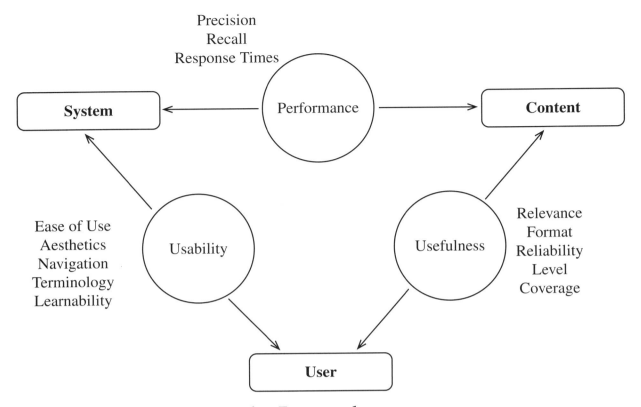

Figure 2-3 Taylor's User Interaction Framework.

Design	Discovery
Well-structured	Ill-structured
Complex	Simple
Specific goals	Amorphous goals
Initial state understood	Not understood
Assumptions agreed upon	Not agreed upon
Familiar pattern	New pattern
Magnitude of risk great	Not great
Susceptible to empirical analysis	Not susceptible
Internal imposition	External imposition

Figure 2-4 MacMullin and Taylor's Problem Dimensions. Adapted from Susan MacMullin and Robert Taylor. "Problem Dimensions and Information Traits." *The Information Society*, 3 (1), 1984, 102–107.

Taylor argues that information use involves a progression that moves from data to information to knowledge and finally to action. Taylor called this progression the value-added spectrum, shown in Figure 2-5. At the base of the progression are the organizing processes, then the analyzing processes, the judgmental processes, and finally the decision processes. The organizing processes will likely be well known to all librarians, as this has been the primary locus of value-added activities of libraries for decades.

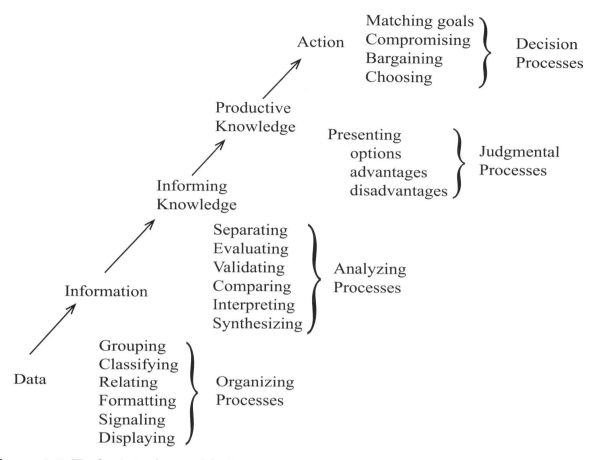

Figure 2-5 Taylor's Value-Added Spectrum Model. Robert Taylor, *Value-Added Processes in Information Systems*. Norwood, NJ: Ablex, 1986. p. 6, figure 1.1.

The terms "data," "information," and "knowledge" carry a fair amount of semantic baggage.[8] Data is typically considered as the state or condition that characterizes an entity at some point in time (and the data is usually labeled in way that is appropriate to the context, intent, or type of information system). In information technology terms, each label or attribute is a field, a collection of fields is a record, and a collection of records is a file. Data alone is usually valueless without further processing that adds value in some way. Data becomes information when connections among and between data (or fields of data) are established. Information adds structure and relationships among the data; provides context in that patterns within the data are identified.

Taylor suggests that informing knowledge occurs as synthesizing processes (selecting, analyzing, validating, and so forth as shown in Figure 2-5) are used. Knowledge uses the context and patterns found within information and also establishes casual links within a data set or among multiple data sets. Taylor then suggests that judgmental processes (choices are presented, and benefits and risks are considered) are then used to present information and informing knowledge in order that people can move to productive knowledge. And from productive knowledge, action is taken when decision processes are applied.

Clearly, the boundaries between data, information, and knowledge are not well defined; yet, the notion of a relationship or hierarchy among the three concepts is quite clear.[9] The data–information–knowledge–wisdom (DIKW) hierarchy is not a recent development. The poet T. S. Eliot alluded to this from his 1934 poem "The Rock."[10] Eliot was inquiring about the wisdom lost in knowledge and the knowledge lost in information.

Russell Ackoff, a pioneer in information management, came up with definitions that have been widely adopted and cited:[11]

- **Data** are symbols (numbers, letters, and other specialized shapes)
- **Information** is data that are processed to be useful and provide answers to "who, what, where, and when" questions
- **Knowledge** is the application of data and information, providing answers to "how" questions

Problem Dimension	*Description*
Assumptions agreed upon vs. not agreed upon	Whether the problem situation pertains to a topic area or body of knowledge which has a set of consistent rules/laws/principles from which inferences can be made or not
Assumptions explicit vs. not explicit	Whether assumptions about the problem situation are well articulated or not
Complex vs. simple	Whether the problem situation has an easily defined solution path or not
Design vs. discovery	Whether the problem situation pertains to inventing something rather than finding something
Familiar vs. new	Whether the problem situation is procedural/well-established rather than unfamiliar/novel
Initial state understood vs. not understood	Whether the interrelationships among the contributing factors of the problem situation are well understood or not
Internal vs. external imposition	Whether the problem situation is imposed internally by the organization or is imposed externally from outside the organization
Magnitude of risk great vs. low	Whether the consequences of failing to resolve the problem situation are high or not
Specific vs. amorphous goals	Whether the problem situation has well-defined and directed results rather than amorphous, unclear direction
Susceptible to empirical analysis vs. not susceptible	Whether the problem situation requires empirical evidence for problem resolution or judgment calls to be made
Well structured vs. ill structured	Whether the problem situation can be solved by application of logical/algorithmic processes or not

Figure 2-6 Taylor's Problem Dimensions. Adapted from Robert Taylor, *Value-Added Processes in Information Systems*. Norwood, NJ: Ablex, 1986. pp. 42–45.

Obviously, the notion of the DIKW hierarchy as a clean step-by-step movement upward toward wisdom is fallacious (since we all know that wisdom and knowledge are messier, discontinuous, and hard to come by). The more likely analogy is the use of a helix where we are constantly circling back to better understand something so that we may progress upward toward the goal of wisdom.

Taylor suggested 11 possible ways to classify problems—see Figure 2-6. Developing a perspective on the resolution of problems, Taylor asserted that there are two components. First, the way people typically use information to solve their problems (Taylor identified eight classes of information use—see Figure 2-7). The second relates to how information is presented to assist people discover solutions to their problems (Taylor identified 19 information traits across 9 perspectives as shown in Figure 2-8).

From the information professional's perspective, Taylor's primary contribution was the development of his value-added model, shown in Figure 2-9, with 6 user criteria and the 23 ways in which value is added. The six broad user categories—ease of use, noise reduction, quality, adaptability, time saving, and cost saving—represent ways a user might evaluate an information system. The relative priority of one value criterion over another will vary depending on the person, situation, information needs, and other user-centered concerns. One day a customer might be interested in noise reduction and another day he or she might be concerned about speed (time savings) and ease-of-use value.

Information Use	*Description*
Conformational	Information is used to verify another piece of information
Enlightenment	Information is used to develop a context or make sense of a situation
Factual	Information is used to determine the facts of a phenomenon or event
Instrumental	Information is used to find out what to do or how to do something
Motivational	Information is used to provide confidence to keep going
Personal or political	Information is used to develop relationships, status, reputation or for personal fulfillment
Problem understanding	Information is used for better comprehension of particular problems; more specific than enlightenment
Projective	Information is used to predict what is likely to happen in the future

Figure 2-7 Taylor's Information Uses. Robert Taylor, in Progress in Communication Sciences, Volume X. Brenda Dervin and Melvin Voight (Eds.). Norwood, NJ: Ablex, 1991, pg. 230.

Information Traits	Description

Aggregation
    - Census
    - Clinical
	Information is based on a population
	Information is based on a single case study or sample

Data
    - Hard
    - Soft
	Information is empirically derived
	Information is drawn from inference

Diagnostic
    - What
    - Why
	Information describes what is happening
	Information describes why something is happening

Focus
    - Diffuse
    - Precise
	Information is broad and multi-perspective
	Information is exact

Methodology
    - Qualitative
    - Quantitative
	Information is descriptive
	Information is measurable and represented numerically

Solution
    - Multiple
    - Single
	Information provides a number of solutions to a problem situation
	Information provides a single desired best solution to a problem situation

Specificity of use
    - Applied
    - Theoretical
	Information is immediately useful in an instrumental sense
	Information provides insights as to how/why something works/behaves

Substantive
    - Descriptive
    - Operational
	Information describes the content and meaning of a phenomenon
	Information describes how to do something

Temporal
    - Current
    - Forecast
    - Historic
	Information is present-based
	Information is future-based
	Information is past-based

Figure 2-8 Taylor's Information Traits. Adapted from Susan MacMullin and Robert Taylor. "Problem Dimensions and Information Traits." *The Information Society*, 3 (1), 1984, 99–101.

Every librarian and information professional will recognize most, if not all, of the activities that add value according to Taylor.

Many librarians, archivists, and museum staffers will assert that the organization and cataloging of an organization's collection is the primary added-value activity. This is an inward-looking perspective about the value of the cultural organization and is old school in its perspective. According to Eleanor Jo Rodger, the only perspective about value that counts is that of the customer:

> Being valuable is not about our professional values; in the paradigm of the value of . . . libraries we are the producers, not the consumers of our services. Our personal sense of what is valuable doesn't matter unless it matches that of our customers.[12]

Obviously, there are some in our profession who see themselves as personal custodians and institutional guardians of traditional values, while others believe that information professionals should be working to create value for their customers. As Gary Deane has noted,

User Criteria of Choice	Interface (Value Added)	System (Value-Added Processes)
Ease of Use—System elements that reduce the challenges when using a system.	**Browsing**—Facilitates scanning an information neighborhood. **Formatting**—The presentation of data/information that simplifies scanning. **Interfacing**—Making the system more intuitive. **Interfacing I (Mediation)**—Assisting the user in getting answers. **Interfacing II (Orientation)**—Help the user understand and gain experience. **Ordering**—Organizing the information content (for example, presenting names in alphabetical order). **Physical Accessibility**—Making access to information resources easier.	Alphabetizing Highlighting important terms
Noise Reduction—Providing the appropriate amount of information can be accomplished by: 1) Exclusion (withholding information), 2) Inclusion (supplying additional information), and 3) Precision (supplying the best information).	**Access**—Providing information that is wanted or needed. **Access I**—Identification by a physical description and location. **Access II**—Subject description (index terms, descriptors, or names). **Access III**—Provide summaries, abstracts, graphs, charts and formulas. **Linkage**—Provide links to items and resources external to the system. **Precision**—The capability to assist users in finding exactly what they want. **Selectivity**—Limit what is retrieved/displayed based on the choices of the user.	Indexing Vocabulary control Filtering

1 Martin Eppler. Managing Information Quality: Increasing the Value of information in Knowledge-Intensive Products and Processes. Second Edition. New York: Springer, 2006.

Figure 2-9 Taylor's Value-Added Model. Adapted from Robert Taylor. *Value-Added Processes in Information Systems*, Norwood, NJ: Ablex, 1986. p. 50.

Quality—In a wonderful book about managing information quality, Martin Eppler asserts that there are sixteen criteria that can be used to assess information quality: comprehensiveness, accuracy, clarity, applicability, conciseness, consistency, currency, correctness, convenience, timeliness, traceability, interactivity, accessibility, security, maintainability, and speed.[1]	**Accuracy**—Error-free transfer of information. **Comprehensiveness**—The completeness of coverage. **Currency**—Providing timely information as well as up-to-date access vocabularies. **Reliability**—Consistency of performance over time. **Validity**—Allowing the user to judge the soundness of information.	Quality control Editing Updating Analyzing and comparing data
Adaptability—Capabilities that respond to the users needs and requests.	**Closeness to the problem**—System capabilities that assist in solving a particular problem. **Flexibility**—Ways of working dynamically with information. **Simplicity**—Providing the clearest and most lucid information. **Stimulatory**—Provides context to encourage use of a system or the staff of an organization.	Provision of data manipulation capabilities Ranking output for relevance
Time Savings—Speed of the response time of a system.	Response speed	Reduction of processing time
Cost Savings—System design and capabilities that save money for the user.	Cost savings	Lower connect-time price

Figure 2-9 (Continued)

It is customers, one at a time, who defines a library's value. This value is realized in the usefulness, the quality, and the availability of the library's products and services, as well as in the customer support that accompanies them. It is also found in the image that the library presents to the customer, an image that must be carefully defined and managed by the library.[13]

Yet, as we will see in the next chapter, the information environment continues to undergo significant transformation.

And so it would seem to be reasonable to ask several questions:

- Do Taylor's traditional added-value tools and techniques still add the same level of value, or is the value diminished or eliminated in some way?
- What new added-value tools and techniques can be embraced that are perceived to be valuable in the eyes of our customers?

Variations on the Taylor Model

Bob Taylor's model has been the inspiration for a surfeit of articles pertaining to information retrieval,[14] the concept of task,[15] the user interface, the knowledge organization,[16] and the user interface within the Moodle Platform,[17] among other topics. But others have felt it important to extend and improve upon the original Taylor model. Consider, for example, the suggestion by Howard Rosenbaum that it was important to move outside of the confines of the value-added approach and embrace Gibbens's structuration theory, as there are important points of convergence between the two.[18]

In 2008, Mike Eisenberg, from the University of Washington Information School, and Lee Dirks felt that it was important to build upon the foundation of the Taylor model by incorporating some revisions and proposing some additions to the original model as shown in Figure 2-10 (additions to the model are shown in bold).[19] These two authors' principal contribution was to combine "time savings" and "cost savings" into a new category of user choice called "performance." They also introduced a new user choice category called "pleasing" along with proposing some associated "values added"—aesthetics, entertaining, rewarding, engaging, and stimulating. Eisenberg and Dirks felt that their modified value-added model could be applied in at least three ways:

1. Developing new systems and tools.
2. Refining/improving existing tools.
3. Studying competitive offerings.

Eisenberg and Dirks continued their work of extending the original Taylor model and more recently introduced the "TEDS framework"—Taylor, Eisenberg, Dirks, and Scholl—that permits the analysis of information system capabilities compared with specific user needs and use scenarios.[20] This reformulated value-added model has been connected with the concepts of *personae* and *scenarios*, and the model has been expanded to 40 values-added activities. The authors suggest that the extended TEDS framework

User Criteria	Values Added	System Processes
Ease of Use	Browsing **Simplicity** Mediation Orientation Ordering Accessibility	Alphabetizing Highlighting **Formatting** **Simplifying**
Noise Reduction	Item Identification **Classification** **Summarization** **Order** **Referral** Precision Selectivity **Novelty**	Indexing Controlled vocabulary Filtering **Selection** **Hyperlinking** **Semantic connecting** **Search**
Quality	Accuracy Comprehensiveness Currency Reliability Validity **Authority**	Quality control Editing Updating Analyzing **Selecting**
Adaptability	**Contextuality** Flexibility Simplicity **Privacy**	Data manipulation capabilities **Sorting** **Customizing** **User profiling** **Informed consent** **Choice**
Performance	Time Savings Cost savings **Security** **Safety**	**Bandwidth** **Parallel processing** **Server size** Response speed **Resource allocation/sharing** **Common protocols, business practices** **Encryption** **Password protection**
Pleasing	**Aesthetics** **Entertaining** **Rewarding** **Engaging** **Stimulating**	**Design** **Interactive** **Gaming** **Reinforcing**

Figure 2-10 Eisenberg and Dirks Adaption of Taylor's Value-Added Model. From Mike Eisenberg and Lee Dirks. "Taylor's Value-Added Model: Still Relevant after All These Years." *Presented at the iConference, February 27-March 1, 2008. UCLA, Los Angeles, California*. Available at https://www.ideals.illinois .edu/bitstream/handle/2142/15081/PA3-4_iconf08.pdf?sequence=2

allows for the analysis of information in a highly interactive and networked environment. The TEDS framework adds the following value-added concepts to the Eisenberg and Dirks Modified Value-Added Model: formatting/presentation to the user criteria of ease of use; and transaction, trust, feedback, community, individualization, and localization to the user criteria of adaptability.

Perspective

The value-added processes identified and articulated by Taylor and extended in the TEDS framework lead to the library's ability to provide a service that is of value to the customer. In reality, it is not important how much a specific information resource and/or service is used, but rather what is the impact or benefit of the resource or service in the life of the library customer.

Yet in an interesting qualitative study, Judith Broady-Preston and Wendy Swain asked library managers, librarians, and other staff members to try to categorize their service offerings into either the library's core business or additional value-added services (services that are ancillary to the core functions of the organization).[21] Examples of value-added services according to the authors are visitor centers, shops, cafes, and permanent/temporary exhibits. And many customers expect such "added-value services" to be the norm or a core function. Not surprisingly, those that worked in the library had a hard time making or understanding the distinctions between the two concepts. And so, attempting to distinguish between core and value added is probably meaningless from the customer's perspective.

What is important for any library is to be able to understand how the library adds value in the life of the customer recognizing that each customer comes to the library (physically or virtually) with many different needs at different times of his or her life. The traditional value-adding activities performed by librarians and other staff members assume that certain activities continue to add value throughout the life of the customer. But since this is no longer the case, it is much more important to understand how library services benefit the customer in the short term and lead to long-term impact in a community.

Other Models

Tefko Saracevic and Paul Kantor developed a taxonomy and framework, based on the vocabulary of users, for establishing the value that may arise from using library and information services.[22] They suggest that an individual has three possible reasons to use a library or information service: (1) to work on a task or project, (2) for personal reasons, or (3) to get an object or information or to perform an activity.

They assert that when an individual interacts with a library service, there are three areas of interaction that should be considered:

- *Resources*—Users are concerned about
  - *Availability*—is the desired item, resource, or service obtainable?
  - *Accessibility*—how easy can the resource or service be obtained?
  - *Quality*—how timely, complete, and accurate is a resource or service?

- *Use of resources, services*—customers can be asked to assess:

  - How *convenient* is a resource or service?
  - What challenges are encountered when accessing a resource or service?
  - What *frustrations* are confronted when using a resource or service?
  - How *successful* is the customer when using a resource or service?
  - What level of *effort* is needed to access a resource or use a service?

- *Operations and environment*—customers could assess:

  - How clear and reasonable are the library's *policies and procedures*?
  - Are the *facilities* well organized?[23]
  - How knowledgeable, helpful, and friendly are *staff members*?
  - Is the *equipment* reliable and easy to use?

While these inward-looking library measures are important, Saracevic and Kantor focused on the outcomes, impact, or results that library resources and services have on the organization. In the view of the authors, an "organization" can be defined as an academic institution, a for-profit or not-for-profit concern, or as a community. Having a reason to use the library and interacting with a set of resources or services, the outcomes can be grouped into six categories:

- *Cognitive results.* The library's resources or services have an impact in the mind of an individual. The individual may have

  - Substantiated or reinforced a belief or knowledge
  - Refreshed memory of a fact or detail
  - Changed in viewpoint, outlook, or perspective
  - Gotten an idea with a slightly different or tangential perspective (oftentimes called serendipity)
  - Learned something new

- *Affective results.* Use of library resources or services may influence or have an emotional impact on the individual. The individual may experience

  - A sense of confidence, trust, and/or reliability
  - A sense of happiness, comfort, and/or good feelings
  - A sense of accomplishment, satisfaction, and/or success
  - A sense of frustration and/or failure

- *Meeting expectations.* When using a library resource or information service, the individual may

  - Be getting what was expected, needed, or sought
  - Be getting nothing
  - Be getting too much
  - Have confidence in what was received
  - Be disappointed that his or her expectations were not met—and seek substitute sources or action

- *Accomplishments*. In terms of tasks, an individual

  - Is able to make better-quality decisions
  - Achieve higher-quality performance
  - Is able to point to the next course of action
  - Can proceed to the next stage in a project
  - Discovers knowledgeable people or other sources of information
  - Improves a procedure, plan, or policy

Joanne Marshall, for one, has focused on improved decision-making as an important outcome in some of her studies that examine the impact of library services.[24]

- *Time aspects*. As a result of using library resources or services, an individual may

  - Save time
  - Need to wait for service
  - Waste time
  - Need time to learn how to use a resource or service
  - Experience a service that ranges from fast to quite slow

Several studies have demonstrated the value of information services on the basis of time saved, improved work quality, and increased staff productivity.[25] And Michael Koenig noted a positive correlation between the costs of information services and corporate productivity.[26]

- *Money aspects*. Using the library may save money or assist in generating new revenues. The individual may be able to provide an

  - Estimate of the dollar value of outcomes or impacts obtained from a resource or service
  - Estimate of the amount of money saved due to use of the library
  - Estimate of the customer's cost in using the service
  - Estimate of what may be spent on a substitute service
  - Estimate of value lost where the library resources and services were not available

Other researchers, such as José-Marie Griffiths, Don King and Alison Keyes, have demonstrated that the cost of a professional user's time (and effort) to obtain information from various sources far exceeds the cost of providing library services.[27] Carol Tenopir of the University of Tennessee has been heading up a multiyear LibValue Project designed to identify the financial impacts of library services in academic libraries (visit the project's website for a thorough ROI & Value Bibliography plus copies of papers and presentations—http://libvalue.cci.utk.edu/). And I prepared a summary article exploring the strengths and weaknesses of using ROI as a means of identifying the library's value, especially in the public library arena.[28]

Involving users of library services and collections is a relatively straightforward way to assess the impact or outcomes. It is interesting to note that the first three outcomes (cognitive results, affective results, and expectations) will likely translate in some way to having an impact on the last three results (accomplishments, time aspects, and money aspects).

David Lewis, a thoughtful librarian and dean of the Indiana University–Purdue University Indianapolis Libraries, has suggested that it is more important to focus on what libraries are *for* rather than on what they *do*.[29] Lewis asserts that libraries are the means by which communities and organizations provide information subsidies. These subsidies are important, since if left to themselves, individuals will not or can't acquire the information resources they need to lead productive lives. The result of these subsidies is that libraries provide a public good. In the paper-based world, libraries provided access to scarce information resources by creating and maintaining collections. However, in the digital environment, the value of the physical collections is rapidly diminishing (given the ready availability of licensed digital resources), which suggests that libraries need to know how to add value in ways they have not done so in the past.

Ways Libraries Add Value—The Customer's Perspective

The primary ways libraries add value are through the knowledge, skills, and expertise of librarians (and other trained staff members). The end result is that when someone uses the library collections and services, he or she benefits by

- *Saving time.* While an individual could (or thinks he or she can) perform a task, the professional librarian can often complete the task more efficiently. In almost every case, the cost per hour of librarian time is going to be less than the cost per hour of our customer's time.[30]

In many cases, if a librarian performs a task for a customer, this frees up time for the customer to be performing other and potentially more important activities. Releasing time for library customers has the potential to add real value to an organization.

- *Speed of service.* The speed with which some library services can be provided may be a real benefit, especially in times of crisis or short deadlines. The speed and accuracy of information services in many cases goes beyond simply saving time of the client.
- *Providing a better service through expertise.* Traditionally, libraries have provided added value by being able to provide a higher-quality service than the client might achieve. In many ways, the knowledge, expertise, and skills of librarians are an underappreciated and untapped resource. This is especially true in the area of information retrieval although this value has diminished considerably in the past 10–15 years—especially in the eyes of our customers.
- *Information discovery.* Many librarians, especially librarians located in special and academic libraries, know that they can often locate information and other resources that prove to be of value to the customer that the customer, on his or

her own, would never have discovered independently—due to lack of skills, lack of time, lack of persistence, or lacking the knowledge of where to search.

- *Saving money.* Obviously, being able to borrow materials rather than having to purchase them creates considerable saving for each library customer. The more each customer borrows, the more money he or she saves. Being able to download electronic articles and other eResources made accessible by a library also saves the cost of paying for each article, but the customer also saves considerable time as he or she is able to accomplish this task anytime, anywhere.

The value a library and a librarian may provide will change and shift with time, and as the needs of the customer will also change depending upon the task to be performed, the perception of the library's value in the mind of the customer will also change.

Designing Services around Outcomes

With this understanding, it is possible to be much more responsive to customers and their various needs by designing new services and changing existing services (as well as dropping some services) to provide more value to each of the customers.

Yet, in conversations with librarians, I constantly hear that the value of their activities and the value of the library are all wrapped up in the library's physical collections or the services that complement the collections. However, in a thought-provoking essay, Scott Plutchak makes an important point:

> If we are thinking about the future of librarianship, then we have to be thinking about the purposes for which we have been building those collections. If the end point of librarianship is to build collections, then I think we are facing the end of our profession. You can only stretch the "building collections" metaphor so far in the digital age. But I do not think that is, or ever has been, the end point of librarianship—even when it has, in fact, for some of us, occupied nearly all of our time and attention during our normal working days.[31]

In addition, the manual and automated systems developed by librarians over the last century or so have one common characteristic: tracking the location and transfer of physical objects in and out of buildings. The catalog reveals what the organization owns and can also track its actual current location—on the shelf, checked out, and so forth. But it must also be acknowledged that these systems have real limitations in that they are tracking physical objects and all of the limitations that physicality imposes on systems and processes as noted by David Weinberger in his stimulating book *Everything Is Miscellaneous*.[32] It is true that with the introduction of a web-based discovery service, the limitations of a library's catalog are substantially reduced (but not totally eliminated in my opinion).

The diminished value that existing processes bring to the table has been identified and discussed to some degree in our professional literature. For example, Roy Tennant in two recent blog postings suggested that the evolution from the MARC cataloging standard was going to be confusing, messy, frustrating, and uncertain—and it has been and continues to be.[33] Who can really say why libraries are moving to Resource

Description and Access (RDA)? Roy went on to suggest that there are host of problems with MARC, presented in no logical order, that include the following:

- Lack of standardized statements/declarations when those would be useful
- Inability to unambiguously encode important characteristics
- Overreliance on punctuation for semantic purposes
- Some MARC fields are ambiguous
- Some information is presented redundantly
- MARC has needless complexity
- Lack of sufficient granularity
- Some MARC free-text fields have formatting requirements
- Punctuation in free-text fields is sometimes meaningful, sometimes not
- Some MARC fields are coded with hidden assumptions
- Some MARC fields are semantically complex
- Lack of easy extensibility
- Technical marginalization (MARC is isolated to the library community)
- MARC has a long tail—while the standard has many tags, most are rarely used

Lorcan Dempsey, the head of OCLC Research and Chief Strategist, has argued that library data should work harder . . . for libraries.[34] That is one of the reasons why OCLC has made its WorldCat database available to Google and other search engines. Thus, when you search within Google Books, you see a link along the left-hand side of the screen to "Find in a library." If you click on this link, you will discover what nearby libraries have this book—and how many miles from your present location the library is located.

Rick Anderson, the associate director at the University of Utah Library, has asserted that libraries do not fail to offer value but rather the value of libraries is not recognized and is being diminished due to three problems:

- *Perception matters more than reality*. In reality, the future of the library will be determined by how patrons act (if they use or do not use library services) rather than the value offered by libraries. If students and faculty members believe that they find what they need on the Internet (whether their beliefs are correct or not), the effect on the library is the same.
- *Patrons genuinely do not need librarians as much as they once did*. As more and more quality resources are accessible via the Internet, the use of reference services has declined markedly in research libraries. Clearly, library users (or former users) are finding information without the need to use librarians.
- *Value not valued is not valuable*. Libraries are operating within the constraints of a free market except that the currency is the time and attention of the customer. The customer makes a value judgment to determine whether visiting the library in some way is going to be worthwhile.

Despite the fact that a majority of libraries have moved into the digital environment, many of these libraries Anderson suggests continue to maintain traditional processes and practices in an "increasingly desperate death grip." For example, libraries continue to build physical and digital collections that are "fenced off" from the larger world. These same libraries devote resources to encourage their users to initiate their searching within the boundaries of artificially constrained collections.

Surplus Value

In another article, Rick Anderson makes the point that libraries are plagued by the problem of surplus value.[35] Karl Marx thoroughly explored the concept of surplus value, which he defined as the value workers create, that is, in excess of the wages they earn. Anderson explores the flip side of the same coin and suggests that organizations (including libraries) can add more value to their services than their customers actually want or need. Anderson suggests that libraries are "selling" access to information in exchange for the customer's time and attention (customers need to learn how to use the different user interface of multiple publishers and consolidators). The key for any organization is to deliver the right value in the right amounts (costs are proportional to value) for each customer. And the institution's mission and the customer's behavior best determine "rightness." Libraries have created a number of services that were once highly valued and used, but sadly this is no longer the case for some services. And services that are not used (or rarely used) provide no value in the life of the customer.

Karen Calhoun used the phrase "excess capacity" as a synonym for "surplus value" in her well-regarded report on cataloging practices.[36] That is, catalogers routinely provide more detailed and accurate information about a work than that is needed by scholars and other users of the catalog. And providing this unappreciated surplus value costs a considerable amount of money that could be better spent providing value that the customer actually wants and needs. Expending resources for one activity has an opportunity cost in that the resources could have been used to provide an alternative service.

Summary

In this increasingly digital world that we live in, how do libraries appear from the perspective of the user? Nat Torkington delivered a speech designed to provoke discussion and debate during a conference of the National and State Librarians of Australasia:

> You want a massive digital collection: SCAN THE STACKS! You agonize over digital metadata and the purity thereof . . . And you offer crap access. If I ask you to talk about your collections, I know that you will glow as you describe the amazing treasures you have. When you go for money for digitization projects, you talk up the incredible cultural value . . . But then if I look at the results of those digitization projects, I find the shittiest websites on the planet. It's like

a gallery spent all its money buying art and then just stuck the paintings in supermarket bags and leaned them against the wall.[37]

The library does not create value, but rather the customer creates value through the use of collections and services. As customers learn something through the use of an information resource or service, they must determine how they can use and/or apply the information within the context of their existing knowledge and prior experiences. Ultimately, the goal of each library is to recognize that it is in the value creation business. **Libraries exist to facilitate value creation in the lives of their customers.**

Main idea:	Robert Taylor's value-added model
Opposing view:	David Weinberger's book *Everything Is Miscellaneous*
Key concepts:	Value-added model, data–information–knowledge–wisdom (DIKW) hierarchy, value-added activities
What has changed?:	Libraries no longer have a monopoly over the access to valuable information resources
Catalyst:	The Internet, competition
Open debate:	How can cultural organizations add value when the foundations of technology and society around them are in a constant state of flux?

Notes

1. Ted Nelson. Computer Lib. Chicago: Hugo's Book Service, 1974, p. 76.
2. Shiyali Ranganathan. *The Five Laws of Library Science*. London: Edward Goldston, Ltd, 1931.
3. Lynn Silipigni Connaway and Ixchel Faniel. *Reordering Ranganathan: Shifting User Behaviors, Shifting Priorities*. Dublin, OH: OCLC Research, 2014. Available at http://www.oclc .org/content/dam/research/publications/library/2014/oclcresearch-reordering-ranga nathan-2014.pdf
4. Robert Taylor. *Value-Added Processes in Information Systems*. Norwood, NJ: Ablex, 1986.
5. A search in November 2015 on Google Scholar identified 697 citations.
6. Giannis Tsakonas and Christos Papatheodorou. "Exploring Usefulness and Usability in the Evaluation of Open Access Digital Libraries." *Information Processing and Management*, 44, 2008, 1234–1250.
7. Susan MacMullin and Robert Taylor. "Problem Dimensions and Information Traits." *The Information Society*, 3 (1), 1984, 91–111.
8. Joseph Matthews. "Valuing Information, Information Services, and the Library." *portal: Libraries and the Academy*, 13 (1), 2013, 91–112.
9. Chaim Zins. "Conceptual Approaches or Defining Data, Information, and Knowledge." *Journal of the American Society for Information Science and Technology*, 58 (94), 2007, 479–493.
   See also, Jay Bernstein. "The Data-Information-Knowledge-Wisdom Hierarchy and Its Antithesis." *Proceedings from North American Symposium on Knowledge Organization Volume 2*. Available at http://dlist.sir.arizona.edu/2633/

10. T.S. Eliot. "The Rock," in *T. S. Eliot: The Contemporary Reviews,* edited by Jewel Spears Brooker. Cambridge: Cambridge University Press, 2004, 297.

11. Russell Ackoff. "From Data to Wisdom." *Journal of Applied Systems Analysis,* 16, 1989, 3–9.

12. Eleanor Jo Rodger. "Value and Vision." *American Libraries,* 33 (10), November 2002, 50.

13. Gary Deane. "Bridging the Value Gap: Getting Past Professional Values to Customer Value in the Public Library." *Public Libraries,* 42 (5), September/October 2003, 315.

14. Charles Cole. "A Theory of Information Need for Information Retrieval that Connects Information to Knowledge." *Journal of the American Society for Information Science and Technology,* 62 (7), 2011, 1216–1231.

15. Katriina Bystrom and Preben Hansen. "Conceptual Framework for Tasks in Information Systems." *Journal of the American Society for Information Science and Technology,* 56 (10), 2005, 1050–1061.

16. David Pimentel. "The KO Roots of Taylor's Value-Added Model." *Proceedings of the North American Symposium on Knowledge Organization,* Volume 2. Available at http://dlist.sir.ari zona.edu/2632/

17. Margit Scholl, Peter Ehrlich, Andreas Wiesner-Steiner, and Denis Edich. *The Project TEDS: TEDS Framework Integration into the Moodle Platform for User-Specific Quality Assurance of Learning Scenarios.* Presentation at the 2014 47th Hawaii International Conference on System Science, 1935–1945.

18. Howard Rosenbaum. "Information Use Environments and Structuration: Towards an Integration of Taylor and Gibbens." *Proceedings of the ASIS Annual Conference,* 30, 1993, 235–245.

19. Mike Eisenberg and Lee Dirks. "Taylor's Value-Added Model: Still Relevant After All These Years." *Presentation at the iConference February 27—March 1, 2008, at UCLA, Los Angeles, CA.* Available at http://faculty.washington.edu/mbe/Eisenberg_Dirks_Taylor_Value-Added_Modified_2008.pdf

20. Hans Scholl, Michael Eisenberg, Lee Dirks, and Timothy Carlson. "The TEDS Framework for Assessing Information Systems from a Human Actors Perspective: Extending and Repurposing Taylor's Value-Added Model. *Journal of the American Society for Information Science and Technology,* 62 (4), 2011, 789–804.

21. Judith Broady-Preston and Wendy Swain. "What Business Are We In? Value Added Services, Core Business and National Library Performance." *Performance Measurement and Metrics,* 13 (2), 2012, 107–120.

22. Tefko Saracevic and Paul B. Kantor. "Studying the Value of Library and Information Services. Part I. Establishing a Theoretical Framework." *Journal of the American Society of Information Science,* 48 (6), 1997, 527–542.

    Tefko Saracevic and Paul B. Kantor. "Studying the Value of Library and Information Services. Part II. Methodology and Taxonomy." *Journal of the American Society of Information Science,* 48 (6), 1997, 543–563.

23. At the time of this study, users had only one option—the physical library. Today, a great many of library users visit the virtual library so a related question that should be asked would be: Is the library's website well organized and easy to navigate?

24. Joanne Marshall. *The Impact of the Special Library on Corporate Decision-Making.* Washington DC: Special Libraries Association, 1993.

    See also Joanne Marshall. "The Impact of the Hospital Library on Clinical Decision-Making." *Bulletin of the Medical Library Association,* 80 (2), 1992, 169–178.

25. S. Dresley and A. Lacombe. *Value of Information and Information Services*. Washington DC: Volpe National Transportation Systems Center, 1998.

  See also A. J. Million, Sheila Hatchell, and Roberto Sarmiento. *Proving Your Library's Value: A Toolkit for Transportation Librarie*s. Jefferson City, MO: Missouri Department of Transportation, September 2012.

26. Michael Koenig. "The Importance of Information Services for Productivity 'Under-Recognized' and Under-Invested." *Special Libraries*, 83 (3), Fall 1992, 199–210.

27. José-Marie Griffiths and Don King. *Special Libraries: Increasing the Information Edge.* Washington, DC: Special Libraries Association, 1993.

  Alison Keyes. "The Value of the Special Library: Review and Analysis." *Special Libraries*, 86 (3), 1995, 172–187.

28. Joseph R. Matthews. "What's the Return on ROI? The Benefits and Challenges of Calculating Your Library's Return on Investment." *Library Leadership & Management*, 25 (1), 2011, 1–14.

29. David Lewis. "What If Libraries Are Artifact Bound Institutions?" *Information Technology and Libraries*, 7, December 1998, 191–197.

30. While I acknowledge that this statement is a bit depressing, it indeed is reality. Consider the salary of a lawyer compared with a librarian in a law firm, and consider the salary of a full professor in a university compared with the salary of a reference librarian.

31. Scott Plutchak. "Breaking the Barriers of Time and Space: The Dawning of the Great Age of Librarians." *Journal of the Medical Library Association*, 100 (1), January 2012, 10–19.

32. David Weinberger. *Everything Is Miscellaneous: The Power of the New Digital Disorder*. New York: Holt, 2008.

33. Roy Tennant. "The Post-MARC Era, Part 1: If It's Televised, It Can't Be the Revolution." *The Digital Shift blog*. April 17, 2013. Available at http://www.thedigitalshift.com/2013/04/roy-tennant-digital-libraries/the-post-marc-era-part-1/

  See also, Roy Tennant. "The Post-MARC Era, Part 2: Where the Problems Lie." *The Digital Shift blog*. May 8, 2013. Available at http://www.thedigitalshift.com/2013/05/roy-tennant-digital-libraries/the-post-marc-era-part-2-where-the-problems-lie-part-2/

34. Lorcan Dempsey. "Reconfiguring the Library Systems environment." Guest Editorial. *portal: Libraries and the Academy*, 8 (2), April 2008, 111–120.

35. Rick Anderson. "Peer to Peer Review: The Problem of Surplus Value." *Library Journal*, June 1, 2013, 14, 16.

36. Karen Calhoun. *The Changing Nature of the Catalog and Its Integration with Other Discovery Tools*. Prepared for the Library of Congress. Ithaca, NY: Cornell University Library, March 17, 2006. See also Karen Coyle. The Evolving Catalog: Cataloging Tech from Scrolls to Computers. *American Libraries*, January/February 2016, 48–53.

37. Nat Torkington. "Libraries: Where It All Went Wrong." November 2011. Available at http://nathan.torkington.com/blog/2011/11/23/libraries-where-it-all-went-wrong/

3

The Times Are Rapidly Changin'

The greatest danger in times of turbulence
is not the turbulence:
It is to act with yesterday's logic.

Peter Drucker[1]

How [are we] to comprehend an age in which . . .
we find ourselves enmeshed in a huge information-processing system,
one that seems almost to have a life of its own,
and to be leading us headlong into a future
that we can't clearly see, yet can't really avoid.

Robert Wright[2]

To say that we are living in an age of disruption is stating the obvious and is, in many ways, a tired (but true) cliché. The scale of this disruption is almost impossible to comprehend. Powerful industries such as broadcast television, newspapers, and popular magazines either have lost their power or no longer exist (or are mere illusions of their former glory) as the result of the Internet and its many service offerings. The amount of change that people have had to cope with is simply staggering, and this is true for people in more developed countries as well as people located in third world countries around the globe.

And many people feel that the pace of change has been accelerating in the past two decades (and in many ways it has), yet Grace Kelley warned librarians in 1934, "Any institution which does not change, adapt itself to the times, and become a part of the onward 'drive of change,' will be pushed aside to be left perhaps for a time to make a harmless life of its own."[3] And many contemporary librarians believe that if libraries do nothing and continue to focus on traditional activities, then libraries will become invisible (or irrelevant).

Trends Impacting Society

Many of the factors that influence the course of libraries are now generated primarily from *outside* the library community. The forces impacting society and libraries in particular are grouped into four categories: technology, the Internet, data and information, and the resulting disruption.

Technology Trends

Clearly, one of the biggest impacts that all societies are experiencing is the result of **the integrated chip**—the engine that runs our computers, our cell phones, iPads, iPods, automobiles, appliances, and so much more. As Gordon Moore, one of the founders of Intel, noted more than two decades ago, the number of components on any given chip doubles every 18 months, while the price is held constant or in some cases decreases (this is now known as Moore's law). The result for the end user is that the processing power of any given device doubles every 18–24 months, which accounts for the seemingly endless introduction of the "new and improved" version of almost every electronic device on a similar timeline.

Handheld portable devices are winning. Following the release of the iPhone, the introduction of Amazon's Kindle, the tablet (notably the iPad), and other competing smartphone competitors, there has been a move away from desktop and "open" web resources to value-added, copyright-protected apps (the App Store has had more than 50 billion apps downloaded).[4]

We now live in an anywhere, anytime environment—people expect that content will be conveyed to their handheld mobile devices right now. Today, there are more mobile phone subscriptions than the total U.S. population. Mobile services are no longer considered a luxury but rather a commodity (and some people behave as if a mobile phone is a necessity such as air and water). Thus, information content must be able to be "squeezed" so that it can be delivered to a very small handheld device. Mobile devices are being used as a new means of sustaining, embodying, and creating social networks that bring people together. Lorcan Dempsey suggests that mobile devices alter the consumption patterns of individuals in fundamental ways.[5] People connect and share themselves through "social objects" (photos, videos, music, or other objects) and thus become connectors to content for others.

Our interactions with "machines" will fundamentally change as more devices become connected to the Internet and on and in our bodies. As we increasingly employ devices that monitor our bodies while we exercise (think Fitbit) or simply track us throughout the day (and night), these data will be accessible to others to assist us in leading a more healthy way of life. Other devices and software will take on roles and responsibilities once reserved to ourselves, our family, and our colleagues at work.

Internet Trends

The Pew Research Center's Internet and American Life Project reports that in late 2013, 70 percent of Americans have broadband at home, and only 2 percent still are using dial-up access.[6] And the Census Bureau found in a recent survey that 98 percent of U.S. households live in areas where they have access to broadband Internet connections.[7] This broadband access opens up a whole new world of possibilities, and the amount of traffic devoted to visiting websites (the World Wide Web) is quickly diminishing while traffic devoted to streaming and other uses is gobbling up all available bandwidth.[8]

But don't get the idea that things are slowing down on the Internet—they aren't. Growth continues at astonishing rates. Consider what happens in *a single day*:

- 3.175 billion Internet users worldwide—70% of them use it daily
- 2 million smart phones are sold
- Over 400 billion emails are sent—about 70 percent are spam!
- 1 million active mobile social users added
- 3 million videos shared on Facebook
- 350 million stickers shared on Facebook, over 4 billion likes on Facebook
- Facebook is hit 5 billion times
- Tumblr has 108 million posts
- 70 million photos posted on Instagram, 2.5 billion likes on Instagram
- Over 708 million tweets
- Over 5 billion Google searches
- Over 8 billion YouTube videos viewed
- 1 billion videos watched over mobile phones.[9]

The Internet has been so successful because it was built on a number of important principles that are still as valid today as when they were first conceived. These principles according to Neil Gershenfeild, Raffi Krikorian, and Danny Cohen include:

- Each device uses the Internet Protocol (IP), which avoids the need to introduce additional standards as new devices are connected to the 'Net.
- Two devices do not require a third to communicate with one another.
- Each input–output device has its own identity.
- The use of packets allows for the transmission of data regardless of the physical medium that conveys them—electrical current, radio waves, or light pulses.
- The use of open standards allows for continuing innovation.[10]

The end result is that the Internet is now *the environment* that cultural organizations must consider when planning the future of their service offerings, the ways they communicate with their customers, and how they engage with those interested in the cultural organization using social media. The Internet is compelling because you are in control—you *pull* what you want to see and do. Watching television (even with several hundred channels) is about content that is *pushed* to you.

Developed during the information age, the Internet now contains the largest collection of information known to man with the greatest extent of topics delivered right to you anywhere, anytime, on any device. Libraries, archives, museums, and now the Internet reflect our left-brain attempts to organize, understand, and disseminate information about our world.

The Deeper Web

Only a small percent of what's available online is visible to a search engine. The rest is buried in proprietary databases. It is possible to categorize the content that is accessible via the Internet into three groups:

The public web—This is the web that people see when searching and browsing (Google estimates that it indexes some 30 trillion individual pages [as of March 2013]).[12] Obviously, the number of pages has increased significantly in the past few years.

The deep web—This portion of the web is typically proprietary (requires you to log in with a password). Examples of the deep web include Facebook, Craigslist, and Grainger. While the estimates vary, it is safe to say that the search engines do not see tens of trillions of documents.

The private web—Encompasses a variety of content ranging from corporate intranets, private networks, and some subscription-based services. It is safe to say that the private web "hides" some three to five trillion documents not seen in a search engine.

Simon Waldman created the title of his wonderful book *Creative Disruption*,[11] by combining the concept of "disruptive innovations" (developed by Clayton Christensen in his books *The Innovator's Dilemma* and *The Innovator's Solution*) and Joseph Schumpeter's theory of "creative destruction" as articulated in his book *Business Cycles*.

Web 2.0 is about the human aspects of connectivity and interactivity (Web 2.0 is an overworked phrase, originally created by Tim O'Reilly,[13])—it's about personalization, conversations, and interpersonal networking. Some of the characteristics of the Web 2.0 concept include: as software gets better the more people use it, software is in perpetual beta, user behavior is not predetermined (and thus should be tracked and the software adjusted as you gather data about the interactions of people and the software), a rich user experience is crucial, and content is accessible and people have the right to remix (with some rights reserved or acknowledged).

Online social networks are popular since they enable people to find others and spread information imaginatively among friends and friends of friends. This results in information being pushed to people rather than being pulled as a result of searching. Issues of trust, copyright, liability, risk, and privacy are not fully understood by many people who use social networks so that whatever they post online can have serious ramifications as content once posted rarely disappears. Benkler suggests that we are witnessing the "networked information economy" in which individuals engage in co-ordinated and cooperative activities and that nonmarket mechanisms are playing an increasingly important role in or daily lives.[14]

A word of caution at this point would seem in order. Jaron Lanier, viewed as a visionary by some and an alarmist by others, raises some significant issues in his new book *Who Owns the Future?*[15] Lanier suggests that there are three significant issues that should be discussed:

1. If we treat information frivolously as expressed in the phrase "information wants to be free," it makes it difficult for an increasing number of people to earn a living and self-defeating in the long run.

2. We are living in the world of one-way linking only while Ted Nelson, who invented the concept of hyperlinks, envisioned a world where people could be really creative by combining ideas, and the combination would lead to a second link (with a micro-payment coming back to the creator whenever someone used the creator's ideas or other creations).[16]

3. Lanier argues that the Internet has moved to a series of large platforms, such as Facebook, that he calls "siren servers" that hold billions of people hostages without sharing the wealth they generate with the people that built the platform and control the wealth. Cause for a pause to consider the merits of Lanier's arguments.

The web has become an instrument for participation. Beyond the passive act of receiving information, users can comment, collaborate, create, and publish their own individualized content—in whatever format they want. More important, content does not stand alone—other people can comment, share to others, rate and debate with others who also like to participate at some level. The barriers to free expression have fallen alongside growing engagement with the reuse and recycling of digital objects, often-cultural assets, that many call a "mashup." Among the many ways to participate are:

- *Social bookmarking* allows the saving of bookmarks to a public website and "tagging" them with keywords. Tools such as del.icio.us or CiteULike have become very popular.

- *Wikipedia* is an editable "encyclopedia" with content contributed, edited, and re-edited by others. Wikipedia entries may be found in more than 200 languages—there are more than 5 million English-language articles (as of November 2015).

- *Blogs* have become a huge source of information for many people with more than 100 million blogs worldwide. Technorati, which tracks all things related to blogging, suggests that about 60 percent of bloggers are hobbyists, 18 percent are professionals who supplement their income blogging, 13 percent are entrepreneur's blogging about their industry, and 8 percent are corporate bloggers. Today, many people blog rather than writing peer-review journal articles or writing a book with the result that information is being fragmented.

- *News sites* are morphing into personalized news delivery systems. Sites such as Google News and Yahoo! allow the individual to customize what content he or she sees, while other sites such as Digg and Memorandum reflect the top stories from the user's perspective.

- *Sharing photos and videos* is huge. The amount of content downloaded to such sites as Flickr, Pinterest, Instagram, and YouTube plus the content being shared on Facebook is truly staggering. People share what they download and others rate the content, and join with others interested in the same content to form groups.

Growing power of the individual. As people gain access to a number of options to accomplish a task and an increasing variety of information about each option is available, people become more demanding about everything. Convenience becomes an important overriding factor in how people make decisions. Consider how quickly folks moved to embrace the iTunes store so they could purchase specific music tracks rather than pre-packaged albums.[17]

We are moving into an era whereby everything will be connected on the Internet of Everything. Soon we will see a network of networks, known as interdevice internet-working, where billions and even trillions of devices will be connected together and automatically transmit data. As noted by Robert Metcalfe, a well-known technology pioneer, as more everyday objects, people, and data become connected, the power of the Internet grows *exponentially*. This observation, now known as Metcalfe's law, suggests that the power of the network is greater than the sum of its parts, making the Internet of Everything, sometimes called the Internet of Things, very powerful indeed. A wide variety of sensors use the connectivity of the Internet to measure and report a plethora of data. This data is then used by a variety of software programs and apps to create new types of smart apps and services for our bodies, homes, buildings, cities, transportation and agriculture—to name only a few. Like electricity, the future Internet will be less visible and yet become more deeply embedded in people's lives.

The law of unintended consequences is wonderfully illustrated by the reality that several thousand trees in Melbourne, Australia, receive emails from people who love a specific tree(s) and send greetings and love letters, ask questions, and report problems each year.[18]

The proliferation of microprocessors
and the growth of distributed communications networks
hold mysteries as deep as the origins of life
[and] the source of our own intelligence. . . .

George Dyson[19]

Data and Information

The information landscape is getting denser, deeper, and more diverse. The decreasing costs and increasing availability of digital storage, the ability to digitally tag any physical space or object, the ability to symbolize information in multiple media formats, and the development of new forms of genetic information means we are collecting more data about ourselves and our world than ever before. The end result is that people now have numerous choices to meet an information need. In addition to having access to a veritable flood of information, people now expect that they will be able to interact with information in multiple ways, reshaping and repurposing it to best fit their needs.

Digital technology **transforms the process of copying** from a cumbersome and inefficient activity in the analog world into a painless, inexpensive, and almost perfect process. One of the by-products of this trend is that creative works are becoming smaller—tracks rather than albums, posts rather than a complete blog, articles rather than an issue of journal, chapters rather than a complete book.

Kevin Kelly suggests that rather than looking at a book as a package that we will, over time, begin to think of each word as an entity that can be linked, cross-referenced, cited, indexed, extracted, annotated, analyzed, remixed, and reassembled in new and creative ways.[20]

The value of data is in its reuse and transformation. Many websites provide open access to their data and tools with the expectation that others will find new and creative uses for their content (sometimes referred to as a mashup). On the web, a mashup refers to the use of content from more than one source to create a new enriched service. The content or data are made available by a website using an open application programming interface or API.

In addition, websites capture information about your preferences and use that information to recommend other related and complement products or services. Buy a book on Amazon and see what other books might be of interest (based on the purchasing habits of others). Travel to another city and receive offers of discounts for hotels and car rentals. Websites spend a lot of time analyzing click data so that they can learn, test, and engage their customers.

The web also knows where you are using information from your smartphone and other personal devices. Combining your location with your preferences allows businesses to send you "instant" discount coupons as you wander in a store or drive by a Starbucks.

The nature of information itself has forever been changed from the domain of the experts, as evidenced by publications in peer-review journals, to a world where everyone can create and cocreate information. The Internet is the first medium that encourages and fosters both one-to-one communication and communication to and within a group (many-to-many). We can choose what information we receive, and it also comes to us from friends and colleagues.

_____

The moment we are living through,
the moment our historical generation is living through,
is the largest increase in expressive capability in human history.

Clay Shirky[21]

_____

Friends, friends of friends, colleagues, and individuals we encounter online who have similar interests are the source of information for a vast majority of people. Whether through chat, Flickr, Facebook, or other social networking sites, relationships develop online, enabled by the exchange of text messages, photos, music, profiles, and so forth. Given that people are constantly connected to each other and share a significant amount by creating, mixing, and recreating information, people take existing content, add their own views and creativity, and republish it in a variety of ways. Access and exchange of information happens in real time, 24/7 in the always-on environment that we live in today.

We are leaving the Information Age and entering the Recommendation Age. Today information is ridiculously easy to get; you practically trip over it in the street. Information gathering is no longer the issue—making smart decisions based on the information is now the trick. Recommendations serve as shortcuts through the thicket of information.[22]

For the individual, everything presented online is competing for our attention leading inevitably to **competition** and **confusion** between information providers (commercial and otherwise) and offerings by libraries.

The manner in which information is being delivered is being shaped by the "Google effect."[23] Google's success can be accounted for, in part, because it is:

- *Simple*. The crisp, clean (read empty), and simple search screen still sets Google apart from its competitors.
- *Intuitive*. Google requires no assistance, no prior knowledge, and most importantly no training to use it effectively. Google has removed the complexity of the search process so the search process is easy and intuitive.
- *Ubiquitous*. Google is merely a click away in most people's browser, and for many, it is the default opening screen. No need to log in but simply enter a search phrase and off you go.
- *Relevant*. The "PageRank" relevancy rankings developed by Google are clearly "good enough" as less than ten percent of users move beyond the first screen.
- *Fast*. Results of searches are retrieved with astonishing speed, which people have come to expect.
- *Free.*

While the use of Google may upset librarians who know of its limitations, clearly the real world of "free, convenient, and good enough" information trumps "requires some effort, less convenient, and excellent" information most of the time. The availability of this vast array of online information resources has led to the reality that online information must compete for attention leading to both competition and confusion between commercial information providers and library offerings. In short, convenience trumps quality every time (well almost always).

There is an increasing trend to disintermediation. As Luke Tredinnick noted in his informative book *Digital Information Culture*:

> The credibility of cultural artifacts in the modern age was in part influenced by the indexical association between content and form, and incorporated a conferred credibility forged in the link between the original creative act and the mechanical reproduction that acted as a kind of shorthand in the evaluation of individual artifacts or information . . . with the separation of material and form, this extrinsic means of validating knowledge has become more problematic.[24]

Publishers are being asked to explain the value that they bring to the relationship between author and reader, and this value is clearly declining as evidenced by the substantial increase in the number of self-published pBooks (print books) and eBooks.

The **volume, variety, and velocity of information** have fundamentally changed the rules of the game. We no longer sip from a water fountain that we turn on and off (as we do when we decide to visit a library) but rather are confronted with attempting to take a drink from a very large fire hose (the Internet) that delivers information in a continuous and unrelenting flood.

Attention is scarce, information is abundant. As network resources proliferate and social media platforms continue to evolve to take advantage of these information resources, the time or attention that people can pay to any one service is going to decline. People have an increasing number of choices that compete directly or indirectly with the library, its resources, and its services so that ease of use or convenience is taking on an ever-increasing role on the network.

Some of the less well-known competitors include "black market" journal articles sharing sites, use of Twitter to request a "free" journal article or industry report, online textbook sharing sites, software programs to override digital rights management from eBooks, and BitTorrenting sites.[25] Well, the list goes on and on.

But can we trust information we find on the Internet. With more and more content being posted in a born-digital format—documents, photographs, videos, audio files (songs)—that are still just strings of binary code (bits), the question that arises is: are we seeing what we believe we are seeing (or hearing)?. These bits can be easily altered using a variety of tools such as Photoshop. And so people develop a sense of truthiness. Farhad Manjoo develops the wide range of truthiness in a fascinating book *True Enough* in which he notes:

> Truthiness means you choose. But you're not deciding a reality; you're also deciding to trust that reality—which means deciding to distrust the others. Whatever you choose, you're making a decision to form a particularized trust. This is the essence of the new medium.[26]

The need to memorize information is rapidly disappearing. According to such writers as Clive Thompson,[27] David Brooks,[28] Peter Suderman,[29] Dan Tapscott,[30] and Nicholas Carr,[31] the Internet has become a replacement for rather than simply a supplement for our own personal memory. Given the speed with which we can retrieve information anytime, anywhere, we are off-loading information onto silicon.

Could it be we are heading toward a future where knowing is obsolete? Sugata Mitra explores this vital question, originally posed by Nicholas Negroponte of MIT fame, in a wonderful TED talk.[32] Mitra's big idea is to develop self-organizing learning environments where children around the world can explore and learn from one another using resources and mentoring from the cloud. His idea is simple—when you need to know something, you can find the answer in a few minutes using resources available on the Internet.

Digital text is fundamentally different from regular text. The stable context imposed by the physicality and uniformity of printed materials, such as books, is being reduced. Printed journals are being torn apart as people typically encounter an article that has been downloaded rather than a recent issue sitting in their to-read pile. The bindings of books are being shredded as folks happen upon individual chapters, charts, figures, and paragraphs accessible without the surrounding text. Texts from a wide variety of sources are gathered together by Internet search engines and made accessible in response to a specific query. Social networking sites identify connections between texts or parts of text based on their popularity and user behaviors. The result is that one text is likely to encounter a different set of adjacent texts depending on a wide variety of factors rather than being constrained by the production of a book or journal article. Texts and other digital artifacts are more often reused, recontextualized, and resituated. This repositioning of texts involves constant chaos as additional digital works are added, transformed, or deleted.

And as people use hyperlinks, the value of the digital artifact is re-energized as the result of the wider audience that the link makes possible. The meaning of a digital artifact may be changed or emphasized as the result of the interaction with other similarly linked items. The resulting pile of interlinked digital artifacts means that each item is subject to different contexts of discovery. In short, Luke Tredinnick suggests that:

> The distinction between text, non-text and context is withering. The meanings of texts are shifted from their semantic content to the spaces between different cultural forms locked in perpetual dialogue.[33]

Liberating knowledge from the world of atoms. Given the vast array of digital resources available on the Internet, it is important to recognize that we are no longer constrained in the ways we organize and describe these resources, as David Weinberger explores in considerable detail in his very entertaining and thought-provoking book *Everything Is Miscellaneous: The Power of the New World Disorder*.[34] David has suggested that the constraints of the physical world disappear in the digital world and that the tools and techniques that used to be effective are no longer valid. In short, we have moved from atoms to bits, and predetermined methods used to organize things and information are no longer necessary in the digital arena. Now we can reorganize knowledge from multiple perspectives to suit our changing needs. David asks a really important and fundamental question for librarians: Is it important to organize something for others, or let them create their own systems of organization?

_____

Discovery consists of seeing what everybody has seen and thinking what nobody has thought.

Albert Szent-Gyorgui[35]

_____

Capturing our data. As we move about the network, we leave very clear tracks of where we have been and what we do while visiting each website. These valuable data are gathered and used in a wide variety of ways ranging from improving the website by improving the online user experience (the domain of information architecture), suggesting what else might be of interest (Amazon recommendations), encouraging our participation by making it easy to rate goods and services, post reviews, and even shape our search experience (one Google user will see different results from another Google user entering the same search request)! This is accomplished as each website that we visit leaves a host of cookies that capture and report data about what we do. The cost of visiting many websites is that we exchange information about ourselves, and some companies, such as Google and Amazon, are really good about translating that directly into money (lots of money).

Distance matters less, but geography still matters. As more and more content is digitized, the separation of information from a physical container will continue. In addition, as more people work together in geographically separated teams, online tools are used to facilitate communication and to foster a sense of teamwork. Being "together apart" is becoming a more familiar aspect of both our working and personal lives (as we use tools such as Skype to stay connected). Yet, geography will continue to have an impact since it shapes our level of access individuals and groups will have to digital networks—pricing, legal constraints, and information technology infrastructure are still influenced by physical geography.

Place matters for everyone at some point in time. Consider how frequently you use your handheld digital device (smart phone) and are interested in finding a gas station, a bathroom, a restaurant, a metro station, a . . . . Using the global positioning system (GPS), your handheld device is able to locate you, and then a website or app uses this information to gather and present relevant information to you. In some cases, you can point your phone at a restaurant and immediately "see" reviews and the menu.

Every digital camera automatically records the latitude and longitude (GPS) coordinates of each photo. This information can subsequently be used in apps and websites for a variety of purposes.

Poor-quality copies of the original are an inferior substitute for the "original." Consider

'The Milkmaid', one of Johannes Vermeer's most famous paintings, depicts a scene of a woman quietly pouring milk into a bowl. During a survey the Rijksmuseum discovered that there were over 10,000 copies of the image on the Internet—mostly poor, yellowish reproductions. As a result of all of these low-quality copies on the web, [. . .] "people simply didn't believe the postcards in our museum shop were showing the original painting. This was the trigger for us to put high-resolution images of the original work with open metadata on the Web ourselves. Opening up our data is our best defence against the 'yellow Milkmaid'."[36]

Disruption Trends

This relentless parade of **scientific breakthroughs and advancing new technologies is unfolding on many fronts**. And it is clear that technology has had and continues to have a unique role in powering growth and transforming economies. Adopted technologies become embedded in capital—both physical and human—and contribute to improving the productivity of organizations. However, technology often is also disruptive, unseating older ways of doing things and rendering old skills and organizational processes irrelevant.

Manual Castells claims that the "network society" refers to interconnected nodes of organizations and individuals who have socially identified themselves through economy, society, or culture.[37] Castells suggests that the Internet-based network society arose as a result of three factors: (1) the information technology revolution, (2) the capitalism and statism restructuring, and (3) the 1960s' social movements of Europe and the United States.

The combination of digital information and information technologies is disrupting the marketplace. Almost 30 years ago, Michael Porter and Victor Millar asserted that the information revolution was affecting organizations in three vital ways:[38]

1. The rules of competition are changed as industry structure and rules of the game are changed.

2. Organizations now have new ways to create competitive advantage and thus leave their rivals in the dust.
3. Whole new market segments emerge that challenge industry leaders.

The early 20th-century economist Joseph Schumpeter suggested that a process of "creative destruction," which rearranges industry structures and replaces existing companies with newer entrants, often accompanied significant advances in national economies. More recently, Harvard University's Clayton Christensen has developed a theory of "disruptive innovation," which explains the demise of established players in an industry while seeing new firms and technologies arise quite quickly. Disruptive innovation transforms a product or service that historically has been fairly expensive (so only a few could afford it) by making the product or service more affordable and accessible thus expanding the market to many more people.[39] In short, this theory of disruptive innovation explains why things and services get easier to use, faster, and cheaper.

Illustrations of disruptive innovation abound—Napster, Amazon, and the Apple Store have led to the demise of Tower Records, Musicland, Virgin Records, and other record stores; small personal computers grew to replace most mainframe and minicomputers; digital photography made film obsolete in less than 20 years; Craigslist has had a huge negative impact on newspaper revenues for ads to sell almost everything; Netflix clearly provides a more convenient and valuable service (whether you receive DVDs in the mail or stream videos) than Blockbusters (especially the onerous late fees!)—which no longer exists; well, you get the idea, we could go on and on. These services are successful in part because they aggregate supply and demand. That is, they reduce the time and effort required to get things done by providing a service that connects multiple fulfillment services, and the service is so appealing that it creates additional demand.

One of the overwhelming forces driving the Internet is that it is possible to significantly reduce transaction costs within an organization and between people and organizations. Barriers that once constrained organizations have now been lifted in how we communicate, conduct research, share data and information, conduct commerce, and create communities. The worldwide competitive environment has forced companies to specialize on what they do really well that adds value and outsourcing other supportive activities such as information technology, human resources, finance, administrative processes, and operations management. For example, Netflix outsources its IT operations to Amazon. The end result is that the Internet scales—to reach worldwide audiences and to reach a single individual. Libraries must recognize the possibilities of Web scale and develop new innovative services.[40]

Ray Kurzweil, a longtime inventor and pioneer in digital technology, has observed that the law of accelerating returns occurs; **when technology becomes digital, the pace of change becomes exponential**.[41] Since the opening of the Internet to everyone in the early 1990s with the introduction of the .com suffix to Web addresses, we have witnessed explosive growth and the introduction of a wide range of appealing services. And while early Internet users had to cope with 300-baud dialup modems (baud was shorthand for a really slow connection) to the broadband access most of us have today, the amount of innovation and change has been (and will continue to be) quite breathtaking.

Growing power of the individual. As people gain access to a number of options to accomplish a task and an increasing variety of information about the options is available, they become more demanding about everything. Convenience becomes an important overriding factor in how people make decisions. Consider how people quickly moved to embrace the iTunes store so they could purchase specific music tracks rather than prepackaged albums.[42]

We live in a world of lavish choice. People have a tremendous array of choice for downloading content (audio, video, photographs, text-based files, and others) as well as a range of devices to playback this content (computers, iPods, cellphones, MP3 players, PDAs) that provide real user control. The result is that people expect more choice, more control, and more personalization.

People can find just about anything they want online—books, images, journal articles, videos, and music—from the really obscure to the very popular. People can also buy a wide range of products from such sites as Amazon and eBay. In addition, there are a huge number of niche sites that provide content, products, and service—so many in fact that nobody or no single website can track them all. This plethora of choices, when aggregated, is referred to as the "long tail."

> The theory of the Long Tail can be boiled down to this: Our culture and economy are increasingly shifting away from a focus on a relatively small number of hits (mainstream products and markets) at the head of the demand curve, and moving toward a huge number of niches in the tail. In an era without the constraints of physical shelf space and other bottlenecks of distribution, narrowly targeted goods and services can be as economically attractive as mainstream fare.[43]

The long tail actually contradicts the 80/20 rule—80 percent of use comes from 20 percent of a collection, or 80 percent of use comes from 20 percent of our users. Since online content incurs the same costs whether there is huge or small demand, it turns out that almost all content is viewed or downloaded each month. Consider the subscription-based streaming music service Rhapsody that offers more than 750,000 tracks. All of Rhapsody's top 100,000 tracks are streamed at least monthly—and the same is true for the top 200,000, 300,000, and 400,000 tracks. The same is true for Amazon book sales, Netflix movie streaming (and DVD viewing), among many other examples.

Amazon recently announced an All-You-Can-Read service—Unlimited Kindle—that provides access to over 600,000 eBook titles for the price of $9.99 per month. Admittedly, this requires you to use a Kindle or download the Kindle app, and it does not provide titles from all publishers, but this is a great example of a disruptive service that will likely affect every library.

Yet the availability of this massive flood of information, some call it an information glut, information chaos, or information overload, has introduced new challenges for all of us. Neil Postman argues that few problems arise from insufficient information, and that a host of problems arise with too much information.[44] And while civilization has had several hundred years to adapt and thrive as a result of the invention of the printing press, each of us as individuals and civilizations as a whole is struggling to make sense of the deluge of information that comes to us each day as well as gaining access to the world of information available instantly at our fingertips.

Lee Rainie, director of the Pew Research Center's Internet Life & American Life Project, has suggested that **we now live in a new information ecosystem** that can be characterized by the following:[45]

- The *volume* of (digital) information grows.
- The *variety* of information sources increases, and the *visibility* of new creators is enhanced in the social media age.
- People's *vigilance* for information changes as attention is truncated while attention is also elongated.
- *Velocity* of information increases, and smart mobs appear.
- *Venues* of people intersecting with information multiply, and the availability of information grows to 24/7.
- The *vibrancy* and immersive qualities of media environments make them more absorbing places to hang out and interact (augmented reality, mirror worlds).
- *Valence* (relevance) of information improves (we create the "daily me" and the "daily us").
- *Voting* on and *ventilating* about information proliferates as tagging, commenting, and rating occur (collective intelligence becomes an important force).

What Are the Implications for Libraries?

Until fairly recently, the quality of a library was judged by the depth and breadth of its physical collections. With the advent of digitization of existing physical collections as well as the ever-expanding born-digital content, traditional library collections are now forming only one aspect of service delivery. As noted by Peter Brophy and others, the availability of the traditional plus the digital library has seen a distinct shift from the notion of the library as principal information provider to the library as one among many sources of information, competing with Internet search engines, independent information resources, and community involvement in the information environment.[46] Clearly, for many people, the book and other physical materials in a library collection "are no longer the common currency for information exchange in our present society and culture."[47]

As noted earlier, almost all of the factors influencing and shaping the direction of libraries are now generated from outside the library sector. Even a quick look at all of the many Internet-based services that are competing head-to-head for the attention of library users and nonusers alike reveals that libraries exist in a very competitive environment.

Consider, for example, the following.

Providing access to digital content is not a new idea, yet libraries are continuing to grapple with their users about how to access these materials and what restrictions are placed on the digital content. Many libraries continue to demonstrate that users must engage with the predetermined rationality and order imposed by the library (in the form of its website design and the ways in which the user can engage with this content) in order to gain access as libraries try to subsume digital materials with traditional print-based organizational practices.

Interesting, Gobinda Chowdury suggests that after more than 10 years of developing the digital library, researchers believe that digital libraries are content collected on behalf of user communities, while the librarians consider digital libraries as institutions or services.[48]

To what extent can libraries manage change themselves? As changing library space (the Information Commons, the Knowledge Commons) and the role of the library in the larger organizational context are being considered, the ability of the library to embrace change and innovation is being called into question. Embracing innovation implies risk, and libraries have long been risk-adverse organizations taking the long view of things. Yet, recently the Association of Research Libraries issued a report that suggested, "very few research libraries should have more than half of their infrastructure devoted to physical collections."[49] Organizational structures organized around physical collections do not have flexible, fast-moving adaptable processes ready to embrace change. And as we move further into the online environment, online technologies offer much hope. Consider, for example, the New York Public Library's ability to quickly innovate online, where "the logic of delivering what users want leads inexorably to trying to give them the best digital experiences in the world."[50] Biblion, a storytelling app, presents a slice of the NYPL's 1939 World Fair collection. The library has also developed software to support crowdsourcing projects including transcribing old menus and geo-referencing old maps.

Digitization influences perceptions. The perception that "everything is available on the web" may have its genesis in the speed with which Google has digitized 20 million books. And Google is still in the process of digitizing even more books (moving quickly toward 30 million). But that is not to say that Google's efforts have been widely applauded. The many lawsuits surrounding the project have yet to reach any kind of resolution given the rejection of the initial settlement. Siva Vaidhyanathan, among others, explored a variety of issues surrounding *The Googlization of Everything (and Why We Should Worry)*.[51] Siva acknowledged the value of the digitization project for Google but argued that libraries, and especially university libraries, have a different and more altruistic mission that has not been acknowledged or protected. The participation of a large number of academic and national libraries has provided Google with a unique and valuable asset—providing online access to the full-text content of these books. The participating libraries singed on to the project without exploring or stipulating in an agreement that concerns about image quality, metadata standards, search options, preservation concerns, and long-term sustainability of the resulting database. Libraries have existed and hopefully will continue to exist for a long time; yet, few corporations can claim to have lives that extent beyond a century.

And other groups are also actively involved in the digitization of books and other materials. Publishers and vendors work to ensure that their electronic journals and aggregated databases are visible using Google Scholar and other search tools, which contributes to the perception that "everything is available on the Internet." And some libraries have ongoing digitization projects to add even more content to the web. And people volunteer to place books that they have digitized on the *Internet Archive* so that the contents are available for all. The implication of this for any library is quite significant and means that **the value of the local (nonunique) collection is being, and will continue to be, marginalized**.

Eli Neiburger, associate director of the Ann Arbor District Library, gave a provocative online talk. The "official" title of Eli's presentation was *Libraries at the Tipping Point: How eBooks Impact Libraries*, while the "unofficial" title —*Libraries Are So Screwed*— gained prominence in the library press.[52]

In summary, Eli's proposition suggested:

Libraries are screwed, because we are invested in the codex, and the codex has become outmoded. It's not just a change of text delivery format, it's a move away from content that is ownable and shareable, and that's a problem when your organization is in the business of owning and sharing content.

The brand of libraries is the book temple. Come to the book temple and get yourself some books. Avid library users know that there's more to it, but . . . our values and our operation parameters and even our physical facilities are all built around the codex. If the eBook is the future of text distribution, then we're really screwed, because we are unlikely to ever have the access to these markets and the flexibility with our purchases that we currently have with the codex market.

The real problem is that the value of library collections is rooted in the worth of a local copy. The localness of something loses most of its embodied value when you can retrieve information from Australia or South Africa in 300 milliseconds. Who cares if it's local or not? You can have it immediately. The notion of a copy loses most of its embodied value when there's no longer a difference between transmission and duplication. When you're dealing with digital objects, to transmit it is to duplicate it. If you know where it is, you'll always have it. There are already more cell phones in the world than there are people, and in this century most humans are going to have persistent Internet access in their pocket. In an inter-networked world, when you can download anything from anywhere, the idea of having a local copy only makes sense to a hoarder.

There may not always be new material made available in formats that libraries can purchase. This has already started. No digital native is going to get excited about waiting to receive a digital object, and what's the sense in making someone give something back to you when you still have it even after you gave it to them? Finally, the user experiences available to people who choose not to bother trying to use the library will only provide increasingly appealing value, which puts us in the situation where all this is happening as taxpayers are having to decide what municipal services they can live without. We are so screwed.

Discovery happens elsewhere. As Lorcan Dempsey has observed, people find items of interest using Internet search engines, RSS aggregators, recommendations found on various websites, and personal resource networks created as a result of using social networking sites. Almost no one will seek out a library website to gain access to resources (unless reminded to do so in some way).[53] At the same time, libraries are interested in having their digitized special collections, learning and research materials often found in repositories, or learning management systems being visible to Internet search engines. This represents a real challenge as libraries move from focusing on their local collections and the tools used to provide access to those collections to a much broader venue. This reality of an abundance of information resources and scarcity of attention to attend to it has been called the Dempsey Paradox (in the good old days, researchers and faculty members were required to take the time to visit the library to use the local collections for their researcher and teaching efforts).[54]

Libraries are not in the flow. Increasingly, people are organizing their work (whether learning, research, or work) using a range of tools found in network environments and libraries, and their resources are not even on the horizon. Thus, libraries need to create library services around the workflow of students, faculty, entrepreneurs, and moms with small children, seniors, and so forth. Software applications demand the ability to interact with other applications—RSS feeds, web services, apps, and so on. People are increasingly adding content to content and then sharing with others. Mix and remix are the order of the day.

Access licenses rather than ownership are becoming the norm. A greater proportion of library budgets is devoted to licensing electronic content (eJournals, eResources, and eBooks) rather than purchasing content. This disturbing trend has several implications: licensed content must be paid for each year rather than purchasing once, and more and more of the library's budget is earmarked for annual licensing charges. Additionally, annual price increases for licensing electronic resources will usually exceed the annual rate of inflation.

Libraries are moving from just-in-case to just-in-time collections. In times past, libraries purchased materials (books, audio, video, and many other formats) since the time and effort to find and purchase these materials when needed were more expensive and time consuming. For academic libraries, as much as 50 percent of the books that were purchased were never borrowed despite the one-time and ongoing costs of providing access to the collections (the just-in-case insurance policy). Now access to many kinds of collections is easy, and the costs to the user are negligible. This means that almost any book can be purchased (in many cases, in both pBook and eBook formats) at any time and delivered quite quickly.

Thus, libraries are increasingly moving to the just-in-time delivery mode since past use is the best predictor of future use (books users select are more likely to get used in the future). Our professional literature refers to this trend as patron-drive acquisitions, customer-driven acquisitions, and demand-driven acquisitions.

Summary

Today libraries are standing at a crossroads with several roads leading into the future obscured by a bewildering array of new technologies.

The fundamental nature of information has changed quite dramatically as shown in Figure 3-1. When people are finding what is on the Internet is in fact "good enough" then libraries must offer services that are very difficult to copy. Kevin Kelly has suggested that there are eight things (that provide generative value) that are better than free that organizations (including libraries) might wish to provide:[55]

- *Immediacy*—Can be found in any media and people are willing to "pay" (in some way) a premium for immediacy.
- *Personalization*—Is a result of an ongoing conversation between the service/product provider and the customer. The more the customer is willing to reveal and share, the better the resulting personalization will be for the customer.

- *Interpretation*—Many organizations, such as *RedHat*, now exist to provide support for "free" software.
- *Authenticity*—Some people are willing to pay a premium for an authentic and reliable copy of something. Authenticity in the form of digital watermarks or an artist's stamp and signature attests to the uniqueness and reliability of the product or service.
- *Accessibility*—Many "in the cloud" services exist to ensure that we have access to digital content—when and where we want it.
- *Embodiment*—Many artists, musicians, and others provide access to their work for free but you pay if you want to experience a live performance.
- *Patronage*—Allowing people to pay what they want is, in a way, a form of patronage that generates real value between the provider and the consumer.
- *Findability*—Unfound works are actually valueless and may lead to real frustration. Given the millions of books, images, videos, songs, podcast, apps, and so on, being discoverable is very valuable.

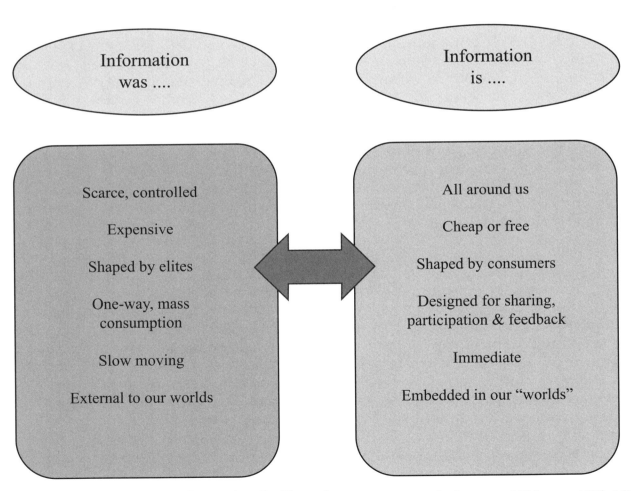

Figure 3-1 Nature of Information Is Changing. Lee Rainie. "The Internet of Things and What It Means for Librarians." Presentation at the Internet Librarian Conference, Washington, DC. October 28, 2014.

Recognizing that significant change is afoot, many libraries have begun to experiment with repurposing space in libraries, new service delivery models, eliminating services that no longer provide real value, streamlining backroom activities (or outsourcing these activities), joining consortia, and so forth. And yet many libraries are continuing to provide traditional library services and building library collections as if there is no need to change.

Yet as Richard Foster[56] pointed out more than 20 years ago, once established organizations (think libraries here) recognize that a competitive threat exists, the typical reaction is to fine-tune the existing model of service delivery—obsolete though it may be—rather than acknowledge that disruptive innovation is occurring and the needed change might be radical rather than incremental.

Main idea:	Change is upon us, and we need to adapt quickly
Opposing view:	We don't need a revolution in cultural organizations; cultural organizations have a track record for successful evolution
Key concepts:	Change, speed of change, technology, the Internet, rules of the game are changing
What has changed?:	The internet
Catalyst:	Other network-level options are capturing the attention of cultural organization customers
Open debate:	How fast should cultural organizations change? In what ways should cultural organizations change?

Notes

1. Peter Drucker. *Managing in Turbulent Times*. New York: Harper Paperbacks, 1980, 86.
2. Robert Wright. "The Web We Weave." *Time*, December 31, 1999.
3. Grace Kelley. "The Democratic Function of Public Libraries." *Library Quarterly*, 4 (1), January 1934, 1–15.
4. Apple competition announcement, 2013. Available at http://www.apple.com/itunes/50-billion-app-countdown/
5. Lorcan Dempsey. "Always On: Libraries in a World of Permanent Connectivity." *First Monday*, 14 (1–5), January 2009.
6. Lee Rainie. *The Changing World of Librarians*. Presented to the Washington, DC, chapter of the SLA Spring Workshop. April 24, 2013. Available at http://www.pewinternet.org/Presentations/2013/Apr/The-changing-world-of-librarians.aspx
7. U.S. Census Bureau. *Computer and Internet Use in the United States* based on the July 2011 Current Population Survey. Washington, DC: U.S. Census Bureau, May 2013. Available at http://www.census.gov/prod/2013pubs/p20-569.pdf
8. Chris Anderson and Michael Wolff. "The Web Is Dead. Long Live the Internet." *Wired*, September 2010. Available at http://www.wired.com/magazine/2010/08/ff_webrip/
9. Data courtesy of Phil Bradley's Weblog. 40 Social Media Statistics, August 26, 2015. Available at http://philbradley.typepad.com/phil_bradleys_weblog/2015/08/40-social-media-statistics.html

10. Neil Gershenfeild, Raffi Krikorian, and Danny Cohen. "The Internet of Things." *Scientific American*, October 2004, 76–81.

11. Simon Waldman. *Creative Disruption: What You Need to Do to Shake Up Your Business in a Digital World*. London: Prentice Hall, 2010.

12. This is the latest published estimate that I could find. John Koetsier. "How Google Searches 30 Trillion Web pages, 100 Billion Times a Month." *Venture Beat* blog, March 1, 2013. Available at http://venturebeat.com/2013/03/01/how-google-searches-30-trillion-web-pages-100-billion-times-a-month/

13. Tim O'Reilly. "What Is Web 2.0: Design Patterns and Business Models for the Next Generation of Software." *O'Reilly* blog, September 30, 2005. Available at http://oreilly.com/web2/archive/what-is-web-20.html

14. Yochai Benkler. *The Wealth of Networks: How Social Production Transforms Markets and Freedom*. New Haven, CT: Yale University Press, 2006.

15. Jaron Lanier. *Who Owns the Future?* New York: Simon & Schuster, 2013.

16. Ted Nelson. *Literary Machines*: *The Report On, and Of, Project Xanadu Concerning Word Processing, Electronic Publishing, Hypertext, Thinkertoys, Tomorrow's Intellectual Revolution, and Certain Other Topics Including Knowledge, Education and Freedom*. Sausalito, CA: Mindful Press, 1981.

17. John Hagel and John Seely Brown. *The Only Sustainable Edge: Why Business Strategy Depends on Productive Friction and Dynamic Specialization*. Boston: Harvard Business Review Press, 2005.

18. Adrienne LaFrance. "When You Give a Tree an Email Address." *The Atlantic*, July 10, 2105. Available at http://www.theatlantic.com/technology/archive/2015/07/when-you-give-a-tree-an-email-address/398210/

19. George Dyson. *Darwin Among the Machines: The Evolution of Global Intelligence*. New York: Basic Books, 1998, 13.

20. Kevin Kelly. "Scan This Book." *New York Times Magazine*, May 14, 2006. Available at http://www.nytimes.com/2006/05/14/magazine/14publishing.html?pagewanted=all&_r=0

21. Clay Shirky. "How Social Media Can Make History." *TED Talk*, June 2009. Available at http://www.ted.com/talks/clay_shirky_how_cellphones_twitter_facebook_can_make_history.html

22. Chris Anderson. *The Long Tail: Why the Future of Business Is Selling Less of More*. New York: Hyperion, 2006, 107.

23. Scott Plutchak. "The Landscape Shifts: New Opportunities for Collaboration Arise as the Primacy of the Traditional Journal Article Fades." *Serials*, 19 (3), November 2006, 184–187.

24. Luke Tredinnick. *Digital Information Culture: The Individual and Society in the Digital Age*. Oxford: Chandos Publishing, 2008.

25. Kathryn Greenhill and Constance Wiebrands. "No Library Required: The Free and Easy Backwaters of Online Content Sharing." Presentation at the VALA Conference, Melbourne, Australia. VALA 2012: eM-powering eFutures. Available at http://www.vala.org.au/index.php?option=com_content&view=article&id=580&catid=87&Itemid=159

26. Farhad Manjoo. *True Enough: Learning to Live in a Post-Fact Society*. New York: John Wiley, 2008, 229.

27. Clive Thompson. *Smarter Than You Think: How Technology Is Changing Our Minds for the Better*. New York: Penguin Press, 2013.

28. David Brooks. "The Outsourced Brain." *The New York Times*, October 26, 2007. Available at http://www.nytimes.com/2007/10/26/opinion/26brooks.html

29. Peter Suderman. "Your Brain Is an Index." *The American Scene*, May 11, 2009. Available at http://theamericanscene.com/2009/05/11/your-brain-is-an-index

30. Don Tapscott. *Grown Up Digital*. New York: McGraw-Hill, 2009.

31. Nicholas Carr. *The Shallows: What the Internet Is Doing to Our Brains*. New York: Norton & Company, 2010.

32. Sugata Mitra. *Build a School in the Cloud*. February 2013. TED Talks. Available at http://www.ted.com/talks/sugata_mitra_build_a_school_in_the_cloud

    See also, Torn Halves. "Sugata Mitra: 'Knowing Is obsolete.' Is it?" *The Digital Counter-Revolution* blog. April 17, 2013. Available at http://www.digitalcounterrevolution.co.uk/2013/sugata-mitra-knowing-is-obsolete/

33. Luke Tredinnick. *Digital Information Culture: The Individual and Society in the Digital Age*. Oxford: Chandos Publishing, 2008, 75.

34. David Weinberger. *Everything Is Miscellaneous: The Power of the New World Disorder*. New York: Holt, 2008.

35. Quote appears in *The Scientist Speculates: An Anthology of Partly-Baked Ideas* (J. Good, Editor). New York: Basic Books, 1962, 94.

36. Harry Verwayen, Martijn Arnoldus, and Peter Kaufman. *The Problem of the Yellow Milkmaid: A Business Model Perspective on Open Metadata*. White Paper No. 2. Paris: Europeana, November 2011, 2. See also The Yellow Milkmaid Syndrome blog, available at http://yellowmilkmaidsyndrome.tumblr.com/

37. Manual Castells. *The Rise of the Network Society: The Information Age: Economy, Society, and Culture, Volumes I-III*. New York: Wiley, 1996.

38. Michael Porter and Victor Millar. "How Information Gives You Competitive Advantage." *Harvard Business Review*, July–August 1985, 2–13.

39. Clayton Christensen. "Disruptive Innovation Explained." *HBR Blog Network*, March 6, 2012. Available at http://blogs.hbr.org/video/2012/03/disruptive-innovation-explaine.html

    See also, Clayton Christensen. *The Innovator's Dilemma: The Revolutionary Book That Will Change the Way You Do Business*. New York: HarperBusiness, 2011.

    Clayton Christensen. *The Innovative University: Changing the DNA of Higher Education from the Inside Out*. San Francisco: Jossey-Bass, 2011.

    Clayton Christensen. *The Innovator's Solution: Creating and Sustaining Successful Growth*. Cambridge, MA: Harvard Business School Press, 2003.

40. OCLC. *Libraries at Webscale*. Dublin, OH: OCLC, 2011. Available at https://www.oclc.org/content/dam/oclc/reports/worldshare-management-services/libraries-at-webscale.pdf

41. Ray Kurzweil. "The Law of Accelerating Returns." *Kurzweil Accelerating Intelligence* Blog. March 7, 2001. Available at http://www.kurzweilai.net/the-law-of-accelerating-returns

42. John Hagel and John Seely Brown. *The Only Sustainable Edge: Why Business Strategy Depends on Productive Friction and Dynamic Specialization*. Boston: Harvard Business Review Press, 2005.

43. Chris Anderson. *The Long Tail: Why the Future of Business Is Selling Less of More*. New York: Hyperion, 2006, 52.

44. Neil Postman. *Technopoly: The Surrender of Culture to Technology*. New York: Alfred Knopf, 1993.

45. Lee Rainie. *How Libraries Can Survive in the New Media Ecosystem: They Can Be "Friends" in People's Social Networks*. Presentation to the Catalonian Library Association's biennial meeting at the Universidad Complutense de Madrid, May 21, 2010. Available at http://www.pewinternet.org/2010/05/19/how-libraries-can-survive-in-the-new-media-ecosystem/

46. Peter Brophy. *The Library in the Twenty-First Century*, 2nd ed. London: Facet Publishing, 2007.

47. Matthew Brack. *Bridging the Gap: Library Digital Collections, Innovation and the User*. Dissertation submitted in partial fulfillment of the requirements for the degree of MA in Digital Asset Management, King's College London, 2012. Available at http://www.nsla.org.au/sites/www.nsla.org.au/files/publications/Bridging%20the%20Gap%20-%20Matthew%20Brack.pdf

48. Gobinda Chowdury. "From Digital Libraries to Digital Preservation Research: The Importance of Users and Context." *Journal of Documentation*, 66 (2), 2010, 207–223.

49. Tyler Walters and Katherine Skinner. *New Roles for New Times: Digital Curation for Preservation*. Washington, DC: The Association of Research Libraries, March 2011, 57. Available at http://www.arl.org/storage/documents/publications/nrnt_digital_curation17mar11.pdf

50. Alexis Madrigal. What Big Media Can Learn from the New York Public Library. *The Atlantic*, 20, June 20, 2011. Available at http://www.theatlantic.com/technology/archive/2011/06/what-big-mediacan-learn-from-the-new-york-public-library/240565/

51. Siva Vaidhyanathan. *The Googlization of Everything (and Why We Should Worry)*. Berkeley, CA: University of California Press, 2011.

52. You can listen to Eli's presentation at YouTube http://www.youtube.com/watch?v=KqAwj5ssU2c&feature=player_embedded You can download Eli's PowerPoint presentation at http://www.slideshare.net/we2aam/ebooks-impact

53. Lorcan Dempsey. "Reconfiguring the Library Systems Environment." *portal: Libraries and the Academy*, 8 (2), April 2008, 111–120.

54. Lorcan Dempsey. "Thirteen Ways of Looking at Libraries, Discovery, and the Catalog: Scale, Workflow, Attention." *Educause Review Online*, December 10, 2012. Available at http://www.educause.edu/ero/article/thirteen-ways-looking-libraries-discovery-and-catalog-scale-workflow-attention

55. Kevin Kelly. "Better Than Free." *The Technium*, January 31, 2008. Available at http://kk.org/thetechnium/2008/01/better-than-fre/

56. Richard Foster. *Innovation: The Attacker's Advantage*. New York: Summit Books, 1986.
    See also, Clayton Christensen. *The Innovator's Solution: Creating and Sustaining Successful Growth*. Boston: Harvard Business Press, 2003.

4

Ways to Add Even More Value

We are called to be architects of the future, not its victims.

Buckminster Fuller[1]

We tend to overestimate the effect of a technology in the short run and underestimate the effect in the long run.

Amara's Law[2]

Libraries Are Obsolete

One of our profession's pre-eminent scholars, David Lankes, was asked to participate in an Oxford-style debate at the Harvard University Libraries and to affirm the proposition: Libraries are obsolete.[3] After considering the topic for some time, David identified a perspective that spans library types and ideology (and scared the hell out of him). David argued that libraries act as institutions of remediation and thus become obsolete. Libraries either were created to fill some deficit in existing institutions or acted to remedy some deficit in the community at large. While this approach may have made sense in times past, today many of these deficiencies fail to resonate with decision makers. Additionally, libraries use valuable resources they ought to be using that will deliver more value to the customer. During the debate, David expanded on this deficit model and suggested that there are a number of deficiencies that should be considered:

- *Access.* Perhaps a majority of libraries were created to share a collection of physical information resources. The benefit to the community was fairly direct in that the library provided access to a set of expensive resources that anyone could use. And yet, ironically, as more people use the library (with a fixed set of resources), access is actually decreased.
- The problem with this model is that today there are a host of websites that let you share resources—consider *LibraryThing, Instagram, Pinterest, Flickr, Facebook,* and *YouTube,* among many others. And while libraries may have begun as sharing institutions, they have since become lending institutions.

- Compared with a deficit approach to collections, a sharing model suggests that a community has abundant resources (ideas, expertise, stories, music, books, photos, and other assets) that can be shared only if the library would build a platform to facilitate sharing.
- *Democracy.* In the first half of the 20th century, public and academic libraries were living Andrew Carnegie's observation that "there is not such a cradle of democracy upon the earth as the Free Public Library." And the development of the federal government's depository library program was designed to overcome a deficit in the public's access to the workings of government. Yet, given the "fiction" that the depository program works with few libraries actually participating, and for those that do, few people even attempt to gain access to resources housed in microfilm cabinets or stored on cramped shelves. Most federal agencies now publish content directly on the department's website, and fewer and fewer documents are now being distributed using the depository library program.
- *Internet access.* In order to help overcome the digital divide, libraries provide Internet access to the disadvantaged and disconnected. Lankes asks whether this is the best solution or whether the money to provide Internet access would be better spent providing Internet access to each individual's home (much like the rural electrification model).
- *Literacy.* Public and school libraries have long held an active role in helping children learn to read. This emphasis on early childhood reading skills was in response to times when public education wasn't so universal. Libraries were, for many, the people's university to remedy the lack of a formal education. Lankes observes that librarians have received very little training in reading instruction or math instruction or science instruction so perhaps the money for literacy programs should be spent in providing better schools. I personally have a real problem with this suggestion as public schools have received a huge influx of funding over the past several decades, and yet the quality of education, by any measure, continues to decline.
- *Information seeking.* Historically, reference librarians assisted patrons in overcoming their deficit in finding high-quality useful information. Yet, reference statistics have been dropping for some time, especially in academic libraries. Given the ease with which people find information using a search engine (Google now has over 5 billion searches a day!), the drop in reference stats should not be a surprise. We no longer need trained librarians to act as search intermediaries to overcome the horrible search interface available on some databases. And we certainly don't need highly skilled reference librarians sitting at a public reference desk waiting for someone to approach asking for assistance. Several alternative models for delivering reference services are available for use.

Interestingly, David Lankes noted that all of the speakers at the debate agreed that librarians aren't obsolete, but libraries may be. One opportunity is for talented librarians to work within organizations to make these institutions more responsive to customer needs. The foundation of the deficit model is that something is broken and the library will fix it (or add little real value in our attempt to fix it). If the message being delivered to our communities is that you are broken in some way, then is it any wonder that financial support for libraries declines year after year? David further suggests that libraries should be showing how libraries add value, which results in positive effects in a community. *If libraries continue to see themselves as lending physical objects (or downloading electronic things), then libraries are going to be in real danger.* However, if libraries move from lending organizations to places of sharing (at a library and online) using a library-provided community portal, then we can offer a real sense of hope for our beloved institution known as the library.

If the old rules and practices that libraries used to add value are increasingly less relevant and valuable, the profession needs a new way to think about how we can transform the library so that the customer perceives the library as a real asset and provides services that add substantial value in the life of the customer.

Rather than thinking of librarians only because we work in libraries, it is important to take a step back and reflect on the value that librarians bring to the table. What is truly unique about what a librarian does and how he or she adds value in his or her interactions with customers? David Lankes suggests in his wonderful and insightful book *The Atlas of New Librarianship,*

The **mission** of **librarians** is to **improve society** through **facilitating knowledge creation** in their **communities**.[4] David organized the *Atlas* around the six major concepts that are highlighted in bold in the mission statement for librarians and uses conversation theory as the foundation to guide the discussion. David asserts that:

- *Mission*—The focus of the mission statement is on librarians and not libraries, the positive effect librarians and the services they provide can have on a community rather than a warehouse of books and other physical materials (and providing access to electronic resources).
- *Knowledge creation*—Knowledge creation is a sloppy iterative process that involves a conversation of some kind—direct face-to-face, via telephone, or email, for example—that allows someone to mold and shape an idea using the "back and forth" as a way to improving an idea or concept.
- *Facilitating*—Librarians facilitate knowledge creation by building a bridge between those involved in the conversation, having sufficient knowledge about the subject area to understand the conversation, providing a platform that allows all of the individuals involved in the conversation to participate freely and safely, and encouraging and supporting those involved in the conversation. In short, facilitating is all about listening and figuring out how to deliver what is needed to keep the conversation going.
- *Communities*—Despite the historical and sometimes artificial nature of boundaries of a community (city limits or students of a university), librarians are really interested in assisting conversations among and between members of a community. Members wish to accomplish a goal, and librarians should be

where people are (in the physical library or in the online virtual world) providing their support, expertise and views so that conversation flourishes.

- *Improve society*—Librarians have an obligation to listen with a conscience, have a voice in the conversation, and a responsibility to guide the conversation especially around such important values as openness, learning, intellectual freedom, ethics, and social justice.
- *Librarians*—While values endure and skills have a limited shelf life, defining the contributions of a profession by the skills that are employed to provide services of value is very problematic. Professionals who are willing to embrace a sense of adventure by engaging their users in a wide variety of ways will become much better at understanding the members of a community and how the library needs to evolve and change in order to better meet their needs.

Scott Plutchak, director of the Health Sciences Library at the University of Alabama at Birmingham, has a similar perspective, "We connect people to knowledge. We bring people together with the intellectual content of the past and present so that new knowledge can be created . . . This is what we have always been about."[5]

Building upon the same theme, Carl Grant has suggested that a librarian's primary value-add is:

We help people create new knowledge by helping them find existing knowledge that is authoritative, authenticated and appropriate for their needs. We put that knowledge in context and provide it without bias. This becomes the foundation upon which they create new knowledge.[6]

Despite the fact that there is a tremendous amount of evidence that the world is rapidly changing, especially changing as the result of the introduction and use of information technology, libraries and what Chris Batt calls other "creating, curating and disclosing institutions—colleges, universities, museums, libraries, and archives among others"—have adopted an insular and myopic view of the world by refusing to consider alternative views of the future.[7] Consider, for example, the question, "If libraries did not exist today, would someone invent them?" And a related question "Would this new invention look anything like libraries do today?"

Key Questions

It is possible to consider a wide range of questions that probably should be addressed if we wanted to really explore the question of needing to invent libraries today. Among these questions are:

- Would we start first with gathering physical containers of knowledge (books, journals, photos, recordings on CD, videos on DVDs)?
- Should we start gathering "born-digital" materials? If so, whom should we ask whether we could obtain a digital copy of—what? Documents, photos, videos, sound recordings, diaries, and so forth? Is permission needed for every document?

- What level of metadata is going to be needed for these born-digital materials? Who should create the metadata—librarians, the creator of the born-digital content, a computer software program, other interested folks?
- Is it necessary to download and maintain a digital copy of something on a "library server" or is linking to the object sufficient? Should the digital copy reside on a library server plus be backed up in the cloud—perhaps in a cloud that is paid for cooperatively by a group of libraries?
- What are the roles or functions of the physical space in a library in a college or university (or a community for a public library) when more and more content is accessible via the Internet?
- What are the things in your community that should be preserved and made accessible in the future? Is this a library's responsibility? A historical society's responsibility? A local museum's responsibility? Should these and other organizations be partnering to ensure the preservation of digital content?
- Is the use of pre-coordinated vocabulary and authority control really necessary in order to develop a catalog?
- Does a library need a catalog containing metadata (when an increasing amount of full-text digital content is available)?
- Should a library catalog focus solely on its collections or should it have a broader outlook (and where do you draw the boundary line of what to include and exclude)?
- Should librarians be found in the library or be dispersed in some way within the larger community?
- Should a group of libraries (within a region or state or several states) create a large warehouse of physical containers and ship desired items directly to the customer (much like Amazon does) in lieu of developing a traditional interlibrary loan service? Should the customer return these items to the library or simply keep them (and pass them on to a friend or family member)? Should a group of libraries manage such a warehouse, or should the libraries outsource the operation to an experienced logistics partner (such as UPS or FedEx)?
- Are existing competitors of traditional library services doing a better job, and should the library even try to provide a specific service (such as videos on DVD, audio tracks on CD, eBooks that are purchased or eBooks that are licensed, or other services)?
- Consider examining the physical and virtual library from the perspective of convenience. Is it possible to improve and simplify the experience for the customer?
- Rather than focusing on retrieving bibliographic records (which are the surrogate of the physical or electronic object), is it possible to consider thinking about retrieving concepts, ideas, or even wisdom?
- How should the library improve its website and online catalog experience given the plethora of data that is available from a tool such as Google Analytics (or other similar tools)?

- How can a library improve access to the ever-increasing number of eBooks, especially self-published eBooks?
- How many library staff members should be devoted to engaging with community members using social media tools? Should these staff members all be librarians, or are a range of skills necessary and thus staff involved with social media may include librarians and nonlibrarians?
- Is organizing a collection of physical containers in call number order (using a specific classification system—such as Dewey Decimal or Library of Congress) necessary? What other organizing options exist?
- Should traditional high-density library shelving be used, or could collections be presented using bookstore merchandising-style shelving?
- Should the library be called a library or . . .? You might want to check with Anythink in Colorado or The Idea Store in London, England.
- How can the library engage with its local community as well as a broader national or worldwide community to deliver a range of new (digital) services never even dreamed of before?

In short, librarians and other cultural organization professionals have the opportunity to carefully examine the perceived value for each of its existing services from the customer's perspective as well as to try to provide even more value to its customers by really understanding its unique value proposition(s) for each customer segment.

One of the realities of every profession and organization, regardless of size or purpose, is that people become very comfortable in what they are currently doing and what they have been doing over the course of their careers. This comfort level might be called a "zone of comfort," and this zone contributes, in part, to the reluctance people have to change. We must recognize how our deeply engrained way of thinking limits our ability to realize that libraries and librarians need to add value in many new ways.

Every time we make a change or take action it is based on a hypothesis or theory and for most cultural organizations that theory is the future will be a continuation of the past. Yet, such a theory is no longer relevant in this age of disruption we find ourselves living in.

We also need to understand and recognize that value is created at the points of intersection between a library's collections and services and our customers. When we think about value creation, too often, we use the lens of the library's perspective (and people use the customer's perspective as shown in Figure 4-1). Our deeply held ways of thinking about the library and how it can add value limit our ability to engage with library customers in new and creative ways. The disconnect exists between the library's perspective and the customer's perspective given the increasing array of choices that people now have using the Internet. Libraries have the opportunity to cocreate value with their customers in new and wonderful ways, but this opportunity is etched in the reality that libraries and librarians are going to have to continue to change and evolve.

Many well-meaning critics of libraries often suggest that the library should be run more like a business. Yet even a quick glance at the Fortune 100 companies at the beginning of any given decade, and subsequently followed up 10 years later, will reveal that a third or more of the companies no longer exist—they have merged, been bought, or even gone out of business. In an interesting article, Arie de Geus found that companies

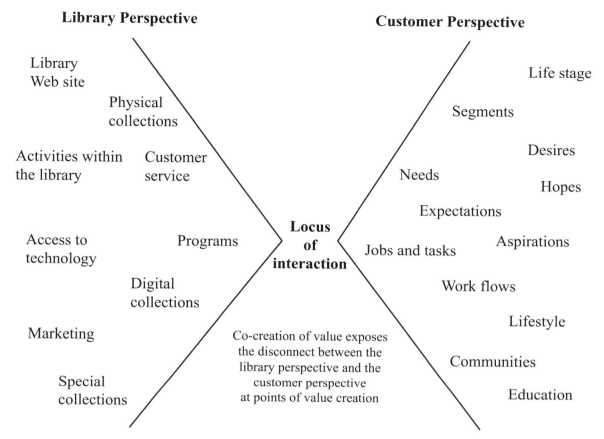

Library Perspective

Library Web site

Physical collections

Activities within the library

Customer service

Access to technology

Programs

Digital collections

Marketing

Special collections

Locus of interaction

Co-creation of value exposes the disconnect between the library perspective and the customer perspective at points of value creation

Customer Perspective

Life stage

Segments

Desires

Needs

Hopes

Expectations

Jobs and tasks

Aspirations

Work flows

Lifestyle

Communities

Education

Figure 4-1 Library Perspective versus Customer Perspective.

that had real longevity—that is, been in existence for more than 100 years—had four similar traits:[8]

- *Fiscally conservative*—The companies always have money in reserve so that when opportunities presented themselves, they could react quickly.
- *Adaptable*—These companies could react to changes in the world around them by learning and being flexible.
- *Keenly aware of their identity*—The top management team as well as all of the employees were aware of their mission and the company's vision. Everyone considered themselves as stewards and of their need to nurture the enterprise for the long term.
- *Embraced new ideas*—These successful firms encouraged experimentation and recognized that really great ideas can come from anywhere—both inside and from outside the organization.

Strategic Planning

Cultural organizations face challenging environments when engaged in the strategic planning process since a majority of nonprofit, service-oriented cultures tend to be resistant to change. And, in reality, most cultural organizations practice a form of long-range planning that starts from a current position and sets very achievable goals and targets for the next three- to five-year time horizon (even if the process is called strategic planning). When an organization is creating a real strategic plan, it identifies the benefits that each customer segment receives and then determines the best way to deliver that value. In short, it is asking the "how" questions: How do we organize our collections? How do we facilitate the browsing of our collections that will really appeal to our customers? How do we deliver value to our online users? Rather, libraries, archives, and museums typically start from the status quo and consider only small incremental improvements of their existing services.

In a classic Harvard Business Review article, John Hagel and Marc Singer argued that there are three different kinds of organizations—innovation oriented, building customer relationships, and an infrastructure organization—as seen in Figure 4-2.[9] Each type of organization employs people with different skill sets, and each has unique competitive, economic, and cultural imperatives. And while a business might try to be all things to all people, really successful companies will select one focus and become the best in that particular domain.

A product or service innovator focuses on meeting the needs of its potential customers in new and creative ways. Apple is a powerful example of a business that innovates developing wonderful intuitive products (iPod, iPad, iPhone, and so forth) as well as new services (iTunes and the App Store). One innovative library is AnyThink in Colorado.

A customer relationship–focused organization wants to develop, nurture, and maintain strong emotional connections with its customers. It does this by asking for permission to accumulate data about their use of a product or service and then making the whole experience better by customizing the service based on the stated (or implied) needs of the customer. Personalization becomes a key focus for the service provider.

An organization that focuses on infrastructure is attempting to be as cost efficient as possible by eliminating activities that do not add value and reducing waste. An infrastructure business tends to have high-volume repetitive activities such as telecommunications, manufacturing, and logistics.

Hagel and Singer went on to suggest that organizations are going to be going through a process of unbundling or separating the organization into its three components—customer relationship management, infrastructure management, and management of innovation—as a result of the Internet making rapid worldwide communication possible. As a result, *nimble organizations* are going to be better able to compete than their more *clumsy counterparts*.

Challenges related to defining, targeting, and measuring something as vague and imprecise as "value" must be confronted, especially when the concept must be applied to intangibles such as service.[10] This is especially true in the case of libraries that have little experience or tradition that identifies the library's value from the customer's perspective.

However, once a library better understands the value proposition from the customer's perspective, the library is better able to deal with reduced financial resources since it knows what delivers the greatest (and the least) value in the mind of the customer. And it is the customer who determines the actual value of an information resource or service—not the library.

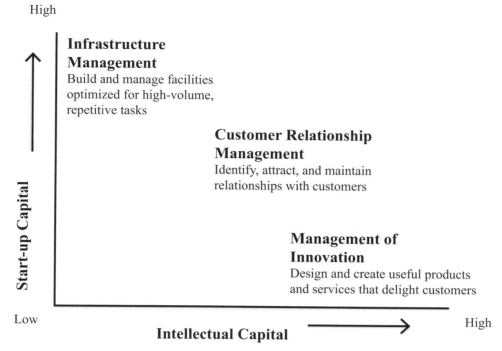

Figure 4-2 Types of Organizations.

Customers are tending to ignore the traditional approach to marketing communications (Hey, check us out with our new XX! You'll like it.) and are increasingly making decisions about what products to buy and what services to use based on the experiences of their peers and from anonymous network-level resources such as Yelp!, reviews on Amazon and other websites. Bill Lee, who blogs on the Harvard Business Review Blog Network,[11] suggested that customer value propositions come in four levels:

- *Level 1—Buyers perceive you as the supplier of a commodity.* These customers focus solely on price and the convenience of acquiring the product or service. This is the least desirable proposition for any organization as people are concerned only about what they can get from you—a one-way relationship. In the case of a library, this would be free content and services.

- *Level 2—Buyers perceive that you are helping them accomplish their job.* These customers focus on outcomes and are delighted that you help them get the job done. Think Apple, Southwest Airlines, or Zipcar for a more current example. Customers likely will perceive librarians as adding value by saving time, providing expert advice or guidance, or gaining access to high-quality content.

- *Level 3—You are able to engage the customer emotionally.* The fact that Southwest encourages its staff to actually have fun while doing their job makes the experience for the customer much more engaging—which promotes loyalty. Rather than a quick visit to the library, the customer is happy to spend time browsing the stacks, attending a program, participating in a book club discussion, or enjoying the experience of being in a community space.

- *Level 4—You help customers build their social capital.* Helping your customers comment on and document their interactions with the library build their own networks and communities. The library serves as a foundation upon which people can build their own social presence.

While it is necessary to think creatively about ways that a library could move to Level 3 or Level 4, the library might acknowledge the contributions of those who are active on the library's website by adding reviews (Amazon identifies its top reviewers and has a Reviewer Hall of Fame—in many cases, the top Amazon reviews are more influential than traditional media reviewers), assist customers in building affiliation networks (some companies create industry councils that are engaged in discussing important industry topics—not specific products or services), build customer status in the community (giving awards in a number of categories annually), and give customers a say in what the library should be doing.

Often libraries are encouraged to market their brand—associating a set of values and qualities with the library. Since brand is focused on the library, brand marketing has an inside-out orientation—the library identifies the attributes it wants to project and communicates that message in a variety of ways. By contrast, the value-added approach begins with the customer. It's about helping people accomplish a specific task or activity; it's about making the customer more productive. This outside-in approach works to understand customers' behaviors, motivations, and needs, which leads to a set of services that will satisfy them (hopefully better than what the competitors offer).

Library customers come in all shapes and sizes with a diverse set of needs and are confronted with a bewildering array of options in the information-seeking landscape. This array of choices is the result of an every-increasing set of competitive options that are available anytime, anywhere using any device. Each library employee should have a clear understanding of how the specific activities that he or she engages are linked to delivering value to existing customers or in attracting new customers.[12]

When using the building blocks of a business model to better understand an existing cultural organizations offering or a planned service, consider these questions:

- What kind of infrastructure do we need to make the operation sustainable and interoperable (at the network level)?
- How do we protect intellectual property while offering open access?
- What is the impact on our customers when we use different channels—website, Flickr, Pinterest, YouTube, Facebook, and so forth?
- What market segments are central to our mission?
- What kind of impact will this planned service have on our organization?
- Do we have the necessary resources, or should we partner with others?
- Should we consider allowing advertising or offering premium subscriptions to help defray the costs of this service?

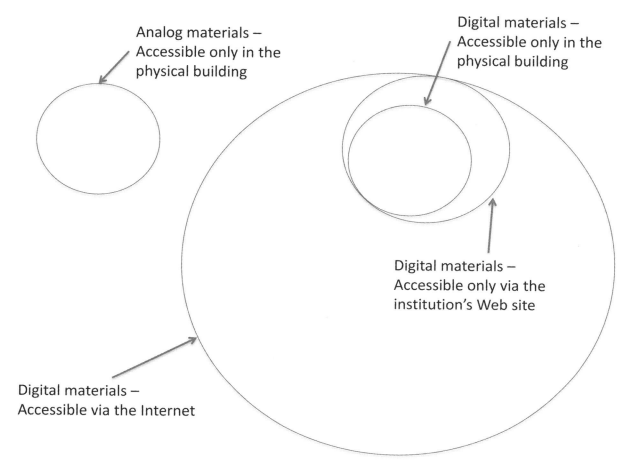

Figure 4-3 Access to Cultural Heritage.

Interestingly, the cultural heritage institutions (museums, galleries, archives, and libraries) in the Netherlands developed a seven-step planning process that incorporates the business model discussed earlier that identifies the customer's value proposition considering the strategies to be used to make these institutions more relevant to people today. The resulting Business Model Innovation Cultural Heritage Roadmap is called BMICE, and it can easily be downloaded.[13]

Figure 4-3 illustrates the potential reach of the collections and services of a cultural heritage institution depending upon the way in which the customer gains access to its resources: from the need to actually be in the library to use analog materials to the use of the organization's digital materials (the customer is located within the building or connected via the organization's website). Of course, the greatest potential access is provided to those who are using the Internet.

The seven steps include:

1. *Business model mapping*—Mapping out the existing business model to assess whether or not particular innovations are desirable and add value.
2. *New value propositions*—Developing an innovative product or service.

3. *Fit and vitality check*—Checking to determine whether the innovation is appropriate and viable from the customer's perspective.
4. *Setting a course*—Deciding whether or not to proceed.
5. *Action plan*—Develop a specific action plan of what will be needed to successfully implement the innovation.
6. *Execution*—Actually making the necessary changes in order to implement the innovation.
7. *Evaluation*—Draw a new business model map with the innovation included and determine whether the implementation has met all expectations.

The Bill & Melinda Gates Foundation has developed the results hierarchy, which is applicable in a number of setting—including libraries. The hierarchy is read from the bottom up, and the input, process activities, and output measures reflect an internal perspective and are focused on how well the library is managing its resources. Measures of outcomes and impacts are focused on identifying measures of change.

Strategic Triangle

Another important model to be aware of is Mark Moore's strategic triangle.[14] This model suggests that the top managers of government agencies and not-for-profit organizations can focus their attention on three key strategic components of management:

- *Creating public value*—in the cultural organization context, by providing access to collections, technology, and services, exhibits and so forth
- *Management of the (political) authorizing environment*—being effective actors in networks of cooperation, competition, implementation, and delivery
- *Building operational expertise to deliver value*—ensuring that the organization is operating in an efficient and lean manner

Creation of public value focuses on management's attention as to what and how the cultural organization should be providing services that add value in relation to its mission. Political management is concerned about the expectations of various political stakeholders ensuring that the library receives the necessary resources to achieve its mission. And operational expertise or management is centered on what processes, systems, and resources must be organized so that value is created in the lives of the library's customers.

It doesn't take much imagination to see the utility and applicability of Moore's strategic triangle model in a cultural organization setting and that public, academic, and other types of libraries do indeed create public value in several ways. Unfortunately, cultural organizations do not carefully consider or write about the ways in which cultural organizations in general, and how a particular organization, add real value in the life of their customers.

One study carefully examined the strategic triangle's impact on program outcomes. The study reviewed the management activities of school administrators in three possible directions: upward to their authorizing environment (school boards), outward to the larger network and policy framework, and downward to their internal managers (school district managers). The research noted that those managers who spent the majority of their time managing outward to the larger external network performed better than their counterparts who focused in the other two directions.[15]

Blue Ocean

The book *Blue Ocean Strategy* divided the world into two camps: the Red Ocean Strategy and the Blue Ocean Strategy.[16] The **Red Ocean Strategy** views the world in a traditional light: an organization competes in an existing market space; the objective is to beat the competition; the focus is on exploiting existing demand; and it aligns the organization's processes and services on differentiation **or** low cost. In a very direct way, "Red Ocean" also symbolizes the very nature of the competitive environment—a for-profit firm may bleed "red ink" (short for financial losses).

On the other hand, the **Blue Ocean Strategy** focuses on looking at the world using the prism of value innovation: create unchallenged market spaces, make competition unrelated (by not competing), create new demand, and structure the organization's activities in the quest of differentiation **and** low cost. The book illustrates these strategic concepts by examining the emergence and growth of such interesting organizations as Cirque du Soleil, Starbucks, Yellow Tail wine, and Southwest Airlines.

The value innovation framework allows you to ask four questions to test an industry's business model:

1. *Eliminate.* What factors that the industry takes for granted should or could be *eliminated*?
2. *Reduce.* What factors can be/should be *reduced* before others in the industry do so?
3. *Raise.* What factors can be/should be *raised* before others in the industry do so?
4. *Create.* What factors can be/should be *created* that the industry has never offered?

One helpful way to view a Blue Ocean Strategy is through the use of a strategy canvas as shown in Figure 4-4. This strategy canvas compares the typical library with both Amazon and Google Scholar and illustrates the ways in which the service offering of each differs. A successful Blue Ocean Strategy will have *focus* (does not attempt to compete across all factors of competition), the *value curve* (diverges from others), and a *compelling tagline* (distilling the value message into an easy-to-understand phrase or sentence). Value innovation is all about creating more value for customers but at a lower cost—breaking the mold of the old value versus cost trade-off.

Clearly, for many libraries, especially libraries that are reducing the footprint devoted to books and other physical collections, a physical space offers many opportunities to engage with their customers and provide real value. Using Figure 4-4 as a starting point, add other value characteristics and alter the value curves I have created. Get creative and think hard about ways your library differentiates itself from other competitors your customers routinely use. The goal is to develop a value curve for the library that is the opposite of your competitors—be low when they are high and high when they are low—except for convenience. Libraries really need to reduce complexity, improve wayfinding, and significantly improve convenience of services. The idea of the value curve is to see the library's competition through the lens of your customers.

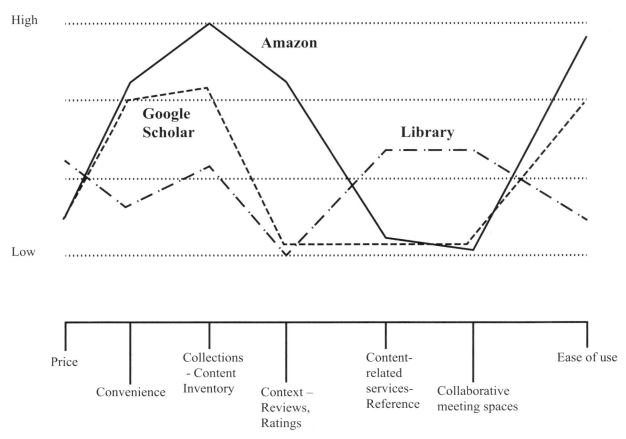

Figure 4-4 Blue Ocean Strategy Canvas. Created by author. Adapted from Blue Ocean www .blueoceanstrategy.com

The authors of *Blue Ocean Strategy* suggest that there are six principles that lead to the successful development of a unique strategy:

Formulation Principles

- Re-create market boundaries.
- Concentrate on the big picture, not the numbers.
- Move beyond the existing demand.
- Get the strategic progression correct.

Execution Principles

- Triumph over key organization hurdles.
- Make execution a part of strategy.

Strategic failure has less to do with formulating a bad strategy and more to do with failing to recognize what is desired by the authorizing environment (funding decision makers), failure in delivering the planned services (organizational capacity), or the service has little or no value in the life of the customer (public value). Robert Kaplan and David Norton have noted that strategic failure is often the result of strategy that is not properly implemented (not tracking the right performance measures, as well as not having all staff members understand or buying in to the strategic plan).[17]

Methods to Add Even More Value

As libraries move from their historical roots of being a "warehouse for dead trees" to an institution that is engaged with its customers, they must abandon many of the ways that they have always added value (since the traditional added-value techniques are no longer "valued" by the library's customers) and find new ways to add value that will have real meaning and be appreciated (and even sought after) by customers of the library.

The concept of paradigms and paradigm shifts, developed by Thomas Kuhn in his well-regarded book *The Structure of Scientific Revolutions*, has been warmly embraced by a great many disciplines as a conceptual tool for understanding the massive changes occurring in our turbulent environment.[18] A paradigm is a mental model that dominates the way people think and act. Yet, a paradigm is clearly a two-edged sword—it helps us structure data so that we can better understand what we see and observe, yet we are also oblivious to change that is occurring around us since some of the data does not fit our particular paradigm. Thus, the very procedures, policies, and organizational forms that have assisted us for years now become the very reason for our inability to react in an appropriate manner to change.

Not since the time of Gutenberg, over 500 years ago, have society and libraries been faced with such a large and fundamental paradigm shift as we change from moving atoms (books and other physical objects) to the digital arena (moving bits and bytes). This is an exciting time to be involved with libraries and delivering services that are of increasing value to our customers. Do we hold on to printed text and other forms of storing and sharing information in a physical form, or do we embrace the data deluge of born-digital (and the digitized analog)? Does it have to be an either-or question?

It is also important to recognize that galleries, libraries, archives, and museums offer a variety of services and types of collections that can bring real value to people's lives. Yet, the type of value may be quite different, depending on individuals and their particular need when they interact with a specific service or collection. Note that the individual may interact with a physical space or in a digital environment. Consider the following types of values:

- *Community value*—People benefit from being a part of a community that interacts with a specific item, collection, or service.
- *Education value*—A resource contributes to its own or other people's sense of culture, education, heritage, or knowledge, and therefore value it.
- *Existence/prestige value*—Knowing that people, both inside and outside a community, prize a resource or collection provides value to an individual.
- *Inheritance/bequest value*—People derive value knowing that resources contributed to galleries, libraries, archives, and museums will be used by future generations.
- *Utility value*—Being able to use a resource now or sometime in the future is a source of value for people. Utility or use value is often divided into direct benefits and indirect benefits.

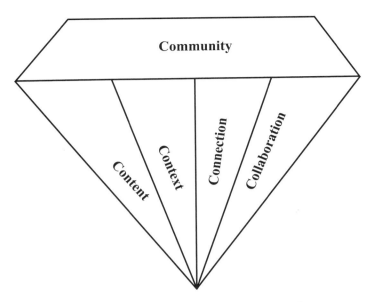

Figure 4-5 The Adding Value Diamond.

In my view, libraries can add even more value, using the "Adding Value Diamond" as shown in Figure 4-5.

When Martha, my wife-to-be, and I were going to look at engagement rings, a helpful jeweler explained that there are four characteristics used to determine a diamond's value—the 4Cs: color, carat, cut, and clarity. In a similar vein, I am suggesting that there are five ways that libraries can add value now and into the future—the 5Cs: content, context, connection, collaboration, and community.

Content

The content found in most academic and public libraries are relatively homogeneous. The amount of collection overlap is quite high, but fortunately, the tail is quite long—almost every library has some content that is unique to their library.

A majority of libraries have, or are planning to, digitized and cataloged all of the unique materials found in a library's special collections. Many libraries around the world have received grants to digitize collections with the result that several tens of millions of pages of content is now accessible via the World Wide Web. The topic of content will be explored in greater detail in Chapter 5.

Context

In the information environment, context has the potential for making a large impact. As illustrated by the writings of Edward Tufte[19] and Richard Saul Wurman,[20] context provides the basis for people gaining a better understanding of information. The point that these two authors make in all of their writings is that any graphic (chart or diagram) must not quote data out of context. Most readers when they look at a chart or diagram will unconsciously ask the question "compared with what?" Similarly, users of cultural organization catalogs or websites like the option of being able to choose related resources.

As will be discussed in much greater detail in Chapter 6, there are a variety of tools and techniques that will allow the cultural organization to add a great deal more context and thus significantly improve the value of services. As seen in Figure 4-6, a search in Wikipedia reveals the many ways in which the word context has been used.

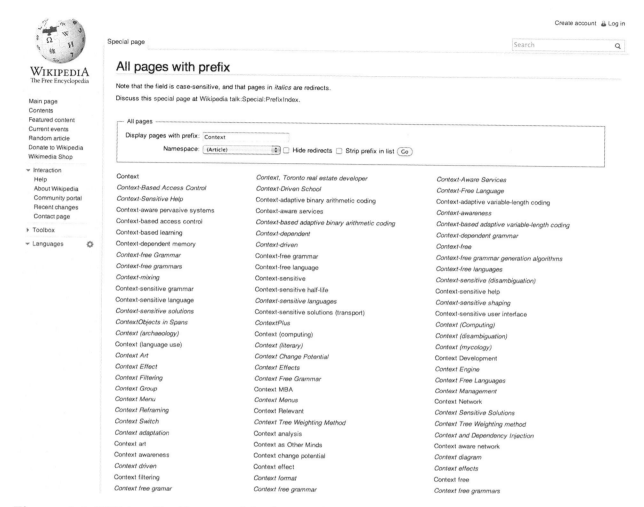

Figure 4-6 Wikipedia Pages with the Prefix "Context." Available at https://en.wikipedia .org/w/index.php?title=Special%3APrefixIndex&prefix=context&namespace=0

Connection

Developing a deeper understanding of customers and their various needs will improve existing services and may lead to creating new services. One approach is for librarians to become much more deeply involved in the day-to-day lives of their users. Some have called this the virtual librarian, the roving librarian, the personal librarian, the embedded librarian, the wandering librarian, the consulting librarian, or simply a "team member." Yet, this concept raises an important question as to scalability. Can some or most libraries afford the costs of sending professional librarians out into the community (and ignoring the tasks that they are currently doing)?

As we will see in chapter 7, librarians can add real value in the life of their customers both by better understanding their needs by gaining a deeper understanding of their day-to-day activities and by having the opportunity to make meaningful contributions. On the web, we all, live in a world of intersecting communities or networks, and it is through these intersections that librarians and other cultural organization professionals will have their greatest impact.

Collaboration

Encouraging the participation of talented individuals to accomplish a wide variety of goals is another way in which the library can add real value. Any group of people, oftentimes called a crowd, can take on any number of roles—as experts, a crowd of ordinary people, a coalition of parties, or a community of kindred spirits. Most likely, the first crowdsourcing project was the development of the first edition of the *Oxford English Dictionary*.[21] Crowdsourcing has been used to accomplish a wide variety of purposes—solve problems, reduce spam, collaborate on projects, raise money, find talented individuals to work on short-term projects, and assist scientists among many other activities.

Chapter 8 provides an in-depth discussion of the power of collaboration and the ways libraries can involve their users in meaningful projects. Yet, the real goal ought not to be the completion of a specific project but rather the development or a much deeper relationship between the individual and the library. And Chapter 9 provides a discussion about the ways in which some libraries and museums are embracing collaboration with their users.

Community

In reality, libraries, archives, and museums serve only a subset of their total community (however that is defined). Individuals who use library services, known as users, customers, clients, patrons among a host of other names, represent some portion of the total number of possible customers (e.g., the students, faculty, and staff on a campus)—including both physical and virtual visitors to the cultural institution. As libraries, archives, and museums move increasingly into the digital world, these institutions have an opportunity to become more engaged with a larger proportion of the total worldwide community. The importance of community is discussed in much greater detail in Chapter 10.

Summary

The ways in which libraries have historically added value are no longer providing sufficient value in the eyes of those who count—our customers. The reasons for this change are many, but the most important revolve around the impact the Internet has had and continues to have as new technologies are introduced and existing technologies are enhanced.

Five topics are introduced that offer libraries, archives, and museums the opportunity to engage with their users in new and interesting ways that will directly and indirectly add value. The five topics have been organized as the 5Cs: content, context, connection, collaboration, and community.

Main idea:	Cultural organizations can create value in new ways beyond the traditional ways they have done so in the past
Opposing view:	Stick to our knitting—focus on keeping control of our data and building collections
Key concepts:	Adding value, unique value proposition, differentiation
What has changed?:	Everything
Catalyst:	Information technology and the always on society
Open debate:	How to add unique value in the life of our customers

Notes

1. Quoted in Steven Sieden. *A Fuller View: Buckminster Fuller's Vision of Hope and Abundance for All*. New York: Divine Arts, 2012, 101.

2. Quoted in PC Magazine's Encyclopedia. Available at http://www.pcmag.com/encyclopedia/term/37701/amara-s-law

3. David Lankes. "Beyond the Bullet Points: Libraries Are Obsolete." *Virtual Dave . . . Real Blog*. April 20, 2012. Available at http://quartz.syr.edu/blog/?p=1567

4. David Lankes. *The Atlas of New Librarianship*. Cambridge, MA: MIT Press, 2011, 13.

5. T. Scott Plutchak. "Breaking the Barriers of Time and Space: The Dawning of the Great Age of Librarians." *Journal of the Medical Librarians Association*, 100 (1), 2012, 12.

6. Carl Grant. "Are Librarians Choosing to Disappear from the Information & Knowledge Delivery Process." *Thoughts from Carl Grant* blog. February 28, 2012. Available at http://thoughts.care-affiliates.com/2012/02/are-librarians-choosing-to-disappear.html

7. Chris Batt. *If We Did Not Have Libraries, Would Someone Invent Them?* Presentation for the 2010 Lucile Kelling Henderson lecture, University of North Carolina, October 5, 2010. Available at http://www.slideshare.net/Chris_Batt/chris-batt-unc-presentation-0510

8. Arie de Geus. "The Living Company." *Harvard Business Review*, March–April 1997, 51–59.

9. John Hagel and Marc Singer. "Unbundling the Corporation: What Business Are You Really In? Chances Are, It's Not What You think." *Harvard Business Review*, March–April 1999, 133–141.

10. Raquel Sanchez-Fernandez, Angeles Iniesta-Bonillo, and Morris Holbrook. "The Conceptualization and Measurement of Consumer Value in Services." *International Journal of Market Research*, 51 (1), 2009, 93–113.

11. Bill Lee. "Building Customer Communities Is the Key to Creating Value. *HBR Blog Network*, February 1, 2013. Available at http://blogs.hbr.org/2013/02/building-customer-communities/

12. Michael Germano and Shirley Stretch-Stephenson. "Strategic Value Planning for Libraries." *The Bottom Line*, 25 (2), 2012, 71–88.

13. *Business Model Innovation Cultural Heritage*. Amsterdam and The Hague: The DEN Foundation, 2010. Available at http://www.den.nl/art/uploads/files/Publicaties/BusModIn_eng_final.pdf

14. Mark Moore. *Creating Public Value: Strategic Management of the Public Sector*. Boston: Harvard University Press, 1995.

   Mark Weinberg and Marsha Lewis. "The Public Value Approach to Strategic Management." *Museum Management and Curatorship*, 24 (3), September 2009, 253–269.

15. Laurence O'Toole, Kenneth Meier, and Sean Nicholson-Crotty. *Managing Upward, Downward, and Outward: Networks, Hierarchical Relationships, and Performance.* Paper presented at the Meeting of the American Political Science Association, Philadelphia, 2003.

16. W. Chan Kim and Renee Mauborgne. *Blue Ocean Strategy: How to Create Uncontested Market Space and Make the Competition Irrelevant*. Boston: Harvard Business School Press, 2005.

   W. Chan Kim and Renee Mauborgne. "Blue Ocean Strategy." *Harvard Business Review,* October 2004, 71–79.

17. Robert Kaplan and David Norton. *The Strategy-Focused Organization: How Balanced Scorecard Companies Thrive in the New Business Environment*. Boston: Harvard Business School Press, 2001.

18. Thomas Kuhn. *The Structure of Scientific Revolutions.* Chicago: University of Chicago Press, 1962.

19. Edward Tufte. *Envisioning Information*. New York: Graphics Press, 1990; *The Visual Display of Quantitative Information*. New York: Graphics Press, 2001; *Visual Explanations: Images and Quantities, Evidence and Narrative*. New York: Graphics Press, 1997; *Beautiful Evidence*. New York: Graphics Press, 2006.

20. Richard Saul Wurman. *Information Anxiety*. New York: Doubleday, 1989; *Information Architects*. New York: Graphics Press, 1997; *Information Design*. Cambridge, MA: MIT Press, 2000; *33: Understanding Change & the Change in Understanding*. New York: Greenway, 2009.

21. Simon Winchester. *The Meaning of Everything: The Story of the Oxford English Dictionary.* Oxford, England: Oxford University Press, 2004.

5

Content

To conceive of knowledge as a collection of information
seems to rob the concept of all its life . . .
Knowledge resides in the user and not in the collection.
It is how the user reacts to a collection of information that matters.

C.W. Churchman[1]

For many, the raison d'être of a library is its collection of books and other materials. Without its collections, a library is unable to provide access to the information to be found in its collections. With the exception of really large research libraries and almost all national libraries, most libraries have a relatively small role to play in the preservation of some small subset of its overall collection.

The principal reason why libraries have developed collections is to provide convenient access to materials "that people want to see *where* they want to see them [emphasis in the original]."[2] Thus, convenient access to collections has had a long tradition in libraries. When the library was (mostly) the only game in town, readers had to come to the library to get and use a book, obtain a photocopy of journal articles, and so forth. And by implication, this meant that the user and the document had to be in the same place at the same time.

The selection of materials to add to a collection is constrained by the physical space that is available. Every poor decision about what to collect (and retain) costs time and money as well as the library incurring an opportunity cost since something else (potentially of more use value) could have been purchased. Yet, in today's Internet world, the costs of storing digital content are quite low (and the opportunity cost for storing digital content is approaching zero).

Libraries built systems to manage the accessibility of physical content by:

- Building collections of relevant content
- Managing the physical space where the content was housed
- Developing systems to make the process of accessing the content easier
- Developing tools to make locating the content easier

The physicality of the physical collections meant that only one person could use a specific resource at one time. This one user-at-a-time limitation has been lifted as we are transitioning to a digital environment where multiple people, located in many different places, can use the same digital document at the same time. And as more and more library content is digitized and placed online, there is less value in the library serving as a warehouse and providing access to and controlling the borrowing of materials.

And librarians do not have a sterling track record for protecting the interests and demands of users as measured by collection usage (in large academic libraries, as much as 40% or more of the collections have never been used). For this and other reasons, it is not surprising that many libraries are starting to embrace patron-driven acquisitions.

Thus, it is not shocking to see large academic libraries shift major portions of the little used collection to either an off-site storage facility or to an automated storage and retrieval system (AS/RS). Storage of academic library materials for open shelving is quite expensive (one estimate is about $4.26 per book per year) compared with high-density storage options (about $.86 per book per year).[3]

Yes, at what point does a library stop being a library and remains only as a building if all collections are removed? To my mind, the distinguishing characteristic from a historical perspective of a library is its collection—the processes used to select, deselect, and organize this collection—and its ability to provide access to information and the preservation and transmission of culture. Note that this collection can have a wide variety of formats for storing the information content—although the move to a true digital library is happening with increasing speed.

One of the interesting dilemmas facing libraries is that while digital materials are real and can be viewed, repurposed, and used in many ways, they do not have the same properties of physical items that can be seen and touched. Attempting to provide tools for visualizing a collection of digital content has up until recently, relied on the tried and true library online catalog. The same indexes and the same displays of the online catalog are used to provide access to both digital and physical materials. The end result is that we have failed to provide our users with the tools that they need to visualize and begin to comprehend the breadth and width and depth of our ever-increasing digital collections. One of the fundamental issues that contemporary and future cultural organizations must solve is assisting its customers in gaining a better understanding of what is to be found in a digital library, archive, museum, or gallery.

We can no longer rely on classification systems and the arrangement of materials in a cultural organization to provide some sense of the collection's scope and size as we move into the digital arena.

One way to improve the searching experience is to enhance the bibliographic record with additional content. Cochrane and Markey noted more than 30 years ago that users wanted "the ability to search books tables of contents, summaries, or indexes"—these enhanced records provided more terms to be indexed thus increasing the precisions and recall for the user.[4] More recently, Karen Calhoun and her colleagues noted in a conclusion to a study of online catalogs that "[e]nd users rely on and expect enhanced content including summaries/abstracts and table of contents."[5] And while several studies have consistently demonstrated that enhanced records lead to higher circulation of those materials, it would not seem to be cost effective for a cultural organization to embrace enhanced records at this time (the costs to enhance a record can range from $1 per record to as high as $10 per record (depending upon the process selected).[6]

And bibliographic records, despite their "fullness," are a mere skeleton-like reflection of the real item (look at the robustness that you achieve when you provide full-text searching as in the case of Google Books or the amount of information provided via Amazon). The bibliographic record is a poor surrogate that enables discovery and a preliminary assessment of the usefulness and utility of the item. For example, consider David Verba and Todd Wilkens's book *Subject to Change*. The bibliography record found in a library's catalog is fairly short and compact compared with the lengthy record found in Amazon. In addition to the bibliographic information and cover of the book (what Amazon calls Product Details), the site provides Editorial Reviews, star ratings, Most Recent Customer reviews, what other items customers buy, among other options.

My favorite definition of a library catalog is that it "is a place where bibliographic records get lost alphabetically." And with the shift to the network environment, discovery increasingly happens elsewhere using a search engine (most often Google), while the local library catalog reflects access to content at the institutional level. And the library catalog is also becoming lost (if it is not found in a search engine). Given the option of searching bibliographic records (even enhanced bibliographic records) compared with being able to search every word in more than 30 million digitized books, it is no wonder that people are increasingly turning to Google Books, or sites that provide other book-related information such as Amazon, LibraryThing, Goodreads among a host of other network-level resources.

A majority of the content available online from the library are eResources that are licensed rather than purchased. As such, the library user more often than not does not see the value the library adds through the selection, licensing, and providing access to eResources (electronic journals and aggregated databases). As a result, the contribution of the library (paying for and providing access to the licensed content) is becoming invisible to the user. Walt Crawford has suggested that academic libraries are becoming "little more than subsidized article transfer mechanisms."[7]

In addition to being invisible, the user of these online eResources experiences a great deal of frustration since each online resource has its own user interface that must be learned (and relearned depending upon the interval of time that passes using a specific resource).

Many library catalogs provide a thumbnail image of book covers and, in a sense, evoke their physicality. This return to the physical world as content such as for eBooks is increasingly available only in an immaterial world, which will, for a time, tie the two worlds together. Yet, libraries have been reluctant to experiment with new ways to provide access and promote discovery—especially to digital content.

CASE STUDY

LibraryThing

LibraryThing (www.LibraryThing.com) is a community of 2,003,276 book lovers (as of November 2015) that encourages its members to catalog, discuss, and recommend books and authors to like-minded individuals. Over 100 million books have been cataloged, and users have added more than 122 million tags and almost 2.5 million reviews. In many ways, LibraryThing is a Facebook-like site for people who like books. And after you rate a number of books, it begins to make suggestions that are quite good. In addition to readers, authors, libraries, and publishers use the site.

Customers pay $10 per year (or $25 for life) to catalog their own library and interact with other like-minded book people. You can keep track of what you have read and what books you would like to read. There are thousands of groups that have a particular discussion focus such as Librarians who LibraryThing; Science fiction fans; Read YA lit; Crime, Thriller & Mystery; Hogwarts Express (Harry Potter); Historical fiction; and so forth. The number of participants in each group will vary from several hundred to tens of thousands.

A series of APIs (Application Programming Interface) allow software developers from other sites to tap into the wealth of LibraryThing data to create new and interesting applications. Some libraries have become LibraryThing members and are thus able to display LibraryThing reviews and book covers in the library's online catalog.

CASE STUDY

Goodreads

Goodreads (www.Goodreads.com) has some 40 million members, 1.1 billion books, and an impressive 43 million reviews (as of November 2015). Goodreads is dedicated to help people find and share books they love. After you indicate the titles and genres you have enjoyed in the past, the site provides insightful recommendations. You can also track what your friends are reading and discussing as well as sharing with your friends.

There are thousands of groups on Goodreads that include genre groups, new books groups, author groups, groups from your hometown, just for fun, organizations, student groups, and many, many more. Goodreads reviews can be accessed using an API. About 50 APIs allow other websites and other applications to be more personalized, social, and engaging by using the Goodreads data. Goodreads was purchased by Amazon in 2012.

CASE STUDY

aNobii

aNobii (www.anobii.com) is an online reading community allowing people to shelve, find, and share books. aNobii is Latin for the common bookworm and encourages users to keep track of what they are reading, have read, and want to read. The site connects people with similar reading tastes as well as discovering new and recently reviewed books. There are a number of reading groups, book clubs, and discussion forums that will appeal to everyone.

aNobii was acquired by the Sainsbury, a UK supermarket chain, with additional investments from HarperCollins, Penguin, and The Random House Group. A series of APIs provided by aNobii allow developers from other sites to include book-related information of their site.

Digitization

The amount of digitization that is taking place in libraries, museums, and archives around the world is quite simply staggering to image. Consider this small sample of digitization efforts:

- *Project Gutenberg* volunteers are digitizing mostly books in the public domain including many classic works. As of November 2015, there are over 50,000 free eBooks that can be downloaded.[8]

- The *Library of Congress American Memory Project* is designed to provide free and open access to written and spoken words, sound recordings, still and moving images, prints, maps, and sheet music that document the American experience. Early in 2016, the *American Memory Project* contains some nine million items.[9]

- The Library of Congress also provides access to other really large data sets, sometimes called big data, such as 50 billion tweets, a collection of hundreds of thousands of electronic journal articles, and five billion files in a single institutional web archive.

- The *British Library's* Online Gallery contains some 60 million digitized pages (and plans to digitize an additional 750 million pages over the next few years). The library has digitized three million pages of 18th- and 19th-century newspapers that are all accessible online. Among its most popular works are Handel's Messiah, a selection of Leonardo da Vinci's sketches, *Alice's Adventures Under Ground*, Mozart's musical diary (with audio clips), Jane Austin's early works, Ramayana (17th-century paintings from India), and many more.

- The *National Library of Australia's* Trove site, which provides access to 458,957,616 online resources including books, images, historic newspapers, maps, music archives, and more—as of November 26, 2015.[10] The site is designed to appeal to people from all walks of life—tracing family histories, doing professional or amateur research, teaching, studying, or reading for pleasure. More importantly, it provides a set of tools that allow people to become much more engaged with the content found within Trove.

- The *International Dunhuang Project* provides digital access to resources and artifacts found from archaeological sites along the ancient Silk Road traveled by Marco Polo and many others.

- The *Internet Archive* contains over 3.8 public domain eBook, texts, video, live music, audio files.[11]

- *Google Books* has digitized more than 30 million books (about 20% of these books are in the public domain) and expects to digitize more than 100 million books in the coming decade. In 2010, Google estimated that there are 129,864,880 books in the world—at that time.[12]

- The *HathiTrust*, a partnership of major research institutions and libraries, is working to preserve the cultural record for future generations. The HathiTrust Digital Library contains records (primarily from Google Books) for some more than 6.8 million titles and more than 13 million volumes (as of January 2016)—and more records are being added all the time.[13]

- The national libraries from most countries around the world are involved in various levels of digitizing resources. Several have plans to digitize more than 10 million pages of content over the next 10 years.

- *Gallica*, a site provided by the French National Library, has some 800,000 digitized newspapers, manuscripts, maps, drawings, and books.

- University and college libraries, large and small, in almost all countries have been digitizing content from their special collections.

- Public libraries of all sizes have been involved in preserving and providing digital access to portions of their special collections. Consider the vast array of resources available online at the New York Public Library, the Boston Public Library, the Chicago Public Library, the San Francisco Public Library, to name just a few.

- The state and provincial libraries are making some of their collections available online.

- Most museums, galleries, and historical societies are involved in digitizing portions of their collections.

- And archives have also been busy digitizing portions of their collections.

Recently, a report estimated that it would cost approximately 100 million euros to digitize the content not yet digitized for all of Europe's museums, archives, and libraries. European libraries hold about 77 million titles or almost 2 billion pages and some 7 million rare books; European museums hold 265 million man-made objects and more than 221 million natural objects (about 75 million individual works of art and 350 million photographs), while the European archives hold some 17 billion pages of materials.[14]

The Google Cultural Institute has more than 500 partners (museums, galleries, and libraries) from over 60 countries with more than 6.2 million objects and artifacts online. The website has more than 19 million unique visitors in the last year, and they generated 200 million page views, and visitors typically spend more than 8 minutes on the site each time they visit.[15]

Interestingly, Tom Tryniski, an enterprising individual who is located in upstate New York, has let his "hobby" become an obsession. Tom has digitized over 33,100,000 pages of historical newspapers (as of November 2105), and these are available for searching at his website (www.fultonhistory.com). Using a relatively inexpensive microfilm scanner and a network of PCs, Tom has scanned all of these pages on his own and provides access to the content for free. Tom's quirky personality is immediately apparent when you visit his website, but all that entertainment disappears when you start searching. And Tom's site is quite popular with more than twice the traffic as received by the Library of Congress's historic newspaper site, *Chronicling America*.[16]

So it is obvious that there is no dearth of digital content that people can access anytime, anywhere using a wide variety of devices. The total number of digital items accessible via the Internet is impossible to estimate but surely runs into the tens of millions of items and represents hundreds of millions (if not billions) of pages. Yet, one of the real challenges for anyone interested in a particular topic is that relevant resources are found in multiple locations (websites) and discovering this pertinent content is challenging at best. This distribution of interesting resources is often referred to as "silo" resources.

Clearly, digitizing analog content, which makes these materials accessible and more discoverable and useful in digital form, adds value from the perspective of the user. Yet, for a variety of reasons, the interested user rarely discovers much of this content.

But digitizing lots of content doesn't necessarily lead to lots of people using your site. The National Science Foundation pulled all of its funding for the National Science Digital Library project in July 2011. The funding cut was a simple acknowledgment that the $175 million investment over several years had failed on grounds of sustainability and utility. The original goal of the project was to "provide organized access to high-quality resources and tools that support innovations in teaching and learning at all levels." The science teaching profession was never broadly engaged with the project, and there was no evidence of improved student learning for students who had visited the digital libraries.[17]

Now contrast the multiyear, expensive National Science Digital Library project with the popular and heavily used resources of the *Kham Academy* (www.khan academy.org)—that has received significantly less funding. The *Khan Academy* primarily covers not only math, but also science topics such as chemistry, physics, biology, as well as finance and history, and is quite popular with teachers, students, and parents. Perhaps the best feature of the *Khan Academy*, aside from its excellent instructional videos, is that it responds quickly to comments and suggestions for improvement. In short, the *Khan Academy* is really engaged with its users.

With all of these massive digitization efforts under way, Kevin Kelly has envisioned a world (that he calls the "universal library") in which all of the digitized books become a "single liquid fabric of interconnected words and ideas."[18] Kelly hopes that

As each word in each book is cross-linked, clustered, cited, extracted, indexed, analyzed, annotated, remixed, reassembled and woven deeper into the culture than ever before. In the new world of books, every bit informs another; every page reads all the other pages.

Such a utopian view of the future world as viewed by Kelly is not without its critics as Christopher Rowe argues that such a future is not possible or even desirable.[19] The reality is that there will not be one seamless universal library but rather the typical individual will encounter a patchwork of digital book databases—some accessible to anyone, while others will require payment in one form or another.

Frameworks

One solution to siloed online collections is the use of a larger framework that pulls together the resources from multiple sites and makes them accessible from a single site. For example, the *European Library* provides access to the collections of Europe's 24 national libraries and many research libraries. Users can search more than 200 million records and access more than 24 million pages of full text and more than 7 million digital objects using The *European Library*.[20] The *European Library* delivers digital content monthly to *Europeana*, another mega-site that enables people to explore Europe's museums, libraries, archives, and audiovisual digital collections.[21] The "big idea" of *Europeana* is to aggregate content from numerous sources, improve it in several ways, and make it accessible in meaningful ways.

Another example of a mega-site is the Digital Public Library of America—see Figure 5-1 (www.dp.la). This site will ingest metadata from a wide variety of institutions (libraries, museums, galleries, historical societies, and archives) and point to the actual item (rather than attempting to ingest both the metadata and the digital object itself). A group of librarians and others involved in the formation and development of the DPLA have created a vision:

> The Digital Public Library of America (DPLA) will make the cultural and scientific heritage of humanity available, free of charge, to all. The DPLA's primary focus is on making available materials from the United States. By adhering to the fundamental principle of free and universal access to knowledge, it will promote education in the broadest sense of the term.
>
> The DPLA is concentrating at first on the written record—books, pamphlets, periodicals, manuscripts, and digital texts—but are designing the system such that we can move quickly to other types of materials, such as images, moving images, sound recordings, and the like.
>
> The plan is for the [online open source] platform to provide access to a central store of metadata about collections held by individual institutions and by nodes that aggregate collections from many institutions, distributed all across the Web.[22]

The DPLA represents the efforts of one group of concerned librarians that recognize that libraries must change in the way that they deliver services now and in the future. Since more and more information resides in the cloud, users will increasingly

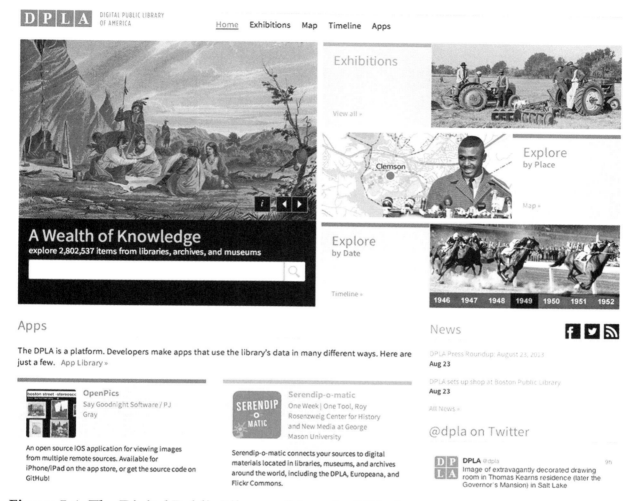

Figure 5-1 The Digital Public Library of America Website. © Digital Public Library of America.

rely upon digital materials being accessible anywhere, anytime. While most will acknowledge that libraries are not going away, libraries must strive to change the services they provide in a digital era. The DPLA will, it is hoped, experiment in ways that digital content from libraries, archives, and museums are displayed and made accessible. As Lorcan Dempsey has observed, we are moving to a shared network environment in which libraries will need to cooperate in order to take advantage of and leverage the visibility of resources that are discoverable at the network level (not the local library level).

Clearly, this vast, almost impossible to visualize, pile of digitized resources provides significant value for humanity in that an individual can search for resources that are going to be helpful and relevant for a particular situation and need. The value is however only latent or represents potential value in that the value will remain locked until it is discovered and used in some manner by someone.

However, challenges surrounding the aggregation model will need to be addressed. For example, a local cultural institution will need to expend time and effort to ensure that the digital objects and associated metadata conforms to required standards before any objects can be made accessible using the Digital Public Library or Europeana or another aggregation site. What benefits does the local institution derive from the increased visibility of their collections? And there is little recognition that cultural organizations metadata, while it serves a variety of purposes, is rarely of interest to the end user.

Another approach is to provide a set of tools that help people explore digitized resources in ways that have not been possible before. One exciting example is the popular *Turning the Pages* tool found on the British Library's website. *Turning the Pages* provides access to 26 wonderful books including Audubon's *The Birds of America*, *Alice's Adventures Under Ground*, a Bible for Ethiopia, and the *Diamond Sutra* (the oldest printed book made in China in 868).

User-Contributed Content

Millions upon millions of people today are "prosumers." First coined by Alvin Toffler in his 1980 book *The Third Wave*, a prosumer is someone who blurs the distinction between a "consumer" and a "producer."[23] Much later (2006), Dan Tapscott and Anthony Williams used the word "prosumption" (production/consumption) and suggested that the mass collaborations of prosumers could help bring success to organizations.[24]

Prosumers engage in a variety of activities belonging to either sphere, regardless of time or location. Prosumers typically embrace Web 2.0 technologies and services such as social networking (Facebook), blogging, podcasting, video on demand, virtual reality (Second Life), sharing photos, videos and tweets, and using Internet-based technologies and mobile communications to stay connected whenever and wherever they desire. Prosumers have a very connected lifestyle.

There are more than 100 million bloggers around the world—more than 62 million bloggers use the *WordPress* system—which is just one of many blogging tools available. More than 409 million people view more than 20.4 billion *WordPress* pages each month (as of November 2015).[25]

It is possible to group prosumers into a series of overlapping groups from a social media perspective as shown in Figure 5-2:

- **Creators** are people who publish on the web (blog, website, video, podcasts).
- **Commentators/Critics** are people who post reviews online, comment on blogs, or contribute in other ways to existing content.
- **Collectors** are folks who read lots of information and may vote or tag pages or photos.
- **Distributors** forward and share content with others.
- **Joiners** are people who have a profile on different social networking sites and visit them with some regularity.
- **Consumers or Spectators** are folks who read online information, listen to podcasts, and watch videos but do not participate.
- **Inactives** are the people who aren't engaged in any of these social activities.

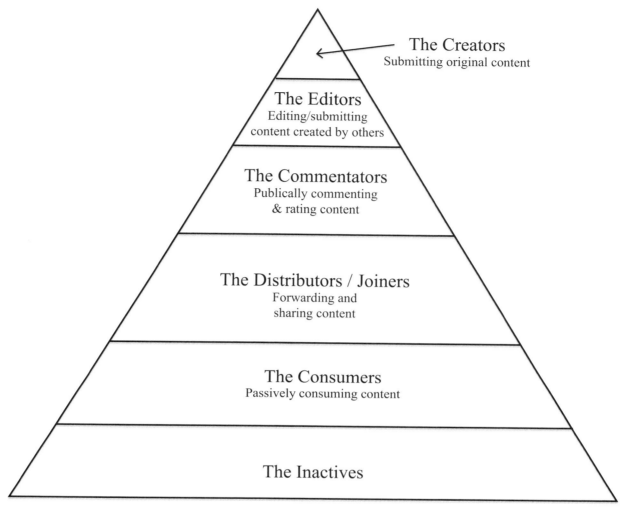

Figure 5-2 The Participation Pyramid.

Overall, less than one-fourth of people are creators, a third are critics, half are joiners, and three-fourths are consumers. Younger age groups are more active than their older counterparts.[26]

Clearly, prosumption is associated with a culture of participation and is assumed to be beneficial while skeptics lament the emerging "cult of the amateur."[27] However, the net effect of the availability of this tsunami of digital content is that the carefully selected content found in libraries is becoming less and less relevant in the lives of those who live and work in any community or on any campus. And the growth of digital content on the Internet is almost beyond comprehension.

Making the assumption that content is the primary focus is simply too shortsighted. Cory Doctorow asserts, "Conversation is king. Content is just something to talk about."[28] The conversations are started and continue around shared blog postings, photos, videos, and so forth. And when a number of people are engaged and discussing ways to get better at something, this form of communication is usually called a "community of practice." And the hundreds of thousands of communities of practice that exist are busy collaborating using tools they find of value on the Internet.

More and more websites are working to establish themselves as destinations (sometimes called platforms) that collect, preserve, and create themed content that focuses on a specific subject. Consider these examples: Rhizome (www.rhizome.org) focuses on new digital media; Mubi (www.mubi.com) collects and preserves classic and independent films; Hulu (www.hulu.com) arranges television content from a number of sources and rearranges them into collections; blogs are aggregated by several sites including The Daily Beast (www.thedailybeast.com), Huffington Post (www.huffington post.com), and the Drudge Report (www.drudgereport.com).

Digital content strategists, called curators in libraries and archives, work to define how content should be positioned, organized, made accessible, and relevant. Does your library "trumpet" its collection strengths (often its special collections) on Wikipedia, Pinterest, YouTube, Historypin, and other sites? Doing so increases the likelihood that others, from around the world, will discover your content and become interested in engaging in a conversation. You can build links between the library and these external content sites as well as linking to other galleries, libraries, archives, and museums that have similar content.

In addition, the cultural organization can use analytic tools, such as Google Analytics, to learn more about the use (or lack thereof) of your website:

- Where people come from?
- How often they share the library's content with others?
- How they share content with others (what social media sites)?
- What are the most popular topics?
- Where do people leave (sometimes called bounce rates)?
- What web pages are not visited at all?

Information Portals

Corporations, government agencies, and other organizations have developed information portals, sometimes called knowledge management platforms or an Intranet, that restrict access to the staff members of a specific organization. The information portal contains a wealth of information placed there by the management team, but it also allows everyone in the organization to contribute content as well as critique, review, and comment on a wide range of topics. The intent of any Intranet is to provide a set of tools that allows experienced and knowledgeable people to share their expertise.

As Lew Platt, the former CEO of Hewlett-Packard, once observed, "If only HP knew what HP knows, we would be three times more productive." This pithy observation resonates with most people who realize that a significant amount of experience, knowledge, and creative ideas exist within any group, and yet for most organizations, this tremendous resource remains untapped. Brian Detlor, building on the work of Robert Taylor and Thomas Davenport's work, has suggested that Intranet developers need to incorporate value-added process in order to improve an organization's

Behavioral/Ecological Component	*Common Design Scenario*
Information Ecology:	
Physical setting	Provide online access to the Intranet so all users can have anytime, anyplace access
Information culture	Present information in engaging ways. Provide links of value on the desktop and mobile device of choice by the user. Ensure that "link rot" is minimized.
Information politics	Ensure that the portal has tools that will facilitate discussion, chat, tagging, so that information hoarding is minimized. Constantly monitor the site to ensure that content that is not being used is removed and that navigation is facilitated.
Information staff	Use library staff to add value by summarizing, filtering, adding metadata, etc. Enlist users to add tags, reviews, ratings and comments.
Information behavior:	
Problem dimensions	Provide multiple perspectives and information summaries that can assist the user in making sense and interpreting information that will assist the user in resolving or bettering understanding their problems.
Information traits	Provide multiple ways to display the same information—quantitative/qualitative, historical/forecasting, and raw data versus charts and graphs.
Information uses	Provide a set of tools that will allow the user to gain access to background information, summary versus detailed information, and general versus specific information.

Figure 5-3 Behavioral/Ecological Framework.

informational context.[29] Detlor has developed an information behavioral/ecological framework as seen in Figure 5-3, which has seven components.

Self-Publishing

The form of the book has changed over time, and most recently the eBook has been developed. Interestingly, some now call the print book a "pBook." The popularity of the eBook has increased as consumers are presented with more affordable options for "reading" an eBook—using an eReader, tablet, or laptop computer. Amazon announced in 2011 that it had sold more eBooks than pBooks for the first time in its history. According to a recent Pew Center Research report, 21 percent of American adults read an eBook in the last year, 68 percent read a pBook, while 19 percent read NO books.[30] Tablet owners and eReader owners report that they read more (eBooks and pBooks) since the advent of the eBook.[31]

In addition to the growing number of eBooks from commercial publishers, more than a million eBooks are available at little or no cost from self-publishers. Not surprisingly, the quality of these self-published eBooks ranges from excellent to quite terrible. However, these self-published eBooks represent another avenue for people to share their ideas and interests with others. While there are literally dozens and dozens of firms to help people self-publish their books, the four largest firms are: Amazon's Create Space, Smashwords, Author Solutions, and Lulu.

One of the real challenges for anyone interested in learning about self-published eBooks is learning about their existence since much of the content is not accessible via a search engine. This is a significant problem for the consumer, the prosumer, and libraries interested in providing access to this voluminous content.

Library-Provided Social Content

Libraries can go way beyond providing the traditional pathfinder or providing access to a reference library via email (or chat or texting or . . .) given we are living in the era of social media. Libraries can be writing a blog about the library or better yet about the community or about an important nearby industry or a popular hobby or recreation activity or . . ., provide access to audio (podcasts) and/or video of story time, author talks, library-provided programs, and so much more. But in addition to stepping up to engage library customers with a library-focused outreach in social media, the library really needs to be where the customer is—whether it is on Facebook, Twitter, Pinterest, LinkedIn, and so forth. If librarians reach out and connect with people in their communities, then the library and its services are going to seem to be more relevant in today's hyperactive age.

A quick search on YouTube for "public library story time" found 9,220 results, "public library tour" retrieved 235,000 results, and so on; well, you get the idea. Is your library posting content to YouTube, Pinterest, Facebook, Twitter, and other social media sites?

Summary

There is an old saying in the traditional media businesses of newspapers, magazines, television, and the movies that "content is king." Creating or providing access to great content is a surefire way to build a great reputation. And for the millions of folks who post photos, messages, comments, and tweets on an ongoing and daily basis using a variety of social media tools, the reality is that almost everyone is creating content about everything they do. We are all publishing content—daily, hourly, every few minutes. Clearly, we have reached a stage where there has been a shift from "content is everything" to "everything is content."

When we look at the rapidly changing world of magazines, newspapers, and others that develop new content on a daily basis, it is surprising how little effort is put forth to curate this quite valuable resource beyond digitizing content and making it accessible in some way. We all need to encourage our users to be involved with the content that we provide access to.

As seen in Figure 5-4, today the value of access to content is found on the network and not at the institutional level (the library and its resources and services). In a world of web scale content and web scale discovery, the only reasonable course of action is to ensure that the library's content (especially unique content from special collections) can be "found" by the search engine crawlers. The automated tools developed over the course of the last 30–40 years have been focused on the need to manage physical collections (and that world is losing ground fast).

As libraries, archives, and museums begin to explore the boundaries between information and knowledge created or vetted by professionals versus that created by those who interact with a cultural organization, those professionals will need to relax in order to better understand the real contributions that can be made by knowledgeable and enthusiastic "amateurs."

Thus, a library must be involved in a wide variety of places so that library staff members have the opportunity to share the content and services of the cultural organization to an audience who are interested. And people actually demonstrate their interest when they "friend" your library or start to "follow" you online. If staff can engage your customers by providing them with valuable and relevant content that the library is providing, you win. People take notice and will recommend your cultural organization to others.

Your cultural organization can post some of library's more interesting content online using Flickr (perhaps some historical or unique photos); YouTube (videos created

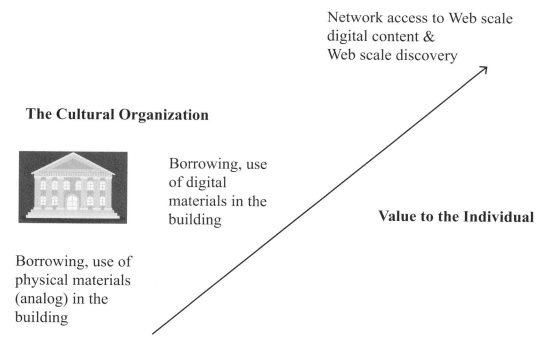

Figure 5-4 Where the Value May Be Found.

by the staff members, teens, and others); Facebook (events and happenings); Pinterest (a content-sharing service that allows you to "pin" images, videos, and other objects to a pin board); a library blog; and so forth. The British Library has released to Flickr over a million images taken from the pages of 17th-, 18th-, and 19th-century books making them free to remix and reuse. Included in these images are illuminated and decorative letters, illustrations, landscapes, paintings, comical satire, and maps.

Clearly, content is very important; yet, in the Internet era, copies of digital content are essentially free. Kevin Kelly, of *Wired* magazine, makes the point however that context is not free, that experience is not free, that packaging is not free, that curation is not free, and alternative output may not be free. Given this, what role may a cultural organization play that adds value to content?

Checklist for Adding Value to Content

	Yes	No
Is staff spending less time acquiring, storing, cataloging, organizing, and providing access to information than they were five years ago?	☐	☐
Has the cultural organization digitized its historical and special collections?	☐	☐
Has your cultural organization re-invented its website in the last year?	☐	☐
Has the organization created entries for its historical and special collections on Wikipedia?	☐	☐
Has your cultural organization posted copies of images on Flickr, on Pinterest?	☐	☐
Has your cultural organization posted videos on YouTube?	☐	☐
Has you cultural organization made its catalog visible to search engines?	☐	☐
Has your cultural organization installed Google Analytics and is using the resulting data to improve its website?	☐	☐

If you answered "no" to one or more of the questions in the checklist, then your library is not doing all it could to add value using content.

Main idea:	Content is very important
Opposing view:	Content in a cultural organization is dead
Key terms:	Collections, content, the network, access, competition
What has changed?:	The Internet
Catalyst:	How does content add value—is access to "stuff" enough?
Open debate:	In the competitive digital environment, how can a cultural organization be viewed as "cool" and having amazing stuff so people return again and again

Notes

1. C. W. Churchman. *The Design of Inquiring Systems.* New York: Basic Books, 1971, 11.
2. Michael Buckland. *Redesigning Library Services: A Manifesto.* Chicago: American Library Association, 1992, 55–56.
3. Paul Courant and Matthew Nielsen. "On the Cost of Keeping a Book, in *The Idea of Order: Transforming Research Collections for 21st Century Scholarship.* Washington, DC: Council on Library and Information Resources, 2010. Available at http://www.clir.org/pubs/reports/pub147/pub147.pdf
4. Pauline Cochrane and Karen Markey. "Catalog Use Studies—Since the Introduction of Online Interactive Catalogs: Impact on Design for Subject Access." *Library & Information Science Research,* 5 (4), 1983, 337–363.
5. Karen Calhoun, Joanne Cantrell, Peggy Gallagher, and Janet Hawk. *Online Catalogs: What Users Want and Librarians Want.* Dublin, OH: OCLC, 2009, v.
6. Debbie Dinkins and Laura Kirkland. "It's What's Inside That Counts: Adding Contents Notes to Bibliographic Records and Its Impact on Circulation." *College & Undergraduate Libraries,* 13 (1), 2006, 59–71. See also, Cherie Madarash-Hill and J Hill. "Electronically Enriched Enhancements in Catalog Records: A Use Study of Books Described on Records with URL Enhancements versus Those Without." *Technical Services Quarterly,* 23 (2), 2005, 19–31.
    Ruth Morris. "Online Tables of Contents for Books: Effect on Usage." *Bulletin of the Medical Libraries Association,* 89 (1), 2001, 29–36.
7. Walt Crawford. *The Big Deal and the Damage Done.* June 2013. Available at www.lulu.com
8. Project Gutenberg. Available at http://www.gutenberg.org/
9. Library of Congress American Memory, Mission and History. Available at http://memory.loc.gov/ammem/about/about.html
10. National Library of Australia Trove. Available at http://trove.nla.gov.au/
11. Internet Archive. Available at http://archive.org/index.php
12. Leonid Taycher. "Books of the World, Stand Up and Be Counted! All 129,864,880 of You." *Google Books Search* blog. August 5, 2010. Available at http://booksearch.blogspot.com/2010/08/books-of-world-stand-up-and-be-counted.html
13. HathiTrust. Available at http://www.hathitrust.org/
14. Nick Poole. *The Cost of Digitizing Europe's Cultural Heritage.* November 2010. London: Collections Trust. Available at http://ec.europa.eu/information_society/activities/digital_libraries/doc/refgroup/annexes/digiti_report.pdf
15. Amit Sood. "The Brave New Digital World." *The Wall Street Journal,* September 16, 2014. Available at http://online.wsj.com/articles/museums-enter-the-brave-new-digital-world-1410905887
16. Jim Epstein. "Amateur Beats Gov't at Digitizing Newspapers: Tom Tryniski's Weird, Wonderful Website." *Reason.com,* March 5, 2013. Available at http://reason.com/reasontv/2013/03/05/amateur-beats-gov-at-digitizing-newspape
17. Jeffrey Mervis. "NSF Rethinks Its Digital Library." *Science,* 323, January 2, 2009, 54–58.
18. Kevin Kelly. "Scan This Book!" *The New York Times,* May 14, 2006. Available at http://www.nytimes.com/2006/05/14/magazine/14publishing.html?_r=3&
19. Christopher Rowe. "The New Library of Babel? Borges, Digitization and the Myth of the Universal Library." *First Monday,* 18 (2), February 2013.

20. The European Library. Available at http://www.theeuropeanlibrary.org/tel4/
21. Europeana. Available at http://www.europeana.eu/portal/
22. The Digital Public Library of America. Concept Note. Available at http://dp.la/wiki/Concept_Note
23. Alvin Toffler. *The Third Wave*. New York: Morrow, 1980.
24. Dan Tapscott and Anthony Williams. *Wikinomics: How Mass Collaboration Changes Everything*. New York: Penguin, 2006.
25. Statistics as of November 2015 provided by WordPress. Available at http://en.wordpress.com/stats/
26. George Van Antwerp. "Creators, Critics, Collectors, Joiners, Spectators, and Inactives." *Enabling Healthy Decisions* blog. August 3, 2010. Available at http://georgevanantwerp.com/2010/08/03/creators-critics-collectors-joiners-spectators-and-inactives/
27. Andrew Keen. *The Cult of the Amateur: How Today's Internet Is Killing Our Culture*. New York: Doubleday/Currency, 2007.
28. Quoted by Clay Shirky. *Here Comes Everybody: The Power of Organizing without Organizations*. New York: Penguin, 2009, 99.
29. Brian Detlor. "The Corporate Portal as Information Infrastructure: Towards a Framework for Portal Design." *International Journal of Information Management*, 20, 2000, 91–101.
30. Krissten Purcell. *Books or Nooks? How Americans' Reading Habits Are Shifting in a Digital World*. A presentation to the Ocean County Library Staff Development Day, May 18, 2012. Available at http://libraries.pewinternet.org/2012/05/18/books-or-nooks-how-americans-reading-habits-are-shifting-in-a-digital-world/
31. Kathryn Zickuhr. *The Rise of e-Reading*. Washington, DC: Pew Research Center, October 12, 2012. Available at http://libraries.pewinternet.org/files/legacy-pdf/The%20rise%20of%20e-reading%204.5.12.pdf

6

Context

All lives need stories near at hand,
and our experiences of narratives
in contextually rich worlds are transformative.

David Carr[1]

During the Middle Ages, Europe and many other parts of the world were periodically visited by cholera (among a plethora of other equally horrible plagues). Despite the best efforts of a wide variety of people, none of the preventive efforts that were attempted to halt the spread of the epidemic had much if any impact. Seemingly, at random intervals, the deaths due to cholera would rise to very high peaks and then to slowly recede to nothing over the course of several months.

The government in England during the 1660s adopted an interesting approach to dealing with the dreaded disease by publishing *Bills of Mortality*, which listed the cause of death each week by precise location. Weekly bills were printed in considerable numbers by an official printer and sold in bookstalls in cities across England (this might also be the first example of open data). So the people of England were aware of the advance and retreat of the various waves of plague as it spread across the nation. Figure 6-1 shows a bill of mortality for the year 1671. Even a quick casual glance at this page will arrest your eyes. Back in the day, they had a lot of reasons why people died. Some of the causes are obvious (stillborn and abortive children, drowned, small pox, and so forth) while other causes are a bit of a mystery (teeth as a cause of death?, convulsion?, swelling?, riling of the lights?, dropfy and tympany?, King's evil?).

John Graunt, who first published *Natural and Political Observations Mentioned in a Following Index and Made upon the Bills of Mortality* in 1662, recognized that there was a fairly constant baseline of mortality in London, which was predictable over time, while the occurrence of the plague would wax and wane over a more limited period of time. Due to his observations and writings, Graunt is considered to be the father of demography, although not a university graduate, and was named as a Fellow of the Royal Society. So Graunt's contribution was to provide *context* with the result that people could better understand the spread of the disease. Thus, it was recognized that it was possible to track and chart public health.

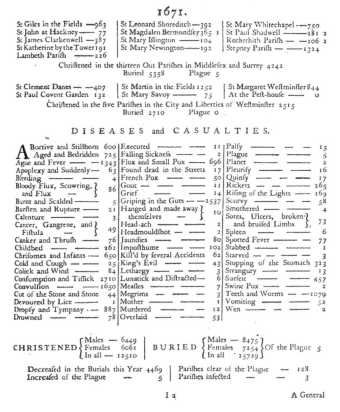

Figure 6-1 A Bill of Mortality. From a Collection of the Yearly Bills of Mortality, from 1675 to 1758 Inclusive. London: A. Millar in the Strand, 1759. Available from Google Books.

At the time of Queen Victoria's rein, people both rich and poor were thrown together on crowded city streets that often ran with raw sewage in the gutters. Street sweepers faced a seemingly endless task of collecting manure that were daily deposited by thousands of horse-drawn vehicles. And certainly the smell of unwashed bodies could be a bit daunting—for rich and poor alike.

On August 31, 1854, the first case of cholera was detected near Broad Street in central London. Cholera is a disease that leads to vomiting, diarrhea, and rapid dehydration, and thus has very high mortality rates. The prevailing theory of the day was that miasma (a poisonous mist or vapor filled with decomposed matter) caused cholera and the Black Death and that little could be done to prevent disease. In reality, however, cholera is contracted by drinking sewage-contaminated water.

Snow created an accurate map of London and plotted the deaths by the address of each death as shown in Figure 6-2 (each death is indicated by the little box or mark in each building). Examining the data in the *Bills of Mortality*, John Snow felt that a particular water pump on Broad Street was the cause of the high rates of cholera in the area. Notice a building (a brewery) just a short distance away that had no deaths—the brewery had its own well, and the workers consumed a fair amount of the product they produced each day! John Snow combined his innate curiosity with the ability to gather data from a number of sources and "connect the dots" to realize that the water pump might be the source of the contamination.

Snow convinced the decision makers to remove the pump-handle on September 7, 1854 "as an experiment", with the result that the number of cholera deaths quickly declined to very low levels as noted in his book *On the Mode of Communication of Cholera*.[2] Snow not only tabulated all of the data by date but also mapped the deaths by location so as to demonstrate the link between the suspected cause of the disease, the water pump, and those who died. In short, Snow provided *context* for the data that he was presenting to the decision makers.

The work of John Graunt, John Snow, and others eventually leads to the notion of probability, statistics, insurance, and epidemiology. Pretty amazing when you think about it. It is also, in my view, yet another example of the law of unintended consequences in that those who decided to publish the *Bills of Mortality* had no idea of the value that was created (or the lives that would be saved) as a result of their decision to share the mortality data.

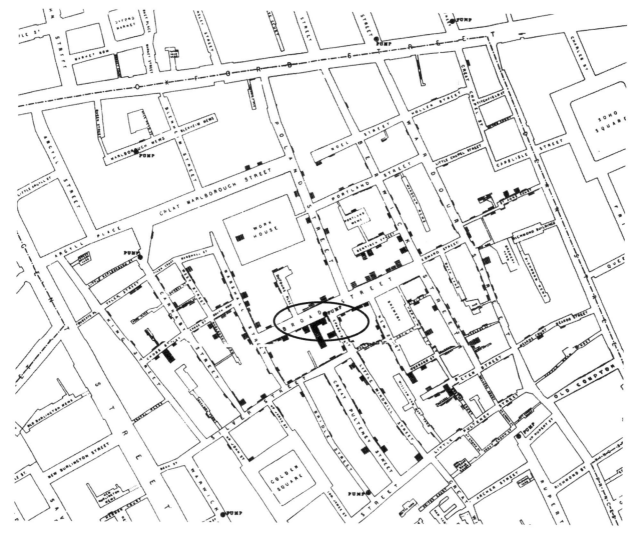

Figure 6-2 Snow's Map of the Spread of Cholera. John Snow. *On the Mode of Communication of Cholera*. London Medical Gazette, 44, 1849, 745–752, 923–929.

Methods to Provide Context

Context is an interesting word and comes from the Latin word *contexere*, meaning to weave together or relate. Many of us would think of context as: (1) the words used to help explain the meaning of a phrase or statement, and (2) the circumstances or conditions concerning an event or action. The real value of context, in my view, is that it provides orientation.

The ability to search digital content is almost a prerequisite for any website. Clearly, search is an effective tool for the delivery of content in response to a specific query, but the mere act of search masks the scope and structure of any collection (of books or other artifacts), thus making an effective search difficult. Clearly, there must be other approaches than search that will assist the user in better understanding the breadth and depth of any digital collection.

Joanna Sassoon has argued that the push for the digitization of cultural and heritage collections and its focus on content risks a decontextualized or superficial view of library, archive, and museum collections.[3] The profession needs to move from a content-centric view of the world (the focus is on organizing and providing access to collections of data and information) to a user-centric view (focusing on providing a distinctive, personalized experience). This can be accomplished only if we provide a new set of tools that facilitates the communication and collaboration among all types of users—scientists, professionals, teachers, students, and the amateur.[4]

It is possible to identify three distinct types of context:[5]

- *Physical context*—Devices can sense their actual, real-world locations
- *Device context*—machines talking to one another
- *Information context*—topics embraced under the concept of information architecture. For more about the field of Information architecture, I would refer you to Peter Morville and Louis Rosenfeld's wonderful book *Information Architecture for the World Wide Web*.[6]

Ultimately, context is all about helping people discover a richer, deeper significance for content.

It is also important to acknowledge that the topic of context discussed in this chapter is not directly related to the concept of context in information seeking. The whole field of information seeking and retrieval research has focused extensively on the role of context in information seeking through a variety of lenses—demographic, social, behavioral, and professional characteristics of users, specific tasks, time, or place of inquiry. In summary, these studies show that users in a specific context have similar characteristics that affect their information seeking and retrieval behaviors. It is also somewhat ironic that despite the presence of literally hundreds of such information-seeking studies, the user interface in the vast majority of library systems has not appreciably changed in more than 20 years.

The circumstances or setting for an event, statement, idea, and so forth help improve understanding. By providing a set of tools that a community (and librarians) can use to provide context to the content that the cultural organization provides, the organization has the opportunity to add real value. Providing context helps people move from considering the content in an abstract manner in order to influence their perceptions of the content as well as influence their tasks and activities.

When thinking about an organizing system that can be applied in a variety of settings, several fundamental questions should be addressed:

1. What is being organized?
2. Why is it being organized?
3. How much is being organized?
4. When is it being organized?
5. Who (or what) is organizing it?

According to Richard Wurman, often called the father of information architecture, there are a finite number of ways to organize information.[7] Each way of organizing information permits a different understanding; each lends itself to different kinds of information;

 and each has different strengths and limitations. These methods of organizing information, which provide *context*, include the following:

Location is useful when comparing and contrasting information that comes from different locales or sources. Location is one useful way of organizing data with significant connections or relationships with other data. Maps are designed to answers a number of questions:

- Navigation—How do I get to . . . ?
- Orientation—Where am I? Where else can I go from here?
- Discovery—What is nearby? What can I do from (or near) here?
- Definition—What are the boundaries?
- Understanding—How do things relate? Are there any discernable patterns?

Richard Wurman produced a series of *Access* travel guides so that travelers could get a better sense of place since each travel guide is organized by geographic relationships. Rather than having a chapter on hotels, restaurants, and so forth, the *Access* travel guide answers a really simple question: "Where am I and what's around me?" More recently, a wide range of geo-based mapping tools (such as Google Maps) has become available to display a plethora of location-based information.

In 1931, Harry Beck, who worked for the London Underground, designed a map of the various underground train routes using different-colored lines running horizontally, vertically, or at 45-degree angles, which has become the basis for most transit maps around the world today. Beck's principal concern was to show passengers how they could move from one station to another and where to change between lines rather than representing precise geographic locations.[8]

Beck's map clearly illustrates how providing context along with content is really appreciated by people. The original printing of Beck's map of the London Underground (700,000 copies) in 1933 was sold out within two months, and a second printing was ordered. The beauty and utility of the map was recognized in 2006 as the second most popular design innovation in the BBC's *Great Britain Design Quest*.

 ***Alphabetical order*** is a frequently used method for organizing a large assemblage of items, such as names in a telephone book, words in a dictionary, entries in an index, and the organization of the fiction collection in public libraries. Any alphabet is an arbitrary sequence of symbols, yet alphabetical order works well since the vast majority of people learn the "alphabet" from an early age. Any other method of organization of words in a dictionary or entries in an index would not serve that purpose or serve it as well.

Given the reality that libraries are "thing" oriented and that these things must be managed and organized, placing things in linear alphabetical order made a great deal of sense—in times past. But things do change, and the cultural organization catalog has moved with glacial speed to become a multifaceted search tool.

The mission of the library is not to gather physical things into an inventory, but to organize human knowledge that has been very inconveniently packaged.

Karen Coyle[9]

Traditional ontologies—a library classification system, for example—work best when the collection is constrained by size and people with expertise who apply the ontology to the collection are trained (and the users of the system become more knowledgeable about how to search through experience and perhaps some training). However, an ontology is not going to work when the collection is quite large, rapidly expanding, and changing shape as new types of content are being introduced minute-by-minute on the Internet. The challenge is further complicated by the dispersed group of amateurs who use the Internet daily and want to gain access to content in new ways.

Interestingly, in the island country of Iceland, the telephone book is organized alphabetically by first name—followed by surnames, occupations, address, and telephone number. Everybody in Iceland is known by their first name as a surname is simply the father's name suffixed with either *son* for boys or *dóttir* for girls. This interesting approach to organization of information works well for a population of 300,000 but probably would not work well when a population exceeds a million or more.

The *Thesaurus Linguae Graecae* provides access to some 10,000 Greek texts. What really adds value, from the users' perspective, is that the Thesaurus provides specialized indexes of value to researchers—an index of Greek root words and editing style, for example.

Yet, perhaps it is prudent to question whether alphabetical order is needed in some or all cases within a cultural organization. Consider the fact that many organizations do not use alphabetical order at all—Google, Amazon, the Open Library, or even OCLC's WorldCat uses relevance as a default. Karen Coyle has made the point that perhaps it is time to no longer design library data for the linear retrieval of the past—that relied so heavily on alphabetical order.

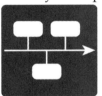

Time works well when a series of events happen over time. Time-lines are used to help orient the visitor in exhibitions, museums, and archives. Time is a well-regarded structure from which to observe and compare changes. Developing a chronological list is another example of organizing objects or information with the side benefit that it avoids any and all judgments about what is important and what is not.

In addition, time is an obvious method for organizing bus and train schedules, for example. The dimensions of time can range from seconds, minutes, or hours to months, years, centuries, or milestones. Several software packages are available to easily develop a timeline for a collection of various items.[10]

The National Library of New Zealand offers a large (3 meter) multi-touch table, called Lifelines, that allows visitors to discover content in the library's collections that relate to their own personal history—the times they have lived in, their family's name, and places in New Zealand they may have visited.[11] The content may:

- Present major events that happened over the course of their lifetime
- Replay popular television shows
- Rediscover popular music from their teen years
- Remind them of toys and books from their childhood
- See photographs from various locations and events
- Read newspaper headlines and view political cartoons from "back in the day"

The users can create a unique timeline and email it to themselves.[12]

Category is an effective way of organizing information or physical objects based on their similarities or common attributes. Types of materials are typically used to organize retail stores and libraries. Category is often emphasized by the use of colors. It is important to communicate to the customer the basis for organizing information by categories.

Hierarchy organizes items any number of ways—for example, by order of importance, from least expensive to most expensive, by magnitude from small to large, and numerical order. Continuum, a synonym for hierarchy, is used to compare things across a common measure—highest to lowest, best to worst, first to last. All rating systems, including the number of stars or numerical rating such as a baseball player's batting average, indicate a value scale. When information is organized in some kind of a continuum, the value scale indicates the most important aspects of the information (in the mind of those who created the continuum).

Hierarchy is created through superordinate/subordinate or parent/child relationships. Within libraries, the Dewey Decimal system is an important and long-held traditional way for organizing collections. Yet, the question must be asked, "Has Dewey (or LC or . . .) become an impediment to better matching customers to the resources within our cultural organizations?"

We typically look at this type of information from left to right or top-down organization. Among the ways to visually represent a hierarchy are the following:

- **Tree structures** are used for high-level mapping or overviews of a system (consider drop-down menus).
- **Nest structures** work best for simple hierarchies (think of a Venn diagram). The child is contained within the parent (and you can add more children—up to a point).
- **Stair structures** are effective for representing complex hierarchies (the child is located below and to the right of the parent). Consider an accordion-style menu or a file system with the + and—to open and close the parent file.

Icons or an image is frequently used to represent a place, thing, concept, philosophy, or idea—especially on websites.

Links provide a well-understood method to inspire people to explore on their own. The link can lead to other useful documents, images, audio or video files, and other relevant material. Links found in great abundance within the World Wide Web provides connections between ideas (as Vannevar Bush, Ted Nelson and Tim Berners-Lee envisioned) and ensures that discovery takes place (often with unexpected and delightful results). And the Web has also linked people in the process as millions of folks have become creators and curators providing access to text (blogs and tweets), photos, images, videos, games and so much more.

Linking between items in the library catalog seems an obvious first step, but few libraries do so (you could link between citations or to items mentioned in a bibliography). Clearly, it would be great to be able to link from the library to content found in the web (some libraries work to improve the accuracy of the content in Wikipedia related to their campus or community). And it would be even better to link from content found on the web to content within the library.

Links are especially important to improve a library's visibility within the search engine environment—this is oftentimes called search engine optimization (SEO). Clearly, uniform resource locators or URL are the currency on the Internet. People exchange links for information, exchange links for influence, and exchange links for goodwill. Links are especially important for computers, and web crawlers record every link on every web page they can find. And remember that "likes" are another form of a link. And as more organizations embrace the concept of open linked data we are seeing a move from a Web of interlinked documents to a Web of interlinked data.[13]

Some libraries and museums have embedded links to other relevant content within their own website or to other content found in other websites. See, for example, the web page from NASA for the Helix Nebula as shown in Figure 6-3A, where the information is tightly controlled and is characterized by the absence of links. Compare

The Helix Nebula: Unraveling at the Seams

Figure 6-3A JPL Website Showing Links. Courtesy NASA/JPL-Caltech.

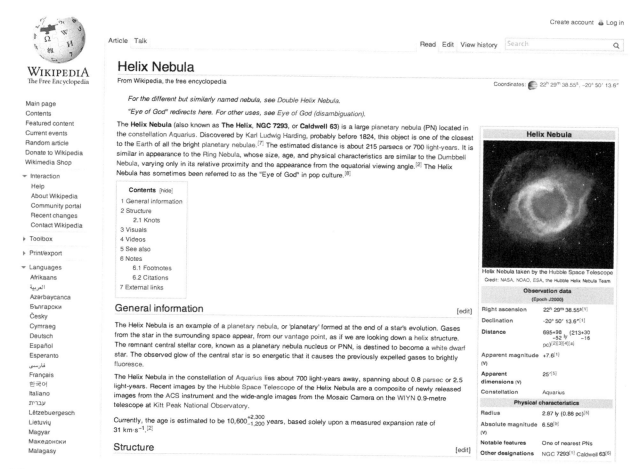

Figure 6-3B Wikipedia Web Page for Helix Nebula. Wikipedia. https://en.wikipedia.org/w/index.php?title=Special%3APrefixIndex&prefix=context&namespace=0

this with the Wikipedia web page for the same content (see Figure 6-3B) where the users find lots of links to facilitate their exploration.

The Google Art Project has digitized more than 32,000 high-resolution images from more than 150 museums, which allows a visitor to compare and contrast art beyond the artificial institutional boundaries that exist due to space and budget limitations. Using Google Art Project website, you can see the three images of Vincent van Gogh's bedroom in Arles—the three paintings may be found in three separate museums (which do not have links to other museums).

As Lorcan Dempsey has observed, people share themselves and connect with others through the use of "social objects" (photos, music, video, links, and other shared interests), and the most successful social networking sites are those that encourage and facilitate the sharing of these social objects.[14] People selectively socialize and disclose information about themselves on these social network sites as they add comments, rate, tag, create playlists, create collections, make recommendations, and so forth. One of the consequences of these activities is that people become a resource for others and become facilitators or connectors with others.

Jodie Wilson described the power of links when after transcribing some letters from World War I soldiers to their relatives back home; she was able to link to histories of the

Links

Eugene Garfield, an American linguist, envisaged a method that has come to be known as citation analysis to quantify the relative importance of a published article (paper). The "counting" tracks the number of times a specific article is cited by others in the following years. Garfield is the founder of the Institute for Scientific Information (SIS) and helped develop the *Science Citation Index, Journal Citation Reports, Index Chemicus* among other products. The *Science Citation Index* led to the development of the impact factor (which has become the de facto standard for measuring the importance of journals).

Larry Page, one of the founders of Google, recognized that a hyperlink was, in essence, a citation and that the web was a huge collection of "articles." PageRank, a not so subtle reference to Larry's discovery, is an algorithm that ranks websites by counting the number and quality of links to the site, and the higher the rank, the more likely the web page will appear in the first page or two of Google search results.[16] Google has expanded this relatively simple concept of counting links, and PageRank now includes more than 200 factors in its algorithm to determine relevancy.

A whole industry, called search engine optimization, has been created to provide advice about ways to ensure that a company or organization's website appears in the first few pages as the result of a Google search (few users will move beyond the first page or two of the search results). Shortly after Google was incorporated in 1998, the simple search box and the highly relevant results being presented first, people quickly moved from its search competitors to Google—today Google is the dominant fixture in the search arena with billions (that's with a "B") of searches being performed each day.[17]

One of the reasons for Google's continuing relevance in the search industry is that users around the world provide information about new and revised websites as they continually adjust (add, edit, and delete) the links from one website to many others.

Tim Berners-Lee and some of his colleagues have suggested some linked data principles that individuals and organizations should follow:[18]

1. Use Uniform Resource Identifiers (URIs) as names for things.

2. Use HTTP URIs so people can look up those names.

3. For each URI, provide useful information using standards such as Uniform Description Framework (UDF).

4. Include links to other URIs, so that more information can be discovered.

The implication for libraries, museums, and other cultural organizations is that we need to stop creating bibliographic and other records as the sole means of adding value and start linking things as our primary objective (while a record is built as a by-product).

regiment the soldiers served in as well as family histories. This, in turn, lead to relatives of the soldiers sharing photos and other information with the library making the content of the letters of even more value to others.[15]

Rather than trusting a predetermined method for organizing information (such as the use of pre-coordinated subject headings), people can rely on a computer to organize the available information using some method (such as Google's relevance ranking). This is known as the **random** or **arbitrary** organization of information.

David Weinberger explores the realities of digital disorder in his book *Everything Is Miscellaneous*,[19] when he suggests:

- Information is valuable when it is thrown into a big digital "pile" to be filtered and organized by users themselves (or the tools that they employ).
- Rather than relying on trained experts, groups of people are inventing their own ways of discovering what they know and want (often using social media to do so).
- Rather than attempting to corral or lock up data as a valuable asset, many organizations are learning to let data and information loose so that it can be remixed and "mashed up" in new and creative ways.

Weinberger suggests that the things taught in library school such as structure, order, precise metadata, and bibliographic control should be thrown out of the window. Rather, as more and more information content becomes accessible as digital content, the old rules no longer apply. Weinberger has asserted that there are three ways to organize information:

1. In the *first order*, things are organized as physical objects. While the way things are organized is not important, there are always real physical limits that get in the way of large collections—consider the millions of books in the Library of Congress or the millions of objects in the Smithsonian. Large institutions, occupying a lot of space, with a large number of staff are a necessary by-product of large collections. By necessity, first-order collections are tidy and require a set of rules with which to operate.
2. In the *second order*, a catalog containing information about the physical objects is created and maintained. The catalog can be organized in several ways (in numerical order such as accession number) or alphabetical by author, subject, and so forth. Yet, the physical nature of the catalog itself will also limit the ways in which someone can approach and learn more about the collection itself. It should be noted that the first two ways of introducing order rely on arranging *atoms* and that atoms can be only in one place at a time.
3. The *third order* relies on the fact that content has been digitized, and the content now exists as *bits* (within a computer system) and removes the limitations imposed by atoms. Thus, not only is the content itself accessible using the Internet, but also the rules governing how a collection is described and used have changed in dramatic and fundamental ways. Information can be in many places at once, does not necessarily fit into neat predetermined boxes, and the real messiness of information is actually a virtue. The third order is all about the *richness of relationships*. The most provocative aspect of this book is that it should be the topic of conversation among librarians about the need for the profession to embrace new ways of looking at our customers and the ways libraries serve them.

Given the now more than 20 years of interacting with and contributing to the Internet, many people are quite comfortable in adding context to information content. Among the ways they go about adding context are adding tags, providing comments, writing (often quite thoughtful) reviews, and rating products and services. Libraries

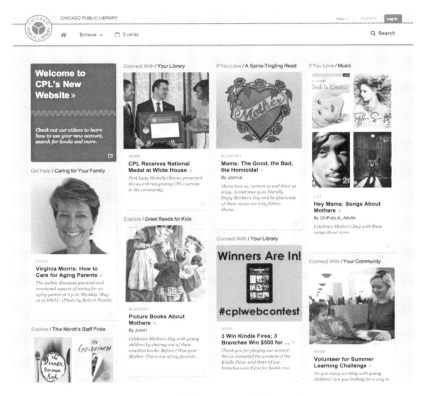

Figure 6-4A BiblioCommons at the Chicago Public Library. BiblioCommons.

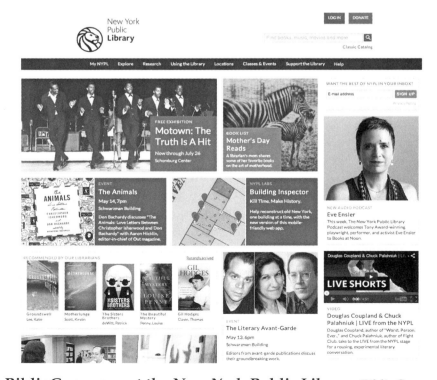

Figure 6-4B BiblioCommons at the New York Public Library. BiblioCommons.

that use the *BiblioCommons* catalog, for example, provide a set of tools that allow their users to add context by adding ratings, reviews, comments, and tags in much the same way as *LibraryThing* or *Amazon* empowers users—see Figures 6-4A and 6-4B. Notice the variety of data about the book that is available to the user including author notes, contents, and reviews from several sources. Following this are comments from other users, links to videos, and the option for a user to add quotes, a summary, and notices.

A **tag** is a term or keyword assigned by anyone to a digital image, a computer file, Internet bookmark, a blog posting, a bibliographic record, and so forth. The process of adding a tag is known as tagging, social tagging, or sometimes labeling. Tags can assist in organizing things, aiding in classification, indicating ownership, noting boundaries, and so forth. Many people find tagging an effective means of attempting to make sense of an information environment, and millions of people are engaged with tagging on a daily basis.

Tags, another form of *metadata* or information about information, are a nonhierarchical method for adding context. A classification system organizes knowledge as a tree-like hierarchical structure using broader–narrower, inclusive–included, superclass–subclass relationships between concepts.[20] Folksonomies or socially constructed tags use vocabulary "folk" use—these tags reflect their natural language and complement the controlled vocabularies used by libraries.

According to Gene Smith, there are seven kinds of tags:[21]

- Descriptive
- Identity
- Ownership
- Opinion

- Self-reference
- Organizing
- Play

Tagging is an individual action performed in a social setting, and this results in an interesting approach to adding value to content. From the library's perspective, the primary benefit of tagging is that the searchability of content is improved, as additional descriptive text is included in the index. For the individual, tagging offers a way to connect directly with the image, photograph, works of art, or video—by tagging or naming them, which is one of the aspects of sense making. In addition, the cumulative impact of all this tagging activity offers the prospect of identifying unique pathways through complex information environments rather than relying on the use of pre-coordinated subject headings found in library bibliographic records. The reality is that each user adds value for the library, for themselves, and for other users by revealing different and unique perspectives and communities.[22] Folksonomy created tags (metadata) when used in combination with traditional controlled vocabularies increase findability and significantly improve searching.[23] The Ann Arbor District Library is one library that integrates tagging within the OPAC itself.

Originally popularized on sites such as *Flickr* and the social bookmarking website *Delicious*, now thousands of sites—from business to news to e-commerce to blogs to social media—encourage users to add tags so that they can be more easily found later on. Note that as of November 2015, *Flickr* has more than 100 million people contributing more than 12 billion photos with several hundred million tags. *Flickr* also provides a tool, *People in Photos*, that allows people to identify by name other individuals found in a photo. Obviously, the Internet allows people to share information with others, and sites that encourage tagging also introduce a community aspect to the creation of data or metadata. Tagging allows communities to name their own resources and concepts in their own terms.

While it is possible to provide a tagging option to users of the library's online catalog (some users might actually take time to add tags to their favorite books), a better option might involve users in a tagging project without them being aware of doing so. The Bibliotheek Harlem Osst, a branch library located in Haarlan—a western suburb of Amsterdam, wanted to come up with a creative way to get its users to describe the books they were reading with phrases such as "boring, great for kids, funny, didn't read it, and exciting." The readers would be contributing knowledge and recommendations for future readers.

The creative solution was to install book drops for each set of predefined tags. The RFID tags identified the book, and the system automatically added the appropriate tag when the item was checked in. The resulting set of book drops made returning items to the library a lot more fun. The end result is that the library's users are directly adding value for future users while being unaware they are doing so.[24] Taking something so mundane as a book drop and turning it into something that adds value (without needing to train the user) and costs so little to implement is a great example of innovative thinking.

It is possible to organize folksonomies into seven types of tags that identify:

1. What or who the resource is about
2. What the resource is, its genre (article, book, photo, video, and so forth)
3. Who owns the resource
4. Categories and subcategories
5. Qualities of characteristics of the resource (funny, stupid, scary)
6. Who contributed the resource
7. Organizational tasks (job search, to read, to forward, and so forth)[25]

Remember that tags are a string of characters and are not always a correctly spelled word.

Some tags conform to a special syntax to define semantic information about the tag making them available for use by a computer program. A *triple tag*, or *machine tag*, has a three-part structure: a namespace, a predicate, and a value. Consider "geo:lat=21.18"— this is a geographic latitude coordinate whose value is 21 degrees 18 minutes. This *triple tag* format is similar to the Resource Description Framework (RDF) model for information. The RDF model triples communicate relationships among and between units of information through subject–predicate–object statements (Jane Austin → author → *Pride and Prejudice*).

The **Semantic Web**, a concept envisioned by Tim Berners-Lee, is a web of data that can be processed by machines. The World Wide Web Consortium (W3C) has developed and promoted standard data formats that support the Semantic Web concept. Berners-Lee expressed this vision as:

I have a dream for the Web [in which computers] become capable of analyzing all the data on the Web—the content, links, and transactions between people and computers. A "Semantic Web", which makes this possible, has yet to emerge, but when it does, the day-to-day mechanisms of trade, bureaucracy and our daily lives will be handled by machines talking to machines. The "intelligent agents" people have touted for ages will finally materialize.[26]

The Semantic Web uses structured data, often called "linked data," based on a model for understanding relationships between "things." The RDF model uses entity–relationship diagrams and expresses information in the form of subject–predicate–object expressions. The fact that libraries transition out of MARC to XML (extensible markup language) means that library metadata would be accessible to web search engine crawlers with the result that library catalogs are more visible during the process of discovery. The goal is to pull data out of existing library or museum silos into a common format so that the data will become more visible and useful to more people.

Websites and documents that use the RDF model create the Semantic Web, sometimes called "Open Linked Data," which facilitates computers being able to parse relationships among data automatically, which results in more effective tools for discovery, visualization, and exploration of information resources. Open linked data can be used to provide context for people, places, concepts, works, organizations and objects.

OCLC has released several data files that employ the RDF model: Faceted Application of Subject Terminology; Virtual International Authority File; and the Dewey Decimal Classification System. For a variety of reasons, the potential of the Semantic Web envisioned by many web luminaries has yet to be achieved.

Recently, the Library of Congress has adopted a new cataloging framework, called BIBFRAME, which will replace MARC and RDA. BIBFRAME has four core classes of information: creative work, instance, authority, and annotation, and is rooted in the principles of the Semantic Web. When libraries have converted their bibliographic (and authority) records into the BIBFRAME model, it will open up library data that for decades have been insular and isolating.[27]

One important step in the broader use of linked data has been Google's development of its Knowledge Graph, which displays specific facts about people, places, historical events, and other topics on the right-hand side of a search results page, as illustrated by Figure 6-5, which is displayed for a search of "Melvil Dewey."

Melvil Dewey

Librarian

Melville Louis Kossuth Dewey was an American librarian and educator, inventor of the Dewey Decimal system of library classification, and a founder of the Lake Placid Club. Wikipedia

Born: December 10, 1851, Adams Center, NY

Died: December 26, 1931, Lake Placid, FL

Education: Amherst College

Children: Godfrey Dewey

Spouse: Emily McKay Beal (m. 1924–1931), Annie R. Godfrey (m. 1878–1922)

Books   View 20+ more

| Dewey Decimal Classifica... | Table 2, Geographic Areas, Gr... | A Classifica... and Subj... 1876 | Summaries DDC 21: Dewey D... |

People also search for   View 10+ more

| S. R. Ranganat... | Charles Ammi Cutter | Paul Otlet | John Dewey |

Figure 6-5 Google's Knowledge Graph.

Taxonomies denuded the cognitive landscape.

Cory Doctorow[28]

When people freely choose tags, the resulting metadata will likely include synonyms (multiple tags for the same concept) and homonyms (same tag used with a different meaning) with the result that searches are less efficient than when using a controlled vocabulary (such as the Library of Congress Subject Headings). However, the terms selected by people directly reflects their vocabularies that are going to be more meaningful to a greater number of people. Since these tags are publicly viewable, they create implicit relationships and paths for navigation between people, objects, and other tags. The categorization that results from this aggregate of tags is known as folksonomy—the combination of folk and taxonomy.[29] The effectiveness of any folksonomy is reliant on the principle of collective intelligence or "the wisdom of crowds," which posits that large, diverse groups of people are capable of solving complex problems. Note that the work of the participants is neither collaborative nor working toward consensus but rather reflects the aggregation of individual vocabularies and thoughts. Most importantly, tagging must reach a "critical mass" of contributions (a large number of users contributing numerous tags) before they really add value from the customer's perspective.[30] Some organizations, such as the BBC, will only allow a tag to be added to its database when it has been used a specific number of times by various users.

Ames and Naaman devised a two-part rationale of tagging motivation: function and sociality.[31] The _function_ dimension focuses on tagging for the purpose of organization and communication. The _sociality_ dimension is focused on tagging to meet individual needs or to engage others. Not surprisingly, the social organization aspect of tagging is what seems to motivate most people who tag.

One study of _Flickr_ found that the tags associated with an individual photo were likely to have context-specific metadata, while the photos in a group-set had tags based on broader concepts that were more relevant to the group.[32] Another study of _Flickr_ tags found little overlap between the tags added by users and the subject headings assigned by librarians.[33] One important concern found with all tagging systems is that a user is unable to move up and down to isolate other more specific or more general terms as tagging, by definition, has no hierarchical organization.[34]

Another study examined the use of Twitter hashtags as a tagging format and found that they can be effectively used both to communicate and to assist in the organization of information and experiences.[35]

A number of libraries have used the LibraryThing for Libraries' APIs to download tags, reviews, ratings, and other content from the _LibraryThing_ website to their library's online catalog.[36] One analysis of the impact of _LibraryThing_ user-generated content found that users were finding four new books using tags for every new book found using subject headings.[37] Rather than embracing the either-or argument, it would seem that the use of folksonomy tags complement, rather than replace, traditional subject headings with the result that the end user benefits significantly. Given that today information sources are more diverse and the web is very participatory, perhaps the idea of the need for authority and control is slowly disappearing.

_____

Joy's Law

No matter what business you're in,
most of the smartest people work for someone else.

_____

Bill Joy[38]

A longer version of a tag is an **annotation**. Annotation can be quite helpful both in creating new information resources and to interpret existing ones. Annotations added by users can be of real value in that they can:

- Engage the broader community—allows people to contribute their knowledge, expertise, and experiences to library content
- Serve specialized groups—highlight resources of interest to specific audiences, for example, teachers
- Acquire diffuse information—capture feedback and insights from users
- Encourage different points of view—knowledgeable individuals can engage in a conversation about views and theories about which others might differ.

Different types of individuals can add annotations. They could be members of a trusted community, members of self-selecting communities (such as folks who participate in blog discussions on a regular basis), collaborating with other "third party" sites that have an interest in your community, or annotations could be added by anybody, anytime.

Among the ways in which an annotation can be created are the following:

- *Abstracts/Summary*—Creating an original abstract or excerpting a portion of the original work (cut and paste) to create an abstract can be easily accomplished. An original summary adds more value than taking the cut-and-paste approach—at least in my experience.

  DeWitt Wallace created a new magazine in 1921 *that* covered a wide variety of subjects by abridging articles so they could be read quickly. Thus, *Readers Digest* was born and by 1929 it had more than 290,000 subscribers.[39] Interesting, Wallace visited the New York Public Library every day for the next two years writing summaries of articles. Four decades later, *Readers Digest* was publishing 40 international editions and had more than 23 million subscribers. Clearly summaries are a popular way to add value.

- *Quoting*—Finding an interesting block of text that provides an interesting or unique perspective is a method that bloggers may use as a starting point for a new blog posting.

- *Re-titling*—Creating a provocative title will often result in an article or blog or . . . receiving more visits than was the case when the original article (and title) were created.

- *Telling a Story*—Stories provide a powerful way in which to add significant context for the user. In a museum, **labels** have been used for a long time to provide the rudimentary framework for a story by typically providing the name of the creator (artist), title and description of the work, year created, and in some cases, the name of the donor. Some museums have added QR codes or provide additional information about a work when someone views the work through the screen of a smartphone. Stories about an item in a collection provide real value that encourages people to connect today and have meaning in the future.

Reviews, an evaluation of a publication, service, product, company, or individual, are having a significant impact as people decide whether to purchase something or attend an event. Not surprisingly, reviews can be found for movies, songs, books, video games, restaurants, products (such as a car, computer hardware or software, and so forth), and services (see Angie's List for one popular site). Reviews are sometimes written by experts, occasionally written by a consumer (someone who has purchased and used a product or service—and hopefully become somewhat knowledgeable about the product or service in the process), and more often than not written by an amateur expressing his or her opinions or anyone in-between.

Reviews are making brands transparent so that people are more willing to trust the comments and observations of total strangers rather than relying on the traditional power of the brand. Yet online review fraud is a reality on such popular sites such as *TripAdvisor* and *Yelp*, but as the number of reviews increase, the power of a fraudulent review is greatly diminished.[40]

Simply allowing customers to add reviews and ratings to a local library system will not really provide very much value since most items in the collection will have no reviews. Thus, libraries need to gain access to a large repository of reviews that are accessible using LibraryThing or other similar websites. A recent start-up, In the Stacks (www.inthestacks.tv) is a place for book discovery, curated by librarians. This is an example of how libraries need to be doing things at scale as Lorcan Dempsey advocates.

Many websites also provide a **rating system** such as the ever-popular five stars (the more you like it, the more stars you select) or the Like symbol (on many websites) or marking a photo as a favorite (as on *Flickr*). *Amazon* combines reviews from its users with a five-star rating system. This popularity rating system is not to be confused with a content rating system that attempts to identify the suitability of television, movies, video games, comic books, and other materials for a particular audience—especially young people.

And almost every blog promotes a discussion by asking for feedback from its readers. These **comments** made by readers of the blog can lead to interesting and stimulating conversations, which others will also find of value.

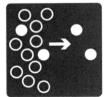

Curation. Upon hearing the word "curation," most of us immediately think of museum curators who have the delightful job of selecting materials from a large collection, usually around a theme, in order to create an exhibit. Great job. But curators have different titles in other fields. Consider editors for newspapers, magazines, and TV news shows—all selecting and organizing content. And now there are millions of individuals curating content on any number of websites and social media sites. And the best curators focus on providing access to high-quality contextual content. But as Troy Livingston has observed:

I think the threat to curators is that if we allow anyone to participate, will that lessen the value of what curators contribute? There's a sense of resistance and fear perhaps in the curatorial profession because of this. I mean, some curators probably hate Wikipedia because there's no oversight. But we're living in a Wikipedia world.[41]

Seth Godin has suggested that curation is important:

If we live in a world where information drives what we do, the information we get becomes the most important thing. The person who chooses that information has power.[42]

In the social media environment, Ross Dawson has suggested five ways millions of curators can be adding value:

- *Filtering*—Identifying good sources of information
- *Validation*—Knowing the expertise and background of your sources
- *Synthesis*—Combining concepts, themes, and ideas—creating a summary
- *Presentation*—Organizing information resources in a way that is understandable and visually appealing
- *Customization*—Revising and remixing to better fit the information to match your audience and their needs[43]

Helping people make sense of the flood of information that is available is a valuable skill for anyone in any organization. Some of the tools employed by many people who write the most popular blogs are:

- *Finding related items* (creating links to related information resources—A bibliography)
- *Illustrating*—Add a drawing or illustration
- *Comparing*—Identify the strengths and weaknesses
- *Evaluating*—Rank and/or rate items
- *Attributing*—Give credit to the original source

Some people, especially for small personal libraries, have found that organizing their collections by color has real appeal—although this is clearly a personal preference and one that would not work well with larger collections in libraries. It is interesting to note that some libraries have allowed some portions to their collections to be reorganized for brief periods of time as an "art installation."[44]

Many libraries and museums have shared some of their photographic content with Flickr with generally very positive results. The Flickr Commons initially involved the U.S. Library of Congress and since has been expanded to more than 30 cultural institutions around the world. While people can search and browse these collections, people can engage the content and enhance it by adding tags, comments, annotate regions within an image, and interact with others who have a similar interest.

Visualization Tools

An emerging and vibrant field is to visualize information and numerical data in ways that people can more quickly understand both the content and the context. We need tools that help us deal with impossible-to-comprehend scale of available information and to present it in ways that are understandable and hopefully provide insight. New insight means assisting people to see something in a new way. The visualization tools being developed meld the fields of computer science, artistic design, statistics, and storytelling.

The appeal of visualization is not surprising given that our brains find it easier to process information when presented as an image rather than as words or numbers. The right hemisphere of the brain recognizes shapes and colors, while the left hemisphere looks at things from an analytical point of view. Trying to grasp the significance of a chart full of numbers requires much more effort and time than having the same information presented in a graphic form. Simplifying things makes it easier to understand and gain insights. And people remember about 80 percent of what they see—and only about 20 percent of what they read.

Visualization allows for the possibility of displaying very large data sets in a way that can reveal patterns and communicate context while preserving the possibility of "diving" deeper into the data if something of interest is found. This is the reason for the appealing nature (and use) of infographics.

When people interact with information, they do so to create knowledge, gain an understanding or insight, or solve problems using the resources in a cultural organization's collection. Increasingly, people are interacting with digital information in a wide variety of settings. As cultural organizations move forward, they need to be mindful that customers will need a broad range of digital tools to help them understand the breadth and depth of available resources. The descriptive information provided by a cultural organization gives some sense of the context for the digital object as expressed in the metadata, uses of semantic markup, hyperlinks, and so forth. However, much information pertaining to the digital object remains hidden and is implicit or latent.

The power of information visualization is that people can interact with the displayed information thus increasing understanding. Among the possible ways to interact with information are:

- *Select*—Gather a subset of data for further analysis
- *Explore*—Show something else
- *Reconfigure*—Consider the information from a different perspective or arrangement
- *Encode*—Show a different representation
- *Abstract/Elaborate*—Show more or less detail (zoom in or out)
- *Filter*—Show something conditionally
- *Connect*—Show related items.[45]

Using visualization techniques can substantially improve our ability to process large amounts of information, identify (hidden) patterns (trends, ranges, comparisons, or surprises), construct mental models, and comprehend complex structures. Thus, visualization tools allow someone to interact much more closely with information in order to gain greater insight. Visually encoded information makes it easier for someone to gain a big picture perspective, identify trends, create mental models, identify key relationships, and develop a deeper understanding about a set of digital objects.

It is possible to group a variety of visualization tools into the following seven categories:

- *Synthesizing tools*—Mind maps, concept maps
- *Modeling tools*—Interactive visualizations, system thinking charts, social network maps, market maps
- *Storytelling tools*—Storyboards, narrative templates, weblogs, and diaries
- *Analyzing tools*—Structured thinking, analytical report templates
- *Recording tools*—Visual presence tools, mind maps
- *Canvassing tools*—Surveying tools, market prediction tools
- *Conversing/Collaborating tools*—people finders, expertise finders, whiteboard/virtual presence tools, wikis.

As the volume of digital data in libraries, archives, and museums continues to grow, questions are being raised as to how to best communicate the scope of a collection as well as how to make this information accessible. Accessing digital materials is useful from the customer's perspective only if people can access in ways that are meaningful to them. People are hungry for tools that allow individuals to construct their own pathways and gain their own understanding of the material rather than relying on a single institution-constructed view. People no longer view or consume cultural content, but rather they reuse it, annotate it, add meaning and context, and create new derivative media forms using a variety of social networking tools and sites.

In addition to a richer, contextualized experience, visualization tools provide the means to begin to understand large, complex data sets, assist in reducing bias in representing events, and making patterns and processes visible.[46]

Displaying Content

More than a decade ago, Ben Schneiderman suggested that designers of information-intensive websites should adopt a "visual information-seeking mantra"—overview first, zoom and filter, then details-on-demand.[47] Using the APIs provided by Flickr, Sam Hinton and Mitchell Whitelaw, from the University of Canberra, developed a Flickr Commons Explorer three-pane interface that displays a word cloud, a single image view, and a thumbnail grid with a central strip providing navigation and orientation as shown in Figure 6-6. The thumbnail grid is an attempt to show everything and can scale from tens to thousands of thumbnail tiles. Moving the mouse pointer over a tile reveals the full image and image title.[48] You can download the interface and play with it (http://creative.canberra.edu.au/cex).

Mitchell Whitelaw, working with the National Archives of Australia, developed a robust and interesting user interface that he calls the "generous interface." The intent is to give the user a sense of the full scope of the massive collections in the archives using this creative interface as seen in Figure 6-7. Given the basic mission of any digital collection is to share, the goal of any interface is to facilitate discovery, provide access

Figure 6-6 Flickr Commons Visual Explorer.

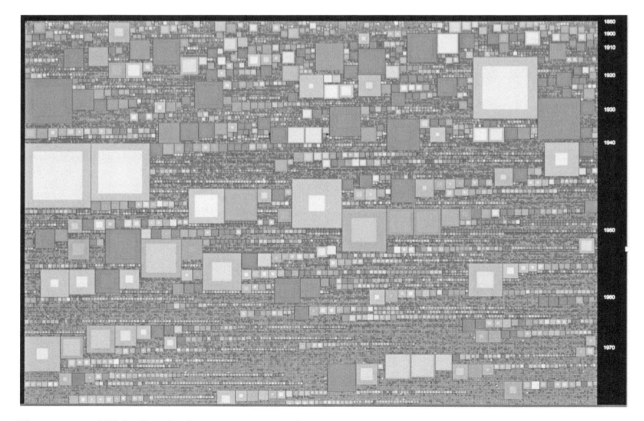

Figure 6-7 Whitelaw's Generous Interface.

to content, and to present an overview of the collection. And the generous interface clearly provides more to see.[49]

Each collection within the archive is called a "series," and in the interface, each series is represented as a square whose area is proportional to both the number of items in the series and the amount of shelf space it occupies. The squares are organized in chronological order—from first to last in (dates are provided to help in the navigation process) while the color represents the agency that contributed the material to the archive. Highlighting one of the squares will reveal links to other preceding or succeeding series.

More recently, Mitchell Whitelaw was asked to develop a new generous interface for *Queenslander*, a pictorial magazine, by the State Library of Queensland, Australia, as seen in Figure 6-8. He added an option that allows visitors to select color as a way to browse the collection as well as a timeline and tags—see Figure 6-9.

Providing visualizations of one or more collections allows the user to gain an understanding of the "big picture." Once this big picture is understood, the user can begin to explore by searching or by browsing (or some combination). Unique characteristics of the collection are hopefully highlighted so that users can explore different paths based on their interests. Clearly, designers of the physical or online space need to encourage exploration and discovery of new and interesting content by providing a set of tools that facilitate serendipity.

Library catalogs have done a really poor job of encouraging the exploration of a library's collection by browsing. And as people wish to interact more and more with online resources, libraries must provide a tool (as a part of the existing online catalog or using a separate tool) that will encourage browsing collections in a visual manner. A great many people are comfortable in using a good browsing interface such as when they use Biblioboard (see Figure 6-10 A–C), the Open Library

Figure 6-8 The *Queenslander* Magazine User Interface. http://www.slq.qld.gov.au/showcase/discover-the-queenslander#/mosaic

Figure 6-9 The *Queenslander* Magazine with a Color Option for Browsing. http://www.slq.qld.gov.au/showcase/discover-the-queenslander#/mosaic

The interior of the home showcases extensive Arts and Crafts detailing in the furniture, lighting and accessories. A grand piano sits in the background.

A front view of the great room shows the massive fireplace as well as the Arts and Crafts detailing.

Figure 6-10 Courtesy of Biblioboard.

(see Figure 6-11), or LibraryThing (see Figure 6-12). And why do we limit ourselves to book covers (back to the library brand as books) when we could use video clips, audio clips, pictures, first page of the journal article itself?

Google developed an experimental infinite digital bookcase (available at http://workshop.chromeexperiments.com/bookcase/) and has organized 10,000 Google Books covers into 28 broad subjects as shown in Figure 6-13. As you move up and down the circular display case, the categories change (in this case, the category is "Business and Investing" as seen by the label at the top of the screen shot). Moving the cursor left and right moves the display of titles. Cool. Clicking on the cover of a book will enlarge it for your inspection—see Figure 6-14. Clicking on the cover opens the book up and reveals a synopsis of the book—see Figure 6-15.

Figure 6-11 The Open Library Browsing User Interface. https://openlibrary.org/

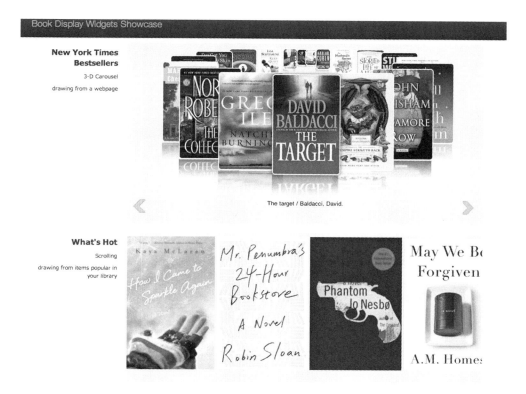

Figure 6-12 LibraryThing Browse Options. © Library Thing.

Figure 6-13 Google's WebGL Bookcase.

3M has developed a visual interface so that library customers can quickly browse the eBooks that are available to download. 3M also provides an app that allows a library customer to view and download available eBooks from the customer's tablet or iPad. Note: Biblitheca acquired 3M Library Systems in late 2015.

The Harvard Library Innovation Lab developed a browsing tool called the "Stack View," which provides visual clues about the character and frequency of use of library materials.[50] The number of pages determines the width of the displayed item, and the greater the color intensity, the more frequently the item has been used.

An interesting website—The Art of Making in Antiquity: Stoneworking in the Roman World (http://www.artofmaking.ac.uk/explore/)—demonstrates the power that can be achieved simply by adding samples that convey what the collection of materials contains—see Figure 6-16. And while the user can browse pre-established categories such as tools, processes, and materials, users can create their own path of

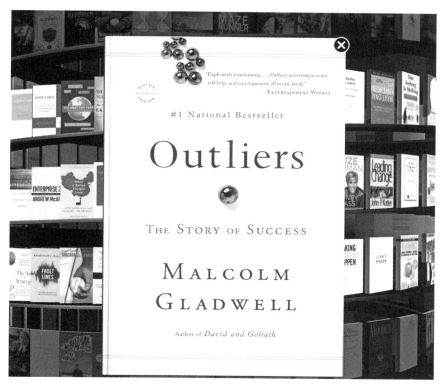

Figure 6-14 Google's WebGL Bookcase Displaying a Book Cover.

Figure 6-15 Google's WebGL Bookcase Showing a Synopsis.

exploration. While search is not ignored, adding samples from the collection provides almost instant context.

Visitors to the Cleveland Museum of Art have the opportunity to interact with "The Collection Wall"—a 40-foot-by-5-foot interactive wall featuring more than 3,500 works of art. The Collection Wall encourages visitors to connect with objects in the collection in new and interesting ways by facilitating discovery and serve as an orientation experience. Visitors can download recommended tours or create their own tour and download digital images, metadata, and comments onto to their iPads.[51] The Collection Wall display changes every 40 seconds grouping works of art by 32 curated views of the collection as well as by theme and type (materials, time period, and technique) as shown in Figure 6-17. The Collection Wall is part of Gallery One, an area adjacent to the entrance of the museum designed to propel visitors into the primary galleries with greater understanding, interest and enthusiasm about the collection. The goal of Gallery One is to provide a fun and engaging environment for all visitors—regardless of their knowledge of art.

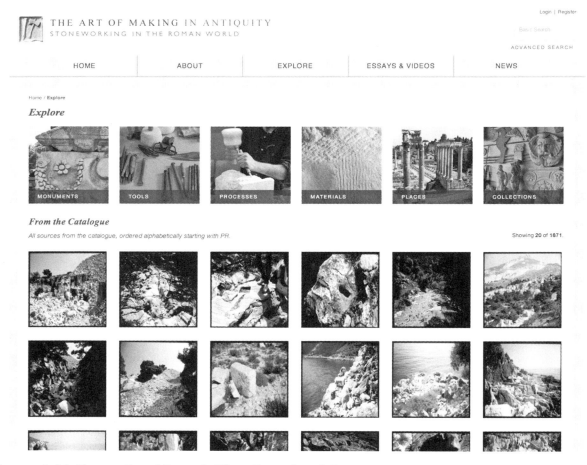

Figure 6-16 Example of Search Plus Sample of Content. With the permission of Wootton, W., Bradley, J., and Russell, B. (2013). "Explore," The Art of Making in Antiquity: Stoneworking in the Roman World. Available at http://www.artofmaking.ac.uk/explore/

Figure 6-17 The Cleveland Museum of Art Collection Wall. Collection Wall, Gallery One. The Cleveland Museum of Art. Image Courtesy the Cleveland Museum of Art.

An interesting visualization tool developed at the University of Calgary, called the Bohemian Bookshelf, aims to support serendipitous exploration of collections. This tool facilitates serendipity by (1) providing five different perspectives or access points to the collection, (2) encouraging curiosity through visually unique perspectives of the collection, (3) highlighting adjacencies among and between items in the collection, (4) providing multiple pathways to explore the collection, (5) supporting previews of items, and (6) encouraging a playful approach to information exploration.[52]

The Bohemian Bookshelf provides five interlinked visualizations of the collection, and when one item is selected, the views of the other four visualizations immediately change. The five visualizations include:

Cover color circle. Each book is grouped by the cover color and is displayed based on its hue and saturation. Each color point in the color circle is represented by a circle with the radius proportional to the number of items with the same color.

Keyword chains. The keyword chains connect items in the collection using keywords. The user can browse the collection moving from one keyword to another.

Timelines. This visualization displays the connection between the time period the book discusses and the publication year.

Book pile. Each book is represented by a square (the same color as the book cover), and the bigger the square, the higher the number of pages. Books with fewer pages are at the bottom of the pile, while the thicker books (with high page counts) are located at the top.

Author spiral. This visualization displays authors in alphabetical order. The author list rolls up into spirals to accommodate larger collections.

Interestingly, users of the Bohemian Bookshelf can move the visualization around to suit their immediate needs and interests. A video demonstration of the Bohemian Bookshelf may be viewed on Vimeo (https://vimeo.com/39034060).

Acknowledging the difficulty of browsing in the online arena, the founders of *Pinterest* worked to remove the organizational structures that the web presumes (directories, pagination, hierarchies) and replace them with a grid of images and words (fixed width and varying length) as shown in Figure 6-18. *Pinterest*, in contrast to most websites, has an infinite scroll—automatically loading more images as the user scrolls down.

Pinterest can best be thought of as a visual social network where people share image collections related to every topic under the sun. With more than 100 million users, *Pinterest* has more than 750 million boards with more than 30 billion individual pins (more than 50 million pins are added daily).

In a comprehensive yet very readable article, Karl Fast and Kamran Sedig identify and discuss 13 task-based visual representation interactions that a digital library can employ that will have great value for the user as seen in Table 6-1.[53] The use of visual representations together with a set of tools that assist the user forms a powerful mechanism for exploring, analyzing, and investigating information. Such tools

Figure 6-18 Pinterest User Interface.

empower the user in problem solving, knowledge creation, decision-making, planning, and sense making.

Visualizing tools are available for free as well as for a fee from a number of sources including Tableau, Swivel, Google, and IBM's Many Eyes website. A wonderful tool called *Trendalyzer*, developed by Hans Rosling and his family,[54] presents large data sets as moving images. You can see Hans Rosling giving several wonderful talks using *Trendalyzer* on the TED website (www.TED.com/search?q=rosling). *Google has purchased Trendalyzer*; the software name has been changed to *Motion Chart* and is now available as a free "gadget" using a Google spreadsheet.

It is also possible to use existing content in new and creative ways. The British Library in conjunction with a game developer sponsored a national contest, called *Off the Map*, to use maps and engraving from the library's archives to craft a new video game. The winning team fashioned a game set in the 17th-century London that was very life-like.

Table 6-1
Task-Based Interactions

Animating—Initiating and controlling motion	*Annotating*—Adding information or meta-information to digital content
Chunking—Grouping independent but related visual elements into a unified visual structure	*Cloning*—Creating a copy, in whole or part, of a digital object
Collecting—Gathering visual elements for future use	*Composing*—Crating a new digital object by putting together independent visual elements
Cutting—Removing elements from a digital object	*Filtering*—Exposing, concealing, or transforming digital elements that possess certain characteristics or match certain criteria
Fragmenting—Separating elements of an object into its component parts	*Probing*—Acquiring more detailed information
Rearranging—Altering the spatial position or orientation of an element	*Repicturing*—Displaying the digital object in a new or different way
Searching—Looking for or ascertaining the position of specific features, elements, or structures in a digital object	

Physical Context

The whole notion of architecture is to design a space (form) that meets the functional needs of the customer (in this case, the cultural organization). However, architects and others are recognizing that it is important to be cognizant of a wide variety of needs and to acknowledge that any design must create a wonderful overall experience. Thus, design that focuses on the overall user experience is called experience design and is driven by the moments of engagements, oftentimes called touch points, between the customer and the building aesthetics, equipment, and staff members. The totality of these touch point experiences drives the customers' perceptions about their memories of the experience. Given that experiences are an affective, personal, and subjective process, designers cannot approach people (customers, users, staff) as objects. Rather, design must recognize the transactive and potentially transformative nature of an experience (whether in a facility or online).

Libraries that have recognized the importance of the overall customer experience include the Anythink Libraries in Colorado; the Cerritos (CA) Public Library; the Idea Stores (tower Hamlets in London, England); the DOK in Delft, Netherlands; the Richmond (British Columbia, Canada) Public Library; the Markham (Ontario, Canada) Public Library; the Singapore Public Libraries; and the British Library among many more. These libraries are concerned about exploring and experimenting with new ways to deliver access to information and services that are more relevant for their communities. The libraries have moved to merchandising of their collections, dropping Dewey, eliminating service desks, embracing social media to raise the visibility of the library, making the online experience one that is so compelling that it continues to draw people back to a website, moving librarians out into the communities that they serve, and so much more.

Summary

Clearly, access to information is not the holy grail. Insight is. **Insight** allows people to see more clearly into complex situations. Insight allows us to move from gathering and analysis to action. So information is the means to an end—and the end is insight. And while we live in a world where information is available 24/7, we find that context helps us to cope and to find insight. Context helps us to determine where and when an information resource or a recommendation to content is appropriate.

Content is something we connect to emotionally,
converse about or learn from . . .
but content without context is useless.

Daniel Eizans[55]

Develop tools that encourage and facilitate participation so that people can add context to content. I believe that two of the most important ways libraries can add real value are opening up their catalogs and encourage people to add tags, reviews, and ratings while also making their resources discoverable by adding links whenever possible to Wikipedia and accessible to web crawlers. As Tim Berners-Lee has suggested, the more links the better.

Libraries, archives, galleries and museums have a difficult and time-consuming task of providing metadata for the wealth of images, audio and video files, digitized newspapers and magazines, and digitized books and other materials found in their collections. The process of digitization has become faster and cheaper through advances in technology with the result that content can be placed online faster than staff members can index them. Obviously, the traditional cataloging and indexing practices are labor intensive and costly. Some libraries are experimenting by placing content online with only a minimal amount of metadata and encouraging people to add other contextual information by adding tags, reviews, comments, and ratings.

Remember that cultural organizations provide a set of tools that enables others to:

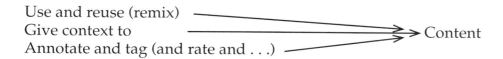

Checklist for Adding Value Using Context

	Yes	No
Has your cultural organization installed a new online catalog (or a new version of an online catalog) that encourages people to add tags, write reviews, rate an item, add a comment, or otherwise engage with the organization's collection?	☐	☐
Does your cultural organization provide a set of tools and time to make yourself a seamless part of the information world of your customers?	☐	☐
Has your cultural organization explored the many ways in which it could add value through the use of context?	☐	☐
Has your cultural organization considered options for eliminating the Dewey Decimal system (or the LC Classification system or . . .)?	☐	☐

If you answered "no" to one or more of the questions in the checklist, then your library is not doing all it could to add value using context.

Main idea:	Context adds real value
Opposing view:	Publishers retain control over context
Key terms:	Context, content, timely descriptive stories
What has changed?:	Internet, social media
Catalyst:	Engagement, community
Open debate:	How to let go

Notes

1. David Carr. *The Promise of Cultural Institutions*. New York: Rowman Altamira, 2004, 57.
2. John Snow. *On the Mode of Communication of Cholera*. London: John Churchill, 1855.
3. Joanna Sassoon. "Documenting Communities: If Digitization Is the Answer, What on Earth Is the Question?" *Connections and Conversations*, Australian Society of Archivists Conference, Port Macquarie, 2006. Available at http://www.archivists.org.au/files/Conference_Papers/2006/Sassoon_ASAConference2006.pdf
4. Gobinda Chowdhury. "From Digital Libraries to Digital Preservation Research: The Importance of Users and Context." *Journal of Documentation*, 66 (2), 2010, 207–223.
5. Peter Lucas, Joe Ballay, and Mickey McManus. *Trillions: Thriving in the Emerging Information Ecology*. New York: John Wiley & Sons, 2012.
6. Peter Morville and Louis Rosenfeld. *Information Architecture for the World Wide Web*. San Francisco: O'Reilly Media, 2006.
7. Richard Saul Wurman. *Information Anxiety: What to Do When Information Doesn't Tell You What You Need to Know*. New York: Access Press, 1989.

8. Ken Garland. *Mr. Beck's Underground Map*. London: Capital Transport, 1994.

9. Karen Coyle. "Think 'Different.'" Keynote Presentation at the Dublin Core 2012 Conference, Kuching, Malaysia. Available at http://www.kcoyle.net/presentations/think Diff.pdf

10. See, for example, *TimelineJS* developed by Northwestern University's Knight Lab, *Timeline-SMILE Widgets* developed by the Massachusetts Institute of Technology, and the Library of Congress *Viewshare*.

11. Andy Neale and Bill Macnaught. *A National Approach to the Sharing of Data and Content*. Presentation at the IFLA 2012 conference held in Helsinki. Available at http://conference.ifla .org/past-wlic/2012/181-macnaught-en.pdf

12. Available at http://natlib.govt.nz/visiting/wellington/the-lifelines-table

13. IMLS. *IMLS Focus: The National Digital Platform*. Washington, DC: The Institute of Museum and Library Services, 2015.

14. Locan Dempsey. "Thirteen Ways of Looking at Libraries, Discovery, and the Catalog: Scale, Workflow, Attention." *Educause Review Online*, December 10, 2012. Available at http://www.educause.edu/ero/article/thirteen-ways-looking-libraries-discovery-and-catalog-scale-workflow-attention

15. Jodi Steelman Wilson. Rescuing Forgotten Voices of World War I: Adding Value to Soldiers' Letters Home. *Indiana Libraries*, 29 (2), 2010, 34–41.

16. Sergey Brin and Larry Page. "The Anatomy of a Large-Scale Hypertextual Web Search engine." *Computer Networks and ISDN Systems*, 30, 1998, 107–117.

17. John Battelle. *The Search: How Google and Its Rivals Rewrote the Rules of Business and Transformed Our Culture*. New York: Penguin, 2005.

18. Nigel Shadbolt, Wendy Hall, and Tim Berners-Lee. "The Semantic Web Revisited." *IEEE Intelligent Systems*, 21 (3), 2006, 96–101.

19. David Weinberger. *Everything Is Miscellaneous: The Power of the New Disorder*. New York: Holt, 2008.

20. Yael Keshet. "Classification Systems in the Light of Sociology of Knowledge." *Journal of Documentation*, 67 (1), 2011, 144–158.

21. Gene Smith. *Tagging: People-Powered Metadata for the Social Web*. Berkeley, CA: New Riders, 2007.

22. Michalis Gerolimos. "Tagging for Libraries: A Review of the Effectiveness of Tagging Systems for Library Catalogs." *Journal of Library Metadata*, 13, 2013, 36–58.

23. Christina Manzo, Geoff Kaufman, Sukdith, and Mary Falnagan. "By the People, for the People": Assessing the Value of Crowdsourced, User-Generated Metadata. *DHQ: Digital Humanities Quarterly*, 9 (1), 2015. Available at http://www.digitalhumanities.org/dhq/ vol/9/1/000204/000204.html

24. Nina Simon. *The Participatory Museum*. Santa Cruz, CA: Museum 2.0, 2010.

25. Scott Golder and Bernardo Huberman. "Usage Patterns of Collaborative Tagging Systems." *Journal of Information Science, 32* (2), 2006, 198–208.

26. Time Berners-Lee and Mark Fischetti. *Weaving the Web*. San Francisco: Harper, 1999.

27. Matt Enis. "Ending the Invisible Library." *Library Journal*, February 15, 2015, 36–38.

28. Cory Doctorow. "Metacrap: Putting the Torch to the Seven Straw-Men of the Meta-utopia." August 26, 2001. Available at http://www.well.com/~doctorow/metacrap.htm

29. Thomas Vander Wal. *Folksonomy*. 2007. Available at http://vanderwal.net/folksonomy .html

30. Steele, Tom. "The New Cooperative Cataloguing." *Library Hi Tech*, 27 (1), 2009, 68–77.

31. Morgan Ames and Mor Naaman. "Why We Tag: Motivations for Annotation in Mobile and Online Media." In *Proceedings of the SIGCHI Conference on Human Factors in Computing Systems*. New York: ACM, 2007, 971–980.

32. Beski Stvilia and Corinne Jörgensen. "User-Generated Collection-Level Metadata in an Online Photo-Sharing System." *Library & Information Science Research*, 31 (1), 2009, 54–65.

33. Elaine Peterson. "Patron Preferences for Folksonomy Tags: Research Findings When Both Hierarchical Subject Headings and Folksonomy Tags Are Used." *Evidence Based Library and Information Practice,* 4 (1), 2009, 53–56.

34. Carrie Pirmann. "Tags in the Catalogue: Insights from a Usability Study of LibraryThing for Libraries." *Library Trends*, 61 (1), 2012, 234–247.

35. Hsia-Ching Chand and Hemalata Iyer. "Trends in Twitter Hashtag Applications: Design Features for Value-Added Dimensions to Future Library Catalogues." *Library Trends*, 61 (1), 2012, 248–258.

36. Anna Richards and Barbara Sen. "An Investigation into the Viability of LibraryThing for Promotional and User Engagement Purposes in Libraries." *Library Hi tech*, 31 (3), 2013, 493–519.

37. Luiz Mendes, Jennie Quiñonez-Skinner, and Danielle Skaggs. "Subjecting the Catalog to Tagging." *Library Hi Tech*, 27 (1), 2009, 30–41.

38. Quoted in Karim Lakhani and Jill Panette. "The Principles of Distributed *Innovation*." *Innovations*, Summer 2007, 97.

39. Steven Rosenbaum. *Curation Nation: How to Win in a World Where Consumers Are Creators*. New York: McGraw Hill, 2013.

40. Itamar Simonson and Emanuel Rosen. *Absolute Value: What Really Influences Customers in the Age of (Nearly) Perfect Information*. New York: HarperBusiness, 2014.

41. Steven Rosenbaum. *Curation Nation: How to Win in a World Where Consumers Are Creators*. New York: McGraw Hill, 2013, 18.

42. Seth Godin. Quoted in Steve Rosenbaum, "Seth Godin: Mark Cuban Is Completely Wrong about Aggregators." *Business Insider* blog. February 10, 2010. Available at http://www.businessinsider.com/aggregation-vampires-2010–2

43. Ross Dawson. "5 Ways to Add Value to Information." *Trends in Living Networks* blog. March 15, 2010. Available at http://rossdawsonblog.com/weblog/archives/2010/03/5_ways_to_add_v.html

44. Rob Giampietro. "On Arranging Books by Color." *The Design Observer Group* blog. August 27, 2006. Available at http://designobserver.com/feature/on-arranging-books-by-color/4677

45. Ji Soo Yi, Youn ah Kang, John Stasko, and Julie Jacko. Toward a Deeper Understanding of the Role of Interaction in Information Visualization. *IEEE Transactions on Visualization and Computer Graphics*, 13 (6), November 2007, 1224–1231.

46. Chris Sula. "Quantifying Culture: Four Types of Value in Visualization," *in Electronic Visualisation in Arts and Culture*. London: Springer, 2013, 25–37.

47. Ben Schneiderman. "The Eyes Have It: A Task by Data Type Taxonomy for Information Visualizations." In *Proceedings of the 1996 IEEE Symposium on Visual Language*, 1996, 336–343.

48. Sam Hinton and Mitchell Whitelaw. "Exploring the Digital Commons: An Approach to the Visualization of Large Heritage Datasets." In *EVA'10 Proceedings of the 2010 International Conference on Electronic Visualization and the Arts*. 2010, 51–58.

49. Mitchell Whitelaw. "Visualizing Archival Collections: The Visible Archive Project." *Archives & Manuscripts*, 37 (2009), 22–40.

    See also, Mitchell Whitelaw. "Generous Interfaces for Digital Cultural Collections." *DHQ: Digital Humanities Quarterly*, 9 (1), 2015. Available at http://www.digitalhumanities.org/dhq/vol/9/1/000205/000205.html

50. http://librarylab.law.harvard.edu/blog/stack-view/. The code can be downloaded from GitHub.

51. Jane Alexander. "Gallery One, the First Year: Sustainability, Evaluation Process, and a New Smart Phone App." Presentation at the Annual Conference of Museums and the Web, April 2–5, 2014, Baltimore, ML. Available at http://mw2014.museumsandtheweb.com/paper/gallery-one-the-first-year-sustainability-evaluation-process-and-a-new-smart-phone-app/

52. Alice Thudt, Uta Hinrichs, and Sheelagh Carpendale. "The Bohemian Bookshelf: Supporting Serendipitous Book Discoveries through Information Visualization." *In CHI 2012: Proceedings of the SIGCHI Conference on Human Factors in Computing Systems*, 2012.

    See also, Alice Thudt. "The Bohemian Bookshelf: Design and Implementation of a Visualization Prototype for Serendipitous Browsing." Project Thesis. Ludwig-Maximilians-Universität München, 2011. Available at http://www.alicethudt.de/BohemianBookshelf/material/ThudtProjectThesis.pdf

53. Karl Fast and Kamran Sedig. "The INVENT Framework: Examining the Role of Information Visualization in the Reconceptualization of Digital Libraries." *Journal of Digital Information* 6 (3), 2005, Article No. 362, 2005–08–08.

54. For more information about the Trendalyzer software, visit the www.gapminder.org website. To be thoroughly entertained while learning more about the powerful ways data can be presented, visit the YouTube site and enter the name "Hans Rosling and watch his TED presentations." You will be amazed.

55. Daniel Eizens. "Context in Content Strategy: Defining Context." *Daniel Eizens* blog. January 12, 2011. Available at http://danieleizans.com/2011/01/context-in-content-strategy-defining-context/

7

Connection

. . . the only way of discovering limits of the possible
is to venture a little way past them into the impossible.

Arthur C. Clarke[1]

Given the increasing competition, especially in the digital arena, what should cultural organizations be doing to become more relevant in the lives of their customers and communities?

For the last century or so, librarians and other cultural organization professionals created places and collections because it was the best way to provide access to the physical materials and related services. But in reality, places and collections are simply tools that are used to fulfill a larger agenda. So the focus should not be so much on our buildings and collections but rather on how to use their talents and skills to assist our customers to succeed and, in turn, help our communities achieve their goals and objectives.

But rather than the one-on-one conversations librarians have historically had (e.g., at the reference desk), librarians now have the opportunity to become engaged with people in new and amazing ways. The Internet-based tools at our fingertips allow authors to become engaged with their readers in more direct ways, and similarly readers can now become authors—in short, people are becoming prosumers. Clearly, one of the striking characteristics of Web 2.0 is the way in which prosumers produce value for companies by adding reviews, comments, ratings, photos, and links without being paid—in effect validating Toffler's vision.

Libraries, traditionally focused on the products of scholarship,
are now prompted to understand and support the processes of scholarship.

Karen Williams[2]

The whole notion of a conversation helps change the mind-set of the ways in which cultural organization professionals can add value as they move from thinking of interactions with customers as transactions to moving toward developing strong and lasting relationships with customers. Professionals connect with their communities using instant messaging, Facebook, Twitter, and other social media tools. In addition to the virtual connections, cultural organization professionals now have more extended conversations with their customers as they move out of the building and interact with customers in their settings—faculty offices, faculty meetings, researcher labs and offices, and classroom settings.

Cameras built into phones are communication devices, and everyday hundreds of millions of photos are shared as a way to create a space for conversations. Whether people are using *SnapChat, Instagram, Kik,* or *WhatsApp,* the end result is that people are engaging others using photos. Libraries can also use this technology to engage with their customers by sharing interesting photos as well as engaging in conversations with photos posted by library users.

―――――

What libraries have all too often focused on in the past
is hardware—buildings, books, journals and rooms.
Librarians get caught up in hardware questions continually—
hardback or paperback, how many PCs, should we buy Blueray discs,
lend Kindles, subscribe to downloadable talking books,
throw out our cassette tapes . . .?
The real value of libraries is not in the hardware.
Your members don't come to the library to find
books, or magazines, journals, films or musical recordings.
They come to be informed, inspired, horrified, enchanted or amused.
They come to hide from reality or understand its true nature.
They come to find solace or excitement, companionship or solitude.
They come for the software.

Hugh Rundle[3]

―――――

The Embedded Librarian

Many librarians have recognized developing a deeper understanding of customers and their needs as an important first step in adding value. The literature is chockfull with stories of librarians becoming much more deeply involved in the day-to-day lives of their users.

Yet, all of this creativity has a real downside as Carl Grant has noted.[4] When people use Google, Google Scholar, or many other popular websites, the one thing that continues to draw people back is the consistency of the user experience—the user interface changes very little. Yet, the user experience as he or she moves from library to library (whether physically or virtually) is marked by significant change and inconsistency. The look and feel is different, the vocabulary and labels are different, the . . . is different. So we continue to ask out users to constantly be unlearning and relearning what is required to perform some fairly routine tasks. Cultural organizations have much to learn from Google and others—simplify the user experience.

David Shumaker and Mary Talley consider that embedded librarians provide services that are directed to the customer not the library, provided to individuals in their working environment, go beyond discovery and delivery of information, and are built on entrusted relationships in the context of the customer.[5] The whole concept of being embedded is that it fosters engagement with library customers, improves communication between both parties, encourages a deeper understanding of the user's work, and allows the librarian to begin to anticipate user needs and to develop meaningful, personalized, and long-lasting partnerships.

Based on a comprehensive review of the literature, Stephanie Schulte suggested that embedded librarians might be involved in a wide variety of activities:[6]

- Embedded in course management systems (discussion board/forum participation, links to library resources, online subject guides)
- Collaboration on course design/assignments
- Co-teaching course (face-to-face or online)
- In-depth research to support student research
- In-depth research to support customer work (grant applications, research projects, competitive intelligence)
- Physical colocation with customers (office hours, permanent office with customers)
- Embedded via social media

Embedded librarians (or whatever their job title may be) will be found in all kinds of higher education institutions as well as health science organizations, corporations, law firms, nonprofits, and government agencies. Generally, profound connections will occur as librarians move from transactions to building relationships. The goal for any library is to foster the act of continued and ongoing engagement (high-quality customer service) rather than looking at each customer interaction as a transaction. Look at the way staff at the Apple Store build rapport, embrace a teachable moment, and encourage playing with new devices. Is this a model cultural organizations might emulate?

Recently, the prestigious UK medical journal *Lancet* published a series of reports that have broad implications for all of academic and medical librarianship. The reports noted a great deal of wasted research dollars that libraries and librarians could help reduce. The recommendations called for improvements in the areas of study protocols, research standards, study registers, literature searching, open access to research, institutional repositories, reporting guidelines, and retracted papers.[7]

Yet, a word of caution is called for. The whole notion of "embedding" librarians, especially for larger libraries, is that it will require significant financial resources, which makes the concept difficult to scale. The real challenge in our world filled with handheld digital devices (smartphones in particular) is how do libraries develop a library app that delivers real value so that the app is not only on millions of devices but also more importantly is used quite frequently.

Innovation

There obviously is no single path that will lead to success. Cultural organization professionals need to embrace change and experiment, experiment, and experiment some more. We need to take risks, try things out, see what happens, ask for feedback, and evaluate the results. Cultural organizations have much they can learn from other organizations (nonprofit and for-profit) so there is no need to reinvent the wheel. Some experiments will be a great success, and others not so hot. Hopefully, we can learn to fail fast. But more importantly, we can learn from both our successes and failures even faster.[8] For every experiment that we do, we should be asking, "What do we hope to learn from this effort?" Ultimately, the goal of a "learning fast" approach to innovation is to embed in the organizational culture the ability to extract the key insights as each project progresses as well as the flexibility and courage to make necessary midcourse corrections.

Brian Mathews has suggested that libraries need to focus on problem discovery rather than immediately moving into problem-solving mode. Brian feels that:

> Problem discovery, more than anything else, is an attitude driven by curiosity and empathy: how can we learn more so that we can do more for our users? Problems are valuable in challenging us to confront *business-as-usual* thinking and to imagine what else is possible.[9]

Brian suggests that it is important to employ a variety of thinking lenses so that we can see problems from a variety of perspectives and enhanced clarity. These thinking lenses might include systems thinking, design thinking, integrative thinking, lateral thinking, agile thinking, and computational thinking.

IDEO, a well-known design and innovation consultancy firm, employs an innovation methodology that produces outstanding results. This process has five phases: discovery, interpretation, ideation, experimentation, and evolution. IDEO focuses on producing human-centered, outcomes-based solutions.[10] Using this process means that more time is spent understanding problems rather than trying to solve them. The focus is always on trying to understand what people are trying to accomplish rather than what they are currently doing.

Clearly, involving the customer in the exploration of ideas and concepts will increase the odds that the hopefully innovative project will be successful. Beyond the traditional means of engaging customers in conversations through the use of focus groups and brainstorming, one interesting approach called Appreciative Inquiry might be used.

Appreciative Inquiry is an approach that asks participants to focus on what works (successes) and encouraging their growth or introducing the idea in your particular organizational setting. The goal is to focus on what creates value for the customer and identify how the organization can encourage that value using a four-step or 4D Model as seen in Figure 7-1. A small group of participants are seated in a "café"-like environment (coffee, tea, water, fruit is available) and asked to respond to several questions. "Good" questions can't be answered with a yes/no or either/or but rather provoke discussion. Generative questions typically start with "what" or "how." For example, "what is the role of the cultural organization in our rapidly changing environment?"

The 4D Appreciative Inquiry Model has four phases:

- *Discovery*—Is about finding out "the best of what is" by asking people to share their own experiences in responding to a guiding question.
- *Dream*—About what might be based on the discussions so far. What qualities and characteristics will make a service the "best" in the world?
- *Design*—What should be the ideal for this community? What colors, sights, and sounds should be present in a room or area to promote the desired behavior?
- *Destiny*—How do we empower participants, what can we learn from the process and the experience so far, and what do we need to adjust to make this project even better?

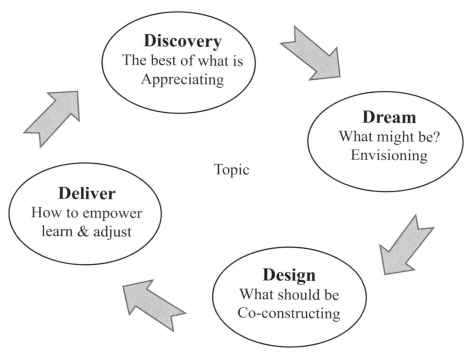

Figure 7-1 Appreciative Inquiry 4D Model.

For more on the Appreciative Inquiry method, see the book by David Cooperrider, Diana Whitney, and Jacqueline Stavros[11] or the work by Diana Whitney and Amanda Trosten-Bloom.[12]

Interestingly, Harvard's Graduate School of Design has created The Library Test Kitchen to prototype library ideas. The Library Test Kitchen is actually a graduate-level course that was offered for the third time in the fall of 2013. The goal is to engage students to redesign an institution that they are a part of.

Projects created by the students in the past three years are all available online (exploring each of these projects is a terrific investment in your time—(visit http://www.librarytestkitchen.org/). Some of these projects include:

- *The Speaking Library*—An online archive of anonymous audio recordings that documents an oral history of the library.
- *Graham Grams*—An edible telegram with a graham cracker and icing printer.
- *Biblio*—A little clam-shaped device that can scan text, suggest related books, and share titles with other Biblio friends.

Librarians from Harvard interact with the students and explore some real fundamental questions: How can librarians connect visitors with invisible digital texts? How can we digitize texts without sacrificing their crucial textual arrangement and scale?

The YOUmedia space, first debuted at the Harold Washington Library in Chicago, and subsequently adopted by other libraries, is a place where young people can create, explore, and express themselves using digital media. The idea is to provide space where teens and preteens can:

- *Hang out*—Talk with one another in informal sessions
- *Mess around*—Experiment with new technologies
- *Geek out*—Teach one another about digital media

The students learn how to capture digital pictures, sound, and video and to integrate their efforts with content from others in a process of remixing and reimagining content. The idea is to involve the young people in a socially connected and interest-driven learning environment so that they are engaged in the process. And to make YOUmedia more successful, the library actively engages the youth in the planning of future programs and activities. The YOUmedia concept is also being implemented in high school and museum settings. One of the key drivers of success is to involve working artists and knowledgeable librarians who can relate with the youth and to serve as role models. YOUmedia attracts a diverse group of teens and encourages a wide variety of activities. An analysis of how the teens spend their time found socializers (hang with their friends), readers/studiers, floaters (use computers and chat with friends), experimenters (use computers and keyboards outside the studio to practice), and creators (interact with staff around a set of shared interests).[13] The StoryLab at the Tacoma (WA) Public Library provides tools and classes for digital illustration, filmmaking, photography, music production, and the like.

Material-dispensing machines (Redbox-style lending machines) can be placed throughout a community or in the library itself to dispense traditional library materials such as books, DVDs, and CDs. The machine can also dispense laptops and other items of value to customers (while the library is open but perhaps not fully staffed). The Contra Costa County Library (CA) calls its dispensing machine "Library-a-Go-Go."

Some libraries provide apps that encourage interaction with the library's website and online catalog. Other apps provide GPS navigation assistance to find items (locations) within the library itself—helping to crack the call number thing.

The Carnegie Library at Pittsburgh has opened up a tiny 235 square foot "branch" library at a neighborhood Public Market that has drawn great interest and crowds. And in San Francisco, continuing with the "small is beautiful" theme, the public library has partnered with a local organization to create a number of "pop-up" libraries in abandoned telephone booths and newspaper racks. In New York City, cubes that can be easily transported and set up in various configurations provide walk-up learning spaces.

The Oak Park (IL) Public Library created an "Idea Box" out of a 9-by-13 foot space in the vestibule of the main library. Each month a new "theme" is introduced, and people are encouraged to create poetry (using magnetic words on a board that is constantly being rearranged), writing their favorite book titles on post-it notes, and so forth. The intent of the Idea Box is to promote lifelong learning through creative play and to have fun.

And, of course, a public library has created a "bookless" branch library, called BiblioTech, in Bexar County (the south side of San Antonio, Texas). One hundred eReaders are available for loan as well as public access computers for people to use. The result has almost overwhelmed staff with almost constant demand.

David Lewis has suggested a fairly radical idea of using an Espresso Book Machine to print books that users wanted and simply give the books to the customer with the expectation that the book would NOT be returned to the library.[14] The customer would be given the option of "taking" an eBook rather than a pBook. David asserts that in 10 years' time, most pBooks will be digitized and accessible online and that print-on-demand machines will be faster, better, and cheaper. The end result is that in many cases, a library could save a considerable amount of money if it simply gave away what people wanted!

Using an Espresso machine, the Sacramento Public Library's *I Street Press* encourages people to print their own content or print out-of-print books.

A Polish architect, Hugon Kowalski, has suggested that a library should be combined with other uses so that people had a number of reasons to visit the facility (and oh, by the way, the library is here so let's drop in). Kowalski has suggested combining the library with a swimming pool (complete with water slides), playgrounds, sport center, or a park on the roof. In addition to partnering with various municipal services, the library might partner with commercial firms to build office buildings, a hotel, or retail space as a way to generate ongoing revenue for the library.[15]

Engaging in Conversations

Libraries have a long tradition of organizing and hosting author talks, artist performances, debates of all kinds, community read one-book projects, and participatory arts projects, among many other types of programs. All of these programs are designed to assist in facilitating a community discussion about relevant and timely topics.

One of the joys of my youth was the opportunity to visit libraries, museums, and galleries on weekends. The high point of the day was having the opportunity of listening to a passionate expert explain about dinosaurs, steam engines, art, and so much more. These knowledgeable individuals were sharing their expertise and their enthusiasm that simply transformed the listening audience. And the best of these experts shared how a particular topic had affected their personal lives. Great stuff!

The New York Public Library has a wonderful event series, called *LIVE from the NYPL*, offering engaging programs. The programs exemplify the library's mission to educate, inform, and inspire the diverse community it serves. *LIVE from the NYPL* provokes conversations, encourages real debates, and provides enticing performances designed to stimulate cultural curiosity. *LIVE* welcomes a variety of artists, creative filmmakers, notable historians, influential leaders, and emerging authors who are shaping the world today.

Launched in 2005, *LIVE* was created when Paul Holdengräber was recruited and asked to "oxygenate" the library.[16] Past *LIVE* performances can be viewed online from the library's website http://www.nypl.org/live/multimedia.

In addition to the more formalized conversations that are occurring in libraries, librarians engage in conversations every day with members of the community. Librarians have the ability to connect people with ideas and information with the end result that people's lives are improved. Librarians can help develop the assets of any community. According to library educator Ken Haycock, libraries need to develop as learning agencies that help build a sense of identity and community. Libraries provide physical space, an online presence, to assist people in using information to make a difference in a community.[17]

The Canton (MI) Public Library (CPL) embraced the notion of community with its strategic plan and connects people with resources and assists in connecting people with each other through its active programming efforts. The CPL was awarded the inaugural LibraryAware Community Award in 2013.[18]

Another way to build conversation and trust is to comment intelligently and fairly frequently to the posting of the members of your community that have blogs or are active using other social media sites. Avoid the obvious "agree totally with what you are saying" (which is your basic "high-five") and come up with a slightly different perspective or reference something someone else had to say (from another blog, or a book or article you recently read), which would hopefully spark some dialogue.[19] Being visible in your community by being out there is really important if the library is going to be a part of ongoing conversations in the community. And follow up with timely and honest reactions so that others will recognize that you are paying attention and are appreciative of others. In short, cultural organization professionals have an opportunity to add real value by starting, joining, and encouraging conversations that are important in the lives of their customers.

One really interesting project, now called the *Human Library*, has been going on around the world for a number of years. The objective is to get strangers to talk with one another about prejudice.[20] The concept is fairly simple and works much like a regular library—readers come to the library and borrow a "book" (in actuality a human being) and enter into a 45-minute or longer conversation. The "books" in the *Human Library* represent groups that are frequently confronted with stereotypes and prejudice.[21]

A *Human Library* requires three types of people:

- Volunteers who serve as "books" who represent stereotype groups—people of color, people from different religious groups, gays, lesbian, Goth, and so forth.
- Readers who wish to engage in an open and candid conversation.
- Librarians who recruit "books" and facilitate the borrowing of "books." By providing access to "living books," librarians are fostering conversations and social interactions that would not likely happen otherwise.

The objective of the *Human Library* is to encourage people to move outside their comfort zone and confront long-held beliefs and stereotypes.

In a wonderful book called *Community*, Peter Block suggests that communities, and by extension libraries, should be shifting conversation from the problems of the community (exhibited by conversations that focuses on fear, assigns blame, and worships self-interest) to the possibilities of the community (conversations based on generosity, possibilities, and gifts).[22] Leadership and transformation can occur within a community when three things happen:

- Shift the context within which people come together.
- Use powerful questions to shape the debate.
- Listen rather than being an advocate or providing answers.

Powerful questions, defined as those that are personal, ambiguous, and stressful, have the potential to open the doors to the future. Block goes on to identify a series of questions that will transform your community including:

- What declaration of possibility can be made that has the power to transform the community?
- To what extent are you invested in the well-being of the entire community?
- What have I done to contribute to the very thing I want to change?
- What risk am I willing to take on to assist in affecting change?

Getting in the Flow

Lorcan Dempsey has written a fair amount about the fundamental change that libraries are experiencing today.[23] In the past, information creation and use was organized around the library, whereas now it is organized around network-level services that support local workflows. Lorcan has recommended that libraries must move in new directions and provide new services so that they are in the workflow of their users. But how is this accomplished? Rather than relying on an institution such as a library, people now turn to other people (typically using social media) as an entry point to information. As John Hagel and his colleagues have noted:[24]

> In a world of accelerating change, the most valuable knowledge is highly distributed and may be embedded in the heads of people who are not well-known and who are difficult to identify.
>
> It's not so much about finding which information is most valuable, as many of those who fret about information overload would have it. Improving return on attention is more about finding and connecting people who have the knowledge you need, particularly tacit knowledge about how to do new things. The danger is that we all get so busy assimilating explicit knowledge that that we have no time to connect people and build relationships through which tacit knowledge flows. We get so busy reading about steampunk, or brewing, or building networks that we don't actually find and connect with and learn from the people who are doing it. It's not so much information that we need as knowledge. And knowledge means people.
>
> These people and the knowledge flows they generate can then become effective filters for information more broadly. By harnessing social media such as blogs, social-network platforms, and wikis, we can begin to rely on these mechanisms to expose ourselves to information that has been curated and passed on by these people. Since we deeply understand their contexts and passions, we can begin to determine when their recommendations are most reliable and increase our return on attention for both the tacit knowledge they offer and the information they recommend to us. Our personal social and professional networks will be far more effective in filtering relevant knowledge and information than any broader social-technology tools we might access.

The authors suggest that there are three levels of pull:

- *Access*—Finding people and resources when and where needed
- *Attract*—Knowledgeable and relevant resources and people to you (typically, people rely on social networks, conferences, unconferences, concentrations of specific talent in relatively restricted geographic locations—Silicon Valley for high-tech talent, Nashville for country music, and so forth)
- *Achieve*—More by learning more effectively (and quickly) and translating that learning into action thereby improving performance

Of course, there are no shortages of network-level services that students, teachers, scholars, and researchers can employ. Consider, for example, such services as *SRRN, arXiv, Mendeley, Citavi, respect, ResearchGate, LibraryThing, Goodreads, Facebook, Twitter, Amazon, Google Scholar*, and *Google Books*. The question then becomes, "How does an individual library (or a group of libraries) become involved with one or more of these services and add real value for a specific group of users?"

Rather than immediately jumping to the conclusion that the cultural organization should start a blog, the organization might want to consider an alternative approach. Identify the blogs and other online social media sites that are popular in your community and begin to follow these sources. As you become comfortable with the content and the ongoing conversation, you can begin to share your point of view by commenting intelligently and frequently as you "put yourself out there." Respond to comments quickly and honestly in such a way that it fosters discussion, and others in the community will begin to trust you.

Interestingly, several libraries post library content several times a day using Twitter and Instagram. For example, the first sentence of a book is posted along with a link to the book in the library's catalog. Or an interesting, and perhaps provocative, quote is used again with a link to the library's catalog. And perhaps most importantly, it is important to talk like a human—let's don't use library jargon. Ask several nonlibrarians to review the content of your website, your online catalog, your . . . to identify words and phrases that have no meaning (or is confusing) for them. Connecting with people in a real and valuable way will bring visibility to the library, museum, gallery or archive.

The real challenge is to recognize that the systems found in libraries that provide access to physical collections (the online catalog) and electronic resources (the library's website, A–Z list of eResources, search for a specific eResource, eBooks) are all isolated within a library-centric view of the world. How can you remember what you are trying to accomplish when you must navigate from one system to another with unique and unwieldy user interfaces in order to accomplish a simple task such as downloading a journal article or checking on a citation? Each of the electronic resources that a user visits is filled with irritating usability failures (too many options, don't understand what a feature will accomplish, jargon, and so forth) so that the journey becomes a real unpleasant experience rather than a smooth flow that enhances the user's productivity.

Customer Service

Providing outstanding customer service is another important way of connecting with your customers. For many organizations, providing a WOW experience is something that differentiates the organization from its competitors—all you have to do is to think of Nordstrom or Zappos. When it comes to customer service, the goal is to reduce customer frustrations. Rather than thinking about customer service as a strategy, it is much more realistic to think of it as a "way of life." Not surprisingly, the key is to think like a customer.

People always ask me, how do you teach core values?
The answer is, you don't.
The goal is not to convince people to share your core values.
It's to hire people who already share your core values.

James Collins[25]

Excellent customer service simply does not happen. Rather library staff members must be trained, nurtured, and mentored. It is better to hire people who like other people (hire the smile), and you can train any skill that may be needed. And remember to celebrate those staff members who have gone the extra mile and provided wonderful service.

Repurposing Space

While particularly noticeable in the academic environment, even public libraries have begun to reposition space around broader goals and less around the management of print collections. So this shift in priorities is encouraging us to think about space less as infrastructure and more about how space supports engagement. Library space is an opportunity to support social interaction around learning, provide access to specialized equipment and expertise, and provide access to communication facilities, exhibits, programs, and so forth that will engage a broader cross section of a community.

Some libraries have moved significant portions of their collections to automated storage and retrieval systems located in specially designed additions to the library or buried beneath the library. Other libraries have moved these collections to dedicated or shared remote service facilities (calling them storage facilities may irritate some people). The result is that libraries have freed up a significant amount of space (sometimes one or more floors) and have taken this opportunity to redesign the space to facilitate interactions between people and between people and specialized services. Sometimes this freed-up space has been renamed using such labels as the "learning commons," "information commons," "scholars commons," and "digital commons". In many cases, libraries use these naming opportunities to raise significant funds to pay for the remodeling.

Apple has been extremely successful with its Apple stores (reportedly, Apple generates more revenue per square foot than any other retailer in the world). The total experience at an Apple store is so pleasing that customers return again and again. Besides being visually appealing and providing a fair amount of space around each product (so two or more people can easily gather around) in each store, the well-trained help is creating an engaging experience for the customer. Apple staff members are less sales-people and are much more problem solvers (although they can and do "ring up a sale" using their iPhone rather than requiring a customer to move to a cash register—do people still use cash?). The strong customer focus permeates everything an Apple staff member does and says. Anthony Molaro, in a blog posting,[26] suggests that the Apple customer focus stands for:

Approach customers with a personalized warm welcome
Probe politely to understand customer's all the needs
Present a solution for the customer to take home
Listen for and resolve any issues of concerns
End with a fond farewell and an invitation to return

Apple invented an entirely new way of delivering value by creating a compelling and engaging customer experience. The leaders of Apple built a prototype of the store using a customer-centric design approach, embraced a willingness to experiment with several options till they got it right in order to determine whether their innovative new business model was going to be a winner.

The end result for the customer is that it is fun to go to the Apple store whether it is to buy something, get a problem solved (notice that you receive assistance at a Genius Bar—not a Trouble Desk), or attend a class to learn how to use a specific device. And Apple trusts their customers since people can purchase a product on their own using their phone or iPad. Simply download an app, connect to iTunes, complete the transaction, and walk out of the store with your purchase. Notice that Apple does not have a security guard. So libraries and other cultural organizations could do far worse if they simply tried to emulate the total customer experience at an Apple store.

Libraries create a connection with their customers when they have created a strong value proposition that really resonates with each customer. Too often, we get caught up in our day-to-day responsibilities and assume that everyone sees the library, its services, and the value of the library as we do. Yet making this assumption is really short changing the library as we must strive to ensure that people understand the importance and value of the library by creating strong connections with each of our customers.

Retail stores that deliver a unique experience are quite popular. Check out any *Build-A-Bear* store, and it's buzzing with energy and laughter as parents (grandparents too) and children work together to make something unique. The end result is an exceptional experience that is memorable and fun.

Libraries have created spaces to provide access to computers that resemble quiet reading rooms. Yet increasingly, people want to gather around a large screen and talk as they work together. Given the widespread use of WiFi, people may want options other than sitting in chairs to use their iPads and laptops.

Scott Walter asks an important question,

When access to content is no longer scarce, what are the services that will stand as the "primary measures of quality" and "distinctive signifiers of excellence" in the academic library?[27]

Scott maintains that there are other characteristics besides size and uniqueness of collections that serve as indicators of excellence including:

- The University of Michigan's Instructor College
- Penn State University's Office of Digital Scholarship Publishing
- University of Washington's Library Assessment Program
- Columbia University's Copyright Advisory Office
- Kansas University's Info Program
- Bowling Green's First-Year Experience Initiative
- Hostos Community College's Literary Magazine Escriba!/Write!
- University of Oklahoma's Knowledge Creation Space
- San Diego Public Library's IDEA Lab
- A group of libraries have created the Library Publishing Coalition
- The British Library has made more than 65,000 19th-century books available and can be printed on demand
- And a host of other examples

A physical space also conveys more than the surrounding—a space conveys ideas, feelings, and states of being. So a library brings together physical and conceptual space in order to link people to ideas, to content, and to each other.[28] And in a physical setting, the functions and activities that can be offered are constrained by the available space. In a digital library setting, there are no obvious constraints other than the imagination of the designer of the user interface.

The traditional library typically asserts a "pull" on potential customers in that the customer must visit the library in order to gain access to its collections, attend a program or performance, interact with a librarian, view an exhibit, and so forth. However, in the digital arena, the library can attract or pull the user to the library's website as well as "pushing" selective content or other information in response to a profile established by the customer.

Bess Sandler, a librarian at Stanford University, noted that users of the physical library often use such emotional terms as "joyous," "immersive," and "beautiful" to describe their interactions with the physical library while using such nonemotional terms as "efficient" and "fast" to describe their interaction with a digital library.[29] Bess makes the point that libraries need to make their online user interface so engaging that users will be using the same emotional terms as "joyous," "immersive," and "beautiful" to describe their interactions with the digital library.

Makerspace

Some libraries are moving from the traditional warehouse-type library to becoming more involved with the community by facilitating cocreation—to provide tools to assist customers produce art, to make parts to repair something, to share their creations with others, or to encourage innovators and entrepreneurs. One option is to set aside an area for a makerspace that likely will include the signature offering of a 3D printer; the space may also include some other low-tech and low-cost equipment such as a drill press, saw, soldering iron, and so forth. A broader definition of the makerspace concept refers to people coming together to share resources, expertise, and enthusiasm. And while a makerspace will likely include at least one library staff member, the efforts of volunteers probably play the most important role in the continued success of a makerspace.

Makerspaces foster play and exploration and facilitate informal learning opportunities due to the peer-to-peer training and nurturing that occurs. People learn by sharing tools and practical experience. The space gives people permission to remake, hack, and tinker to their heart's content. A makerspace might also be called a "Fab Lab" or an "Idea Lab" although, Neil Gershenfeld of MIT's Center for Bits and Atoms suggests that a Fab Lab needs more than a 3D printer—milling machines, a computer-controlled laser, a drill press, and so forth are usually needed. There are numerous Fab Labs located around the world in wonderful and strange settings. Libraries might also consider including a data visualization lab, visual immersion space, and staff who are comfortable manipulating data, especially "big data."

Librarianship is not about artifacts,
it is about knowledge and facilitating knowledge creation.
So what should we be spending our precious resources on?
Knowledge creation tools, not the results of knowledge creation.

David Lankes[30]

Hackerspaces (also called a hackspace or a hacklab) are places where computer programmers, DIY'ers, artists, and makers can congregate, collaborate, and socialize.

Three-dimensional printers start at around $150 and go up from there—the more expensive the machine, the faster an item will get "printed." Some of the libraries involved with a makerspace include the Westport (CT) Public Library, the Fayetteville (NY) Free Library, the Detroit (MI) Public Library, the Martin County (FL) Library System, the Nashville (TN) Public Library, the Chicago Public Library, the Kirkendall (IA) Public Library, the Chattanooga (TN) Public Library, and the Anne Arundel County (MD) Library System.

Chris Anderson says that we are entering a world where manufacturing decentralizes and innovation is moving back to individuals tinkering with ideas in their garages (and in libraries) using 3D printers.[31]

But not everyone is jumping on board the makerspace train. Hugh Rundle, for one, has clearly stated:

The harsh truth is that there is no business case for public libraries to provide 3-D printing. What this is really about is technolust and the fear of being left behind. How many of the librarians clamoring for 3D printers currently provide their patrons with laundry facilities? Sawmills? Smelting furnaces? Loans of cars or whisky stills? I'm guessing none. All these services would be justifiable on the same grounds used to justify 3D printing—individuals would find the service useful, currently they are expensive to buy or rent commercially, and potentially they could be helpful to productivity and the economy. They are also nothing to do with the core business of libraries.[32]

And getting librarians and key stakeholders to have a conversation about exactly "what is the core business of libraries" and what is the "core business of librarians" is what I hope to provoke with this book. The needs in different communities and on each campus of higher education vary, so while the resulting services that are offered will be different, everyone will have a better understanding of how libraries (and librarians) add value!

That there is disagreement about the possible role of makerspaces in a library is very encouraging since it leads us to ask the fundamental question: What is the role of the library in your community? To dismiss the idea of a makerspace out of hand usually means that the librarian is stuck with a fixed image of what a library should be. Clearly, people are exploring and learning in new and creative ways, and this is something that libraries ought to be encouraging in their community. People are creating more content—blogs, music, video, books, art, and so much more—than any other time in the history of the world. People like to be involved, to explore, to try new things out, to create, to make, and to share. In many ways, this is the type of question that the library profession has been answering for years—why does the library provide access to fill in the blank (fax machine, scanner, computer, computer software, printer, toys, tools, 3D printer, and so forth). This is also another manifestation of the "this isn't your parents' (or grandparents') library" discussion that has been ongoing for years.

As Zachary Slobig noted in a recent blog posting:

Libraries—by necessity—are evolving these days. They're no longer just big rooms for storing and lending books. The local library is becoming an inspiration hub and innovation laboratory. Sitting quietly with a book? Sure, that still happens in libraries big and small, but increasingly, libraries are becoming dynamic workshop spaces for creative multimedia learning and doing.[33]

Community Publishing Portals

Some libraries are developing a series of programs that encourage local authors to learn about the opportunities of publishing their work as an eBook. Libraries can bring together author want-to-bes with authors and readers from the local community. In addition to presenting information about self-publishing options, the library can also share best practices with potential and existing authors. Others in the community with complementary talents, such as folks with graphic arts or marketing know-how, can share their experiences.

Libraries have also developed programs to help potential authors learn more about writing, editing, the importance of cover design, and social media marketing. In addition to providing a valuable service for potential authors, developing a community publishing portal is yet another way to connect with people in community who perhaps are not frequent users of the library.

The Douglas County (CO) Libraries has worked to develop its own eBook platform as well as to encourage local authors to publish eBooks and to sell them to the library. The library then treats these eBooks as a regular pBook in terms of lending to customers.

Supporting Economic Development

A number of public libraries have focused on supporting the efforts of local entrepreneurs as they struggle to birth a new business. From the initial concept, the process of bringing a new business to life is challenging, frustrating, and at times seemingly impossible. Some libraries partner with a local Chamber of Commerce, a bank, or a state economic development agency to bring a set of workshops and resources to bear in order to nurture new start-ups. For example, the Sunnyvale (CA) Public Library has a copy of every U.S. patent that individuals can search.

The British Library has created a separate Business & IP Centre to encourage entrepreneurs by providing a continuing series of workshops and knowledgeable librarians to provide assistance. As seen in Figure 7-2, the library teams up with partners (volunteers)

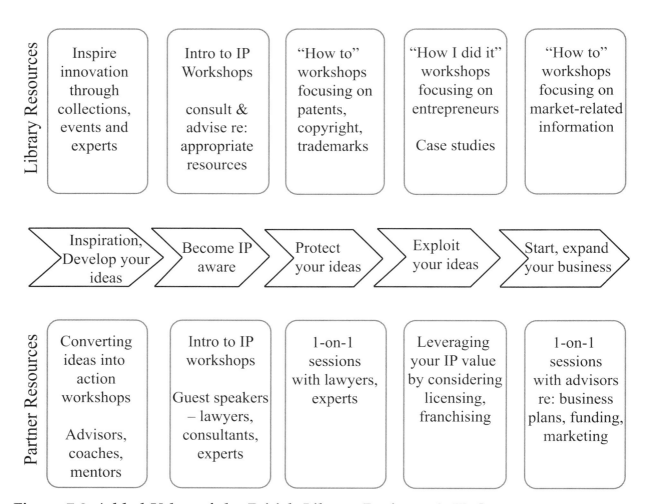

Figure 7-2 Added-Value of the British Library Business & IP Centre. British Library. © The British Library Board.

to provide a comprehensive set of workshops, events, and one-on-one coaching to serve as an incubator for entrepreneurs to start new businesses or expand existing businesses. An evaluation of this business center has found that over a two-year period:[34]

- Eight hundred and twenty-nine new businesses were created.
- An additional 786 new jobs were created.
- Annual revenues for these new businesses totaled 32 million pounds.
- A number of individuals were better able to protect their intellectual property.
- Start-ups fostered through the business center are four times more likely to survive beyond the critical three-year mark than the average London start-up.
- About 10,000 individuals attended workshops and associated events.
- And for every £1 invested in the center, businesses have seen a £22 increase in annual revenues. That's a very good return on investment.

The British Library is now teaming up with six large public libraries throughout England to expand the reach of the Business & IP Centre service.

Catalyst for Civic Engagement

Bill Ptacek,[35] the former director of the King County Library System in Washington, has suggested that in the future, the library will be a concept rather than a place and that it will be:

> More about what it does for people rather than what it has for people. As society evolves and more content becomes digital, people will access information in different ways. Physical items will be less important than they have been up to now. Library buildings and spaces will be used in different ways, and services will be provided beyond the building and virtually. The library as a catalyst for civic engagement will facilitate learning and growth for people of all ages.

The Urban Libraries Council released a report that suggests that public libraries can be leaders of civic engagement in at least five ways:[36]

- *Civic educator*—Raise awareness of civics, civic engagement, and civic responsibility.
- *Conversation starter*—Identify perplexing community issues, create forums for sharing opinions, and develop action strategies to address identified problems.
- *Community bridge*—Bring diverse people, government officials, and leaders of nonprofit organizations together to build stronger communities.
- *Visionary*—Lead efforts to build a broad and inclusive community vision.
- *Center for democracy in action*—Walk-the-walk, talk-the-talk, and act as the place where democracy, civic engagement, and public discourse happens.

The intent is that libraries will become more valued in their communities and thus become the logical place for civic, educational, and social engagement. The goal is to engage people from across the socioeconomic spectrum so that the library can meet their needs whether it's learning about a new technology, learning English as a second language, or supporting students of all ages. The end result is that the library is more broadly engaged and connected with a wider cross section of the entire community.

Two nonlibrarians launched a 10-day open idea forum on Facebook (100 Great Ideas) to gather ideas and foster dialogue concerning the future of Miami-Dade County public libraries. A total of 600 individuals contributed more than 150 ideas that have been grouped into 10 themes: technology tools, mixed space use, leadership, expanded services, partnerships, design and ambiance, and more.[37]

The Douglas County (CO) Libraries has worked quite hard to be an active member of the community by organizing debates about sometimes-controversial topics such as fracking or legalizing marijuana. It provides access to a set of resources representing various sides of the discussion as well as providing a neutral venue for the debates. Douglas County librarians are asked to spend time out of the library and in the community so that the library is more visible and is perceived as a "hub for the community."

Interestingly, the Association of American Colleges and Universities (AACU) have developed a civic engagement VALUE rubric.[38] The AACU encourages institutions of higher education to participate in civic engagement to make a difference in the quality of life in each of our communities.

Summary

Customers do not come to the library for the books, DVDs, music, eResources, computers, or programs. All of these things are simply the means to the end. People come to the library to be inspired, amused, and entertained, or informed. They come to accomplish a task, and in some cases, that is to hide from reality by reading romance, mystery, or other types of fiction. They sometimes come for the solitude or to interact with others. In short, they want a wonderful experience—an experience of their choosing.

Reaching out and engaging in conversations with members of a community allows the library to establish connections and develop social capital. Social capital is, in many ways, much like an invisible bank account in which you can make deposits by listening to and engaging with others. And your social capital bank balance must be sufficiently high before you can even consider asking for a favor or information or . . . from others involved in social media—in short, making a withdrawal of social capital.[39]

The library is there to encourage innovation, learning, and exploration within our communities. People want to become engaged with content, to add context, and to engage with ideas through remixing and sharing their creations with others. And the people within our libraries will help establish the foundation or platform so that all of this innovation can take place? Why it is the librarian.

The library is about making connections—people to other people; people to other institutions; and people to ideas, information, and knowledge. The library is an important node in any community, but we are no longer the center of the information universe. Libraries need to re-image their services and identify how they can best connect with the people in the community they serve. We really need to understand how the library adds unique content and contest in the services it provides.

Traditional libraries may indeed be less relevant in today's world, but as Scott Plutchak has observed, "the need for smart, creative, risk-taking, knowledgeable librarians is greater than ever."[40] Be the change, try things out, explore opportunities that are aligned with the mission of the library, and have fun doing it.

Checklist for Adding Value Using Connections

	Yes	No
Has your cultural organization made the contents of its catalog visible to search engines?	☐	☐
Is your cultural organization where its customers are at the network level?	☐	☐
Does your cultural organization post a minimum of 5–10 tweets per day?	☐	☐
Does you cultural organization have a lot of followers on Facebook?	☐	☐
Does your cultural organization have a blog that generates rich discussion in your community?	☐	☐
Could I find an entry for your cultural organization on Wikipedia?	☐	☐
Will I find images from your cultural organization's collections on Pinterest and/or Flickr?	☐	☐

If you answered "no" to one or more of the questions in the checklist, then your library is not doing all it could to add value using connection.

Main idea:	Cultural organization that embrace experimentation and innovation by engaging with their communities are adding value
Opposing view:	Preserving the traditional cultural organization
Key concepts:	Connection, innovation, experimentation, embracing change, acknowledging change
What has changed?:	Technology, people's needs
Catalyst:	The Internet, handheld devices
Open debate:	How fast should we be changing?

Notes

1. Arthur C. Clark. *Profiles of the Future*. New York: Harper & Row, 1973, 21.
2. Karen Williams. A Framework for Articulating New Library Roles. *Research Library Issues*, 265, August 2009. Available at http://old.arl.org/bm~doc/rli-265-williams.pdf
3. Hugh Rundle. "Libraries as Software—Dematerializing, Platforms and Returning to First Principles." *Information Flaneur* blog. April 4, 2012. Available at http://www.hughrundle.net/2012/04/04/libraries-as-software-dematerialising-platforms-and-returning-to-first-principles/
4. Personal email from Carl Grant. August 20, 2014.

5. David Shumaker and Mary Talley. *Models of Embedded Librarianship: Final Report*. Washington, DC: Special Libraries Association, June 2009. Available at http://hq.sla.org/pdfs/EmbeddedLibrarianshipFinalRptRev.pdf

6. Stephanie Schulte. "Embedded Academic Librarianship: A Review of the Literature." *Evidence Based Library and Information Practice*, 7 (4), 2012, 122–138.

7. **Lancet Waste Series papers**

   Paper 1. Chalmers I., Bracken M. B., Djulbegovic B., Garattini S., Grant J., Gülmezoglu A. M., Howells D. W., Ioannidis J. P., Oliver S. "How to Increase Value and Reduce Waste When Research Priorities Are Set." *Lancet*. 383 (9912), 2014, 156–165.

   Paper 2. Ioannidis J. P., Greenland S., Hlatky M. A., Khoury M. J., Macleod M. R., Moher D., Schulz K. F., Tibshirani R. "Increasing Value and Reducing Waste in Research Design, Conduct, and Analysis." *Lancet*, 383 (9912), 2014, 166–175.

   Paper 3. Al-Shahi Salman R., Beller E., Kagan J., Hemminki E., Phillips R. S., Savulescu J., Macleod M., Wisely J., Chalmers I. "Increasing Value and Reducing Waste in Biomedical Research Regulation and Management." Lancet, 383 (9912), 2014, 176–185.

   Paper 4. Chan A. W., Song F., Vickers A., Jefferson T., Dickersin K., Gøtzsche P. C., Krumholz H. M., Ghersi D., van der Worp H. B. "Increasing Value and Reducing Waste: Addressing Inaccessible Research." Lancet, 383 (9913), 2014, 257–266.

   Paper 5. Glasziou P., Altman D. G., Bossuyt P., Boutron I., Clarke M., Julious S., Michie S., Moher D., Wager E. "Reducing Waste from Incomplete or Unusable Reports of Biomedical Research." *Lancet*, 383 (9913), 2014, 267–276.

8. It would be great if we could have an "unconference" at our professional conferences where we each could take five to seven minutes to present a failure and discuss what was learned. Might be more insightful than the usual "how I done it good" talk.

9. Brian Mathews. "The Art of Problem Discovery." April 2013. Paper presented at the ACRL Conference 2013, Indianapolis, IN. Available at http://www.ala.org/acrl/sites/ala.org.acrl/files/content/conferences/confsandpreconfs/2013/papers/Mathews_Art.pdf

10. IDEO. *Design Thinking for Educators: Toolkit*, 2nd ed. 2011. Available from http://www.ideo.com/work/toolkit-for-educators

11. David Cooperrider, Diana Whitney, and Jacqueline Stavros. *Appreciative Inquiry Handbook: For Leaders of Change*, 2nd ed. Brunswick, OH: Crown Custom Publishing, 2008.

12. Diana Whitney and Amanda Trosten-Bloom. *The Power of Appreciative Inquiry: A Practical Guide to Positive Change*, 2nd Ed. San Francisco: Berrett-Koehler, 2010.

13. Penny Bender Sebring, Eric Brown, Kate Julian, Stacy Ehrlick, Susan Sporte, Erin Bradley, and Lisa Meyer. *Teens, Digital Media, and the Chicago Public Library*. Chicago: Consortium on Chicago School Research, May 2013.

14. David Lewis. "The User-Driven Purchase Giveaway Library." *EDUCAUSE Review*, 45 (5), September/October 2010, 10–11.

15. John Metcalfe. "Would More People Use the Public Library If It Had a Water Slide?" *The Atlantic Cities*. March 19, 2013. Available at http://m.theatlanticcities.com/design/2013/03/would-more-people-use-public-library-if-it-had-water-slide/5019/

16. Drake Baer. "How Conversation Is Making the New York Public Library Roar." *Fast Company Co-Create* blog. January 17, 2013. Available at http://www.fastcocreate.com/1682220/how-conversation-is-making-the-new-york-public-library-roar

17. Ken Haycock. "Building Community Assets." *Next libraries* blog. February 19, 2013. Available at http://www.nextlibraries.org/2013/02/building-community-assets/

18. Michelle Lee. "Community First." *Library Journal*, April 1, 2013, 24–26.

19. Mitch Joel. *Six Pixels of Separation: Everyone Is Connected. Connect Your Business to Everyone.* New York: Business Plus, 2010.

20. For more information about the Human Library, visit http://humanlibrary.org/about-the-human-library.html

21. Ronnie Abergel, Antje Rothemund, Gavan Titley, and Peter Wootsch. *Don't Judge a Book by Its Cover! The Living Library Organizer's Guide.* 2005. Available at http://www.gaidid.ee/system/files/files/Living%20Library%20handbook.pdf

22. Peter Block. *Community: The Structure of Belonging.* San Francisco: Berrett-Koehler, 2008.

23. Lorcan Dempsey. "Libraries and the Informational Future: Some Notes," in *Information Professionals 2050: Educational Possibilities and Pathways*, edited by Gary Marchionini and Barbara Moran. Chapel Hill: School of Information and Library Science, University of North Carolina at Chapel Hill, 2012. Available at http://sils.unc.edu/sites/default/files/publications/Information-Professionals-2050.pdf

24. John Hagel, John Brown, and Lang Davison. *The Power of Pull: How Small Moves, Smartly Made, Can Set Big Things in Motion.* New York: Basic Books, 2010, 173–174.

25. James Collins and Jerry Porras. *Built to Last: Successful Habits of Visionary Companies.* New York: HarperBusiness, 2004, 107.

26. Anthony Molaro. "The Apple Way for Libraries (a Manifesto?)." *The Information Activist Librarian* blog. November 23, 2011. Available at http://informationactivist.com/2012/04/12/ia-greatest-hits-the-apple-way-for-libraries-a-manifesto/

27. Scott Walter. "Guest Editorial. 'Distinctive Signifiers of Excellence': Library Services and the Future of the Academic Library." *College & Research Libraries*, 72 (1), January 2011, 6–8.

28. Jeffrey Pomerantz and Gary Marchionini. "The Digital Library as Place." *Journal of Documentation*, 63 (4), 2007, 505–533.

29. Bess Sadler. "Brain Injuries, Science Fiction, and Library Discovery." Presentation at the Access 2012 Conference in Montreal, Canada. Posted on the *Solvitur Ambulando* blog. October 24, 2012. Available at http://www.ibiblio.org/bess/?p=248

30. David Lankes. *The Atlas of New Librarianship.* Cambridge, MA: MIT Press, 2011, 43.

31. Chris Anderson. *Makers: The New Industrial Revolution.* New York: Crown Business, 2012.

32. Hugh Rundle. "Mission Creep—a 3D Printer Will Not Save Your Library." *Hugh Rundle's* blog. January 2, 2013. Available at http://hughrundle.net/2013/01/02/mission-creep-a-3d-printer-will-not-save-your-library/

33. Zachary Slobig. "Bringing Maker-Style Garage Tinkering into the Local Library." *Good+You* blog. July 20, 2012. Available at http://www.good.is/posts/bringing-maker-style-garage-tinkering-into-the-local-library

34. British Library. *Supporting Economic Growth: 2007–2009.* London: British Library, 2010. Available at http://www.bl.uk/bipc/pdfs/evaluation.pdf

35. Bill Ptacek. "The Library as Catalyst for Civic Engagement." *Library Journal*, 138 (14), September 1, 2013, 30–33.

36. Urban Libraries Council. "Civic Engagement: Stepping Up to the Civic Engagement Challenge." Chicago: Urban Libraries Council, January 2012. Available at https://www.webjunction.org/content/dam/WebJunction/Documents/webJunction/ULC%20Civic%20Engagement%20Report.pdf

37. Rebecca Fishman Lipsey and Francine Madera. *100 Great Ideas: The Future of Libraries.* Miami: 2015. Available at http://www.radicalpartners.net/uncategorized/the-future-of-libraries-100-great-ideas/

38. Association of American Colleges and Universities. "Civic Engagement VALUE Rubric." No date. Available at http://www.aacu.org/value/rubrics/pdf/civicengagement.pdf

39. Laura Solomon. "Understanding Social Capital." *American Libraries*, May 2013, 34–37.

40. Scott Plutchak. "A Bright Future for Librarians: Experimenting Like Crazy." *Journal of the European Association for Health Information and Libraries*, 8 (2), 2012, 26.

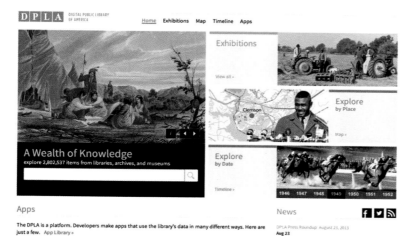

The Digital Public Library of America Web site.

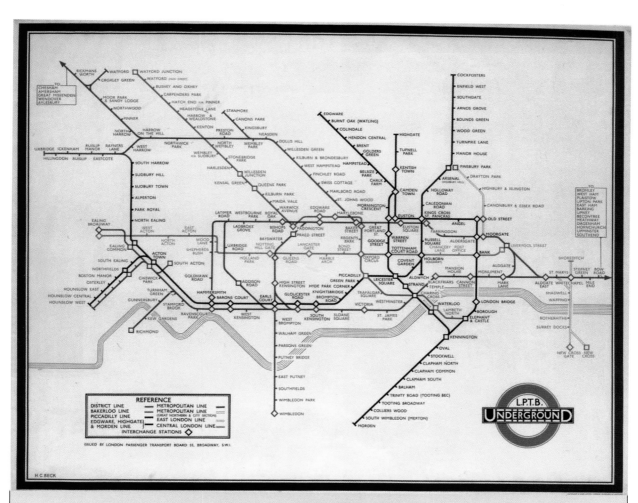

Map of the Underground, Henry C Beck (1933). © TfL from the London Transport Museum collection.

News | Missions | Images | Video & Audio | Education | Public Events | Work at JPL | About JPL

SPACE IMAGES

Enter search text   Search
Advanced Search

Browse by Category

My account: Login Sign up
Share this page:

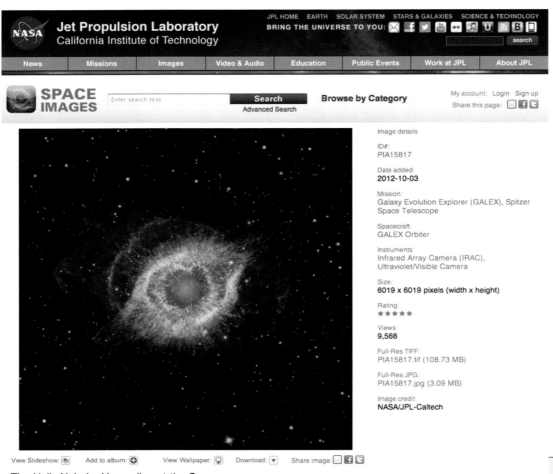

View Slideshow: Add to album: View Wallpaper: Download: Share image:

The Helix Nebula: Unraveling at the Seams

Image details

ID#:
PIA15817

Date added:
2012-10-03

Mission:
Galaxy Evolution Explorer (GALEX), Spitzer
Space Telescope

Spacecraft:
GALEX Orbiter

Instruments:
Infrared Array Camera (IRAC),
Ultraviolet/Visible Camera

Size:
6019 x 6019 pixels (width x height)

Rating:
★★★★★

Views:
9,568

Full-Res TIFF:
PIA15817.tif (108.73 MB)

Full-Res JPG:
PIA15817.jpg (3.09 MB)

Image credit:
NASA/JPL-Caltech

NASA.

Create account   Log

WIKIPEDIA
The Free Encyclopedia

Article Talk

Read Edit View history   Search

Coordinates: 22ʰ 29ᵐ 38.55ˢ, −20° 50′ 13.6″

Helix Nebula

From Wikipedia, the free encyclopedia

For the different but similarly named nebula, see Double Helix Nebula.

"Eye of God" redirects here. For other uses, see Eye of God (disambiguation).

The **Helix Nebula** (also known as **The Helix**, **NGC 7293**, or **Caldwell 63**) is a large planetary nebula (PN) located in the constellation Aquarius. Discovered by Karl Ludwig Harding, probably before 1824, this object is one of the closest to the Earth of all the bright planetary nebulae.[7] The estimated distance is about 215 parsecs or 700 light-years. It is similar in appearance to the Ring Nebula, whose size, age, and physical characteristics are similar to the Dumbbell Nebula, varying only in its relative proximity and the appearance from the equatorial viewing angle.[2] The Helix Nebula has sometimes been referred to as the "Eye of God" in pop culture.[8]

Contents [hide]
1 General information
2 Structure
    2.1 Knots
3 Visuals
4 Videos
5 See also
6 Notes
    6.1 Footnotes
    6.2 Citations
7 External links

General information [edit]

The Helix Nebula is an example of a planetary nebula, or 'planetary' formed at the end of a star's evolution. Gases from the star in the surrounding space appear, from our vantage point, as if we are looking down a helix structure. The remnant central stellar core, known as a planetary nebula nucleus or PNN, is destined to become a white dwarf star. The observed glow of the central star is so energetic that it causes the previously expelled gases to brightly fluoresce.

The Helix Nebula in the constellation of Aquarius lies about 700 light-years away, spanning about 0.8 parsec or 2.5 light-years. Recent images by the Hubble Space Telescope of the Helix Nebula are a composite of newly released images from the ACS instrument and the wide-angle images from the Mosaic Camera on the WIYN 0.9-metre telescope at Kitt Peak National Observatory.

Currently, the age is estimated to be 10,600 +2,300 −1,200 years, based solely upon a measured expansion rate of 31 km·s⁻¹.[2]

Structure [edit]

Helix Nebula

Helix Nebula taken by the Hubble Space Telescope
Credit: NASA, NOAO, ESA, the Hubble Helix Nebula Team

Observation data	
(Epoch J2000)	
Right ascension	22ʰ 29ᵐ 38.55ˢ[1]
Declination	−20° 50′ 13.6″[1]
Distance	695+98 −52 ly (213+30 −16 pc)[2][3][4][a]
Apparent magnitude (V)	+7.6[1]
Apparent dimensions (V)	25″[5]
Constellation	Aquarius
Physical characteristics	
Radius	2.87 ly (0.88 pc)[b]
Absolute magnitude (V)	6.58[b]
Notable features	One of nearest PNs
Other designations	NGC 7293,[1] Caldwell 63[6]

Wikipedia Web page
for Helix Nebula.

Help ∨ Locations Log In

🏠 Browse ∨ 📅 Events

🔍 Search

Welcome to CPL's New Website »

Check out our videos to learn how to use your new account, search for books and more.

Connect With / **Your Library**

NEWS
CPL Receives National Medal at White House »
First Lady Michelle Obama presented the award recognizing CPL's service to the community.

If You Love / **A Spine-Tingling Read**

BLOGPOST
Moms: The Good, the Bad, the Homicidal »
By Joanna

Moms love us, nurture us and drive us crazy. Sometimes quite literally. Enjoy Mother's Day and be glad some of these moms are only fiction: Sharp...

If You Love / **Music**

LIST
Hey Mama: Songs About Mothers »
By ChiPubLib_Adults
Celebrate Mother's Day with these songs about mom.

Get Help / **Caring for Your Family**

EVENT
Virginia Morris: How to Care for Aging Parents »
The author discusses practical and emotional aspects of caring for an aging parent at 6 p.m. Monday, May 12 at HWLC. (Photo by Robert Plumb)

Explore / **Great Reads for Kids**

BLOGPOST
Picture Books About Mothers »
By JulieH
Celebrate Mother's Day with young children by sharing one of these excellent books: Before I Was your Mother This is one of my favorite...

Connect With / **Your Library**

Winners Are In!
#cplwebcontest

NEWS
3 Win Kindle Fires; 3 Branches Win $500 for ... »
Thank you for playing our contest! We've contacted the winners of the Kindle Fires--and three of our branches won $500 for books, too.

Connect With / **Your Community**

NEWS
Volunteer for Summer Learning Challenge »
Do you enjoy working with young children? Are you looking for a way to

Explore / **This Month's Staff Picks**

BiblioCommons at the Chicago Public Library.

New York
Public
Library

LOG IN DONATE

Find books, music, movies and more 🔍
Classic Catalog

My NYPL   Explore   Research   Using the Library   Locations   Classes & Events   Support the Library   Help

FREE EXHIBITION
Motown: The Truth Is A Hit
Now through July 26
Schomburg Center

BOOK LIST
Mother's Day Reads
A librarian's mom shares some of her favorite books on the art of motherhood.

WANT THE BEST OF NYPL IN YOUR INBOX?

E-mail address SIGN UP
Privacy Policy

EVENT
The Animals
May 14, 7pm
Schwarzman Building
Don Bachardy discusses "The Animals: Love Letters Between Christopher Isherwood and Don Bachardy" with Aaron Hicklin, editor-in-chief of Out magazine.

NYPL LABS
Building Inspector
Kill Time. Make History.
Help reconstruct old New York, one building at a time, with the new version of this mobile-friendly web app.

NEW AUDIO PODCAST
Eve Ensler
This week, The New York Public Library Podcast welcomes Tony Award-winning playwright, performer, and activist Eve Ensler to Books at Noon.

RECOMMENDED BY OUR LIBRARIANS

Recently arrived

Groundswell
Lee, Katie

Motherlunge
Scott, Kirstin

The Sisters Brothers
deWitt, Patrick

The Beautiful Mystery
Penny, Louise

Gil Hodges
Clavin, Thomas

EVENT
The Literary Avant-Garde
May 13, 6pm
Schwarzman Building
Editors from avant-garde publications discuss their groundbreaking work.

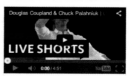
Douglas Coupland & Chuck Palahniuk |
LIVE SHORTS
0:00 / 4:51

VIDEO
Douglas Coupland & Chuck Palahniuk | LIVE from the NYPL
Douglas Coupland, author of "Worst. Person. Ever.," and Chuck Palahniuk, author of Fight Club, take to the LIVE from the NYPL stage for a rousing, experimental literary conversation.

BiblioCommons at the New York Public Library.

Flickr Commons visual explorer.

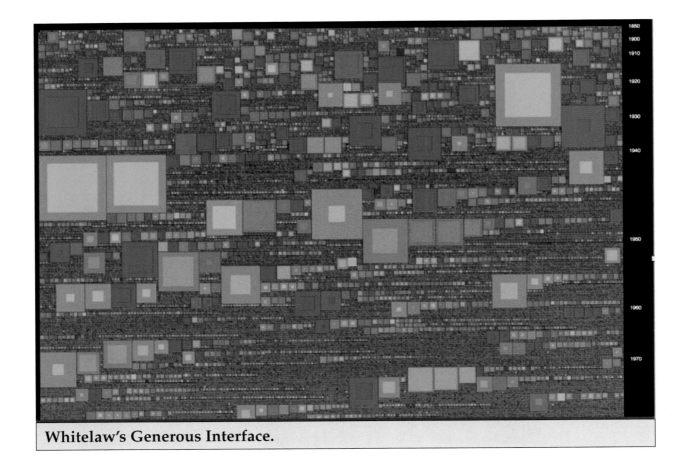

Whitelaw's Generous Interface.

The Queenslander Magazine
User Interface.

The Queenslander Magazine
with a Color Option for
Browsing.

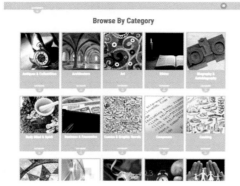

The interior of the home showcases extensive Arts and Crafts detailing in the furniture, lighting and accessories. A grand piano sits in the background.

A front view of the great room shows the massive fireplace as well as the Arts and Crafts detailing.

Biblioboard.

The Open Library Browsing User Interface.

New York Times Bestsellers

3-D Carousel

drawing from a webpage

< The target / Baldacci, David. >

What's Hot

Scrolling

drawing from items popular in your library

LibraryThing Browse Options.

 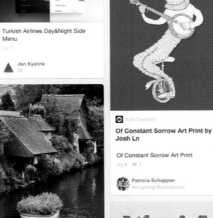    

Pinterest User Interface.

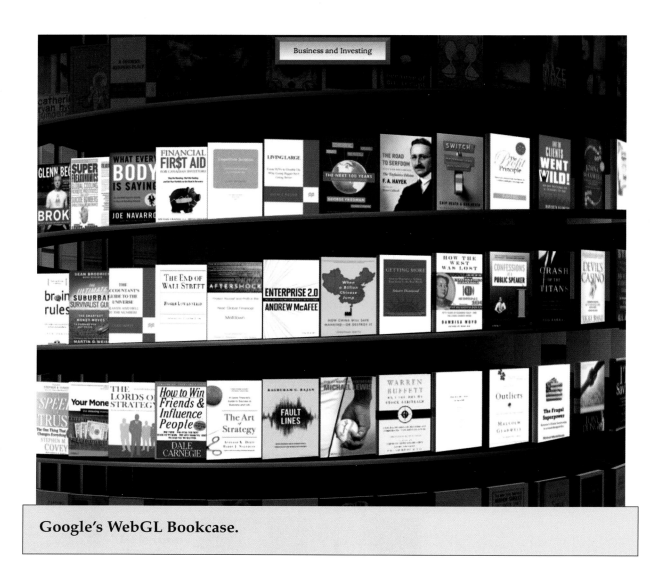

Google's WebGL Bookcase.

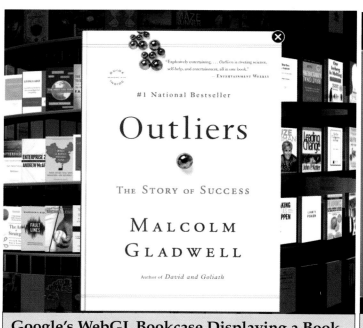

Google's WebGL Bookcase Displaying a Book Cover.

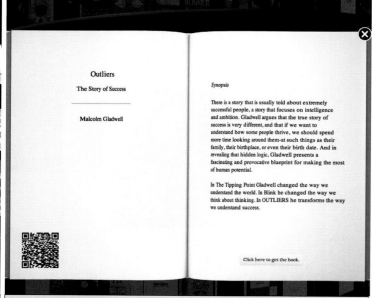

Google's WebGL Bookcase Showing a Synopsis.

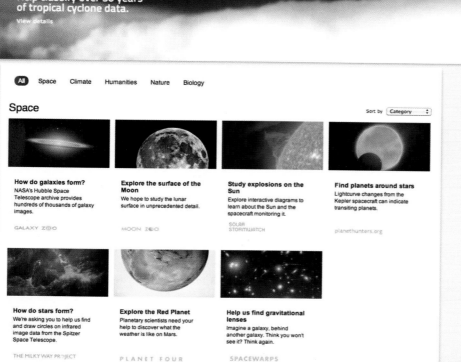

Zooniverse Web Site.

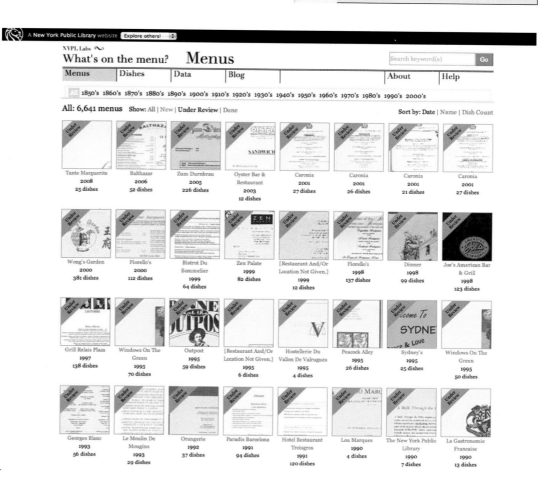

The NYPL What's on the Menu Help Review Page.

NYPL Map Wrapper Page.

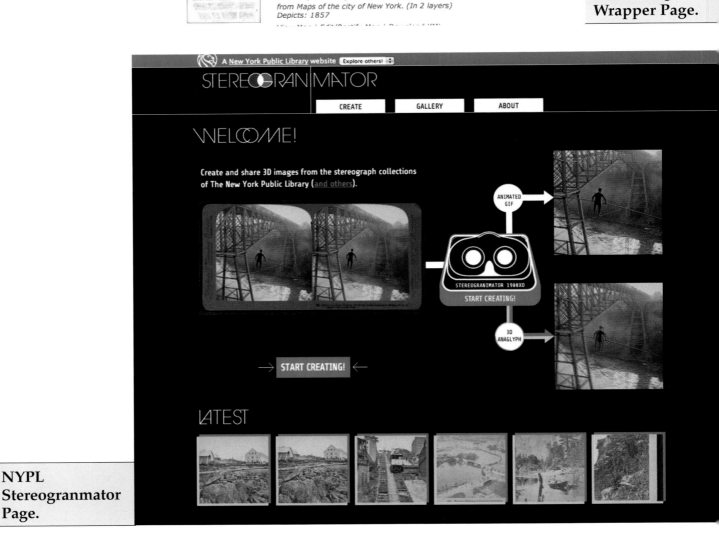

NYPL Stereogranmator Page.

NATIONAL LIBRARY OF AUSTRALIA

It's free and it only takes a minute   **Sign up**   **Login**

 **Trove**

Find and get over 372,699,554 Australian and online resources:
books, images, historic newspapers, maps, music, archives and more

Learn about Trove

A guide to Trove
How to correct newspaper text
How to order a copy of an item

13,880 searches this hour

[   ]   **Search**

☐ Available online   ☐ Australian content   ☐ In my libraries   Advanced search

Contribute

Join the community that's organising
and improving this information resource.

47,268 newspaper text corrections today
1,708 images from users this month
14,176 items tagged this week
1,158 comments added this month
459 works merged or split this month
890 lists this month

Connect to others with similar interests on the
Trove forum

News

Newspaper titles recently added to Trove
Australian visits to Trove for September 2013
Trove at the NSW/ACT Association of Family
History Societies family history fair!

Follow Trove on

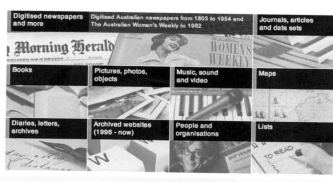

Trove spotlight:

API   Disclaimer   Privacy   Terms of Use   Copyright   Version: 5.5

> **National Library
> of Australia's
> Trove Home
> Page.**

News   « Hide

Welcome to the Flickr Commons! We're bringing
together the members of The Commons with
Flickr users and staff in a space to celebrate,
play with, and carry forward The Commons.

Indicommons: our blog
Commons Participating Institutions

Discussions

NEW Flickr Commons on the new Flickr blog

 This is nice, you can now just view Commons
related posts on the newly updated F...
whatsthatpicture 7 days ago 1 replies

Swedish National Heritage Board - 5 years o...

The Swedish National Heritage Board celebrates
5 years on Flickr Commons on Marc...
Swedish National Heritage Board 2 weeks
ago 5 replies

More discussions

Top Tags

flickrhome   osuarchives   flickrcommons   florida
statelibraryandarchivesofflorida   riksantikvarieämbetet
theswedishnationalheritageboard   collage   ireland
upcycled

Top Contributors

Flickr Commons.

Georeferenced Historical Map from the British Library.

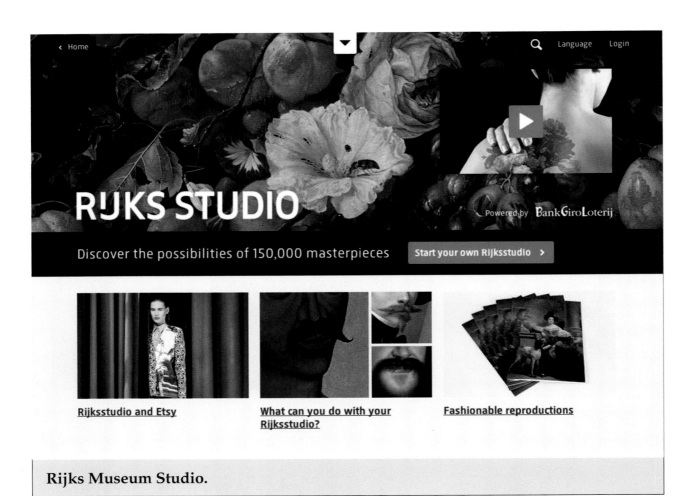

Rijks Museum Studio.

Now in 162,358 Rijksstudios

  Search in Rijksstudio

necklace2
Van Bienen
1 hour ago

necklace 1
Van Bienen
1 hour ago

White tulip in a new dress
Van Bienen
1 hour ago

random inspiration
Petek Sketcher
1 hour ago · 15 works

Joanna Pybus - Shield Suit and Champagne Monster
Etsy
July 8 2014

Modern Crops
Petek Sketcher
2 hours ago · 9 works

Sample of Rijksstudios.

Burgerlijke cultuur in de Nederlanden van de 17e eeuw
Jacqueline Bontje
4 hours ago · 4 works

Favourites
Emily
3 hours ago · 13 works

Paris
Marthe
4 hours ago · 6 works

Muurbehang
Florentine Six
4 hours ago · 15 works

Visita al museo
Caterina V il la
4 hours ago · 18 works

Fashion
Carol Taylor · April 30 2014 · 45 works

Insekten vlinders
Iris Mager
4 hours ago · 5 works

More Sample Rijksstudios.

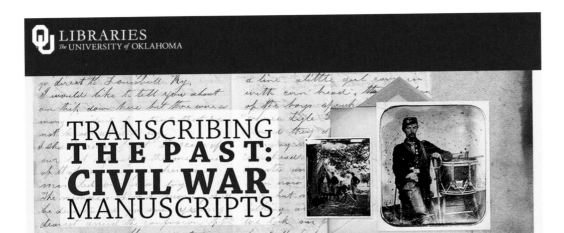

TRANSCRIBING THE PAST: CIVIL WAR MANUSCRIPTS

MENU

Home

About the Project

Transcribe

Get Help

Contact

Login

Transcribing the Past: Civil War Manuscripts

A Crowdsourced Transcription Project to commemorate the 150th anniversary of the U.S. Civil War

Join University Libraries in commemorating the 150th anniversary of the U.S. Civil War by transcribing a Civil War diary and letters. Your transcriptions will make these manuscripts more accessible to researchers everywhere.

My Dear Mary: The Letters of
Lt. Lyle Garrett and Mary Garrett

A Soldier's Life:
The Diary of Charles Kroff

University of Oklahoma's
Transcribing the Past: Civil War Manuscripts.

Blogs | Bookmark/Share | Contact Us

NATIONAL ARCHIVES

Search Archives.gov GO

| Research Our Records | Veterans Service Records | Teachers' Resources | Our Locations | Shop Online |

Citizen Archivist Dashboard

Home > Citizen Archivist Dashboard

One Day...
All of our records will be online. You can help make it happen.

You can become a citizen archivist — just click one of the options below to get started. You can also make suggestions or volunteer in person.

 Welcome   Tag   Transcribe   Edit Articles   Upload & Share   Old Weather

Citizen Archivist Dashboard >

Find Activity by Type:
Tag
Transcribe
Edit Articles
Upload and Share
Old Weather
Enter a Contest
Events
Have Your Say
Make a Suggestion
Volunteer in Person

Find Activity by Site:
Archives.gov
Challenge.gov
Flickr
Tumblr
Wikipedia
Wikisource

Resources:
NARAtions Blog
The Text Message Blog
Research at the National Archives Facebook Page
@USNatArchives on Twitter
Open Goverment

Connect With Us
 Blogs
 Facebook
Flickr
 RSS Feeds
Twitter
 YouTube
More...

National Archives Citizen Archivist Dashboard.

You are not

just an employee, volunteer or board member. You do not merely catalog books, organize periodicals and manage resources. You are the gateway into the mind of the idea people who come to our facilities to find or fuel a spark.

Part WIZARD
Part GENIUS
Part EXPLORER

It is your calling to trespass into the unknown and come back with a concrete piece someone can hold onto, turn over, and use to fuel their mind and soul.

Anything Staff Manifesto.

THE
EXPLORER

confident

seeker

self-directed

optimistic

value: connecting people
with possibility

celebrates adventure
and discovery

motivates people
to explore

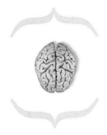

THE
GENIUS

problem solver

expert

advisor

credible

value: the transfer
of knowledge

instills
self-confidence

replaces inertia
with momentum

THE
WIZARD

charismatic

shaman

intuitive

entertaining

value: guide with
wise suggestions

opens peoples eyes
to change

turns skeptics
into believers

Anything Staff Manifesto.

8

Collaboration

Imagine a world where everyone was constantly learning,
a world where what you wondered was more interesting than what you knew,
and curiosity counted for more than certain knowledge.
Imagine a world where what you gave away
was more valuable than what you held back,
where joy was not a dirty word,
where play was not forbidden after your eleventh birthday.

Rick Levine, Christopher Locke,
Doc Searls, and David Weinberger[1]

The OED

The development of the *Oxford English Dictionary*, known familiarly by its initials as the OED, was likely the world's first crowdsourcing project.[2] The goal of this project was to identify all words in the English language and provide example quotations of their usage for each word. In addition, one of the unique features of the OED was to document the earliest usage of each word and to track how the sense of a word (and in some cases, the pronunciation) changed over time. Clearly, this was a project not for the fainthearted as it was estimated that that they would create a dictionary with about 100,000 words and would include well over 200,000 quotations. Starting in 1860, it was originally estimated that the first edition would be published after 10 years of work. In the end, after 70 years of work and the involvement of thousands of volunteers, over six million words were submitted. And while the stories of many of the volunteers make for fascinating reading, the contributions of two American volunteers are particularly noteworthy. Most of the volunteers working on the OED project would create a slip of paper with the word at the top, copy the sentence that the word appeared in, and give the full citation where the sentence was to be found. These slips (in random order usually) were then periodically sent to the OED office at the University of Oxford in England.

The first remarkable American who contributed to OED project was William Chester Minor, who was born to a wealthy family, and served as a soldier-surgeon in the U.S. Army during the Civil War. After the war, he was sent by his family to England, accompanied by his extensive collection of rare books, to convalesce from a serious illness and settled in the small village of Crowthorne, England. Once Dr. Minor started on the OED project, he continually added to his extensive collection of rare books. For each book, Minor would create an extensive index for words that interested him in each of his books (in some cases, it took several weeks to create a precise index for a single book). He would then wait for news from the editors of the OED who would indicate what words they were working on that week. Dr. Minor would then assemble all of the relevant quotations for a specific word after consulting with his index for each book. The word, quotation, and citation would then be written on a separate piece of paper, and the whole bundle of slips would be shipped off to Oxford. The editors would receive the slips in the next day or two, and the project was kept moving (albeit quite slowly). In short, Dr. Minor was acting as if he was an editor and for more than 20 years (working many hours per day) made substantial contributions to the final project.

What was particularly noteworthy about William Minor was that he did all of his work from the Broadmoor Criminal Lunatic Asylum in Crowthorne, England. He had a mental illness and during an attack of paranoid schizophrenia shot and killed a man in London. Given the tremendous amount of free time available to Dr. Minor, he decided to devote his day to working on the OED project, as a way to partially atone for his crime—yet remained a seriously mentally ill individual. Minor apologized to and made reparations to the dead man's widow, and she subsequently visited him regularly at the asylum.

The other interesting American who contributed significantly to the OED was Fitzedward Hall, from Troy, New York, who traveled to India when he was 18 and learned several languages including Sanskrit, Bengali, Hindustani, and Persian. After marrying a daughter of a colonel in the British army, he moved to England and took up a position as a professor of Sanskrit at King's College in London. Some years later, he was involved in an academic row that resulted in his being dismissed from the faculty. He retired to the remote village of Wickham Market, East Anglia, to the north of London and for the next 32 years lived as a hermit (rarely emerging from his cottage). And while an extremely good word detective, Hall's primary contribution was reading and correcting proof pages of the OED as it moved through the production process. Hall worked a minimum of 4 hours a day on the project for more than 20 years and never met the longtime editor of the OED—James Murray.

The contributions of all of the volunteers was acknowledged in the OED, but the motives that drove so many people to contribute so many hours to chronicle the origins of the English language will remain a mystery. The final 10-volume first edition of the OED containing 252,200 entries, more than 1,800,000 quotations, and printed on 15,490 pages is a reflection of the willingness of many people to contribute to a really large and worthwhile project.

Crowdsourcing

Crowdsourcing (as most people would define the term today) involves a group of people striving to achieve a shared large goal by working together collaboratively to achieve what would not otherwise be achievable. Generally, a crowdsourcing activity requires a fair amount of time, commitment, and intellectual effort from an individual than for other activities that he or she might otherwise engage in online.

Jeff Howe and his colleague Mark Robinson in a 2006 *Wired* magazine article coined the term "crowdsourcing," which described the way in which businesses were willing to outsource work to individuals by announcing the opportunity to a large number of individuals via the Internet who would then bid on each opportunity.[3] The article discussed how amateurs were providing competition to professional photographers by using such microstock agencies as *iStockphoto, ShutterStock,* and *Dreamstime;* creating the weekly cable TV show *Web Junk 2.0,* which feature the 20 most popular videos on the Internet; solving challenging technical problems featured on *InnoCentive* or *NineSigma* (an individual who provides a good solution can win from $10,000 to more than $100,000 from the company that posts the challenge); or asking (and paying) people to perform tasks computers are lousy at using *Mechanical Turk* among other options.

David Weinberger has suggested that smart mobs and wise crowds as well as other types of crowdsourcing are the result of the Internet having five specific properties:[4]

1. The Internet is able to connect a great many people.
2. Many different types of people (with lots of different types of knowledge and expertise) use the Internet.
3. The Internet is similar to oatmeal—lumpy and sticky (clusters of networked people naturally form to create communities or neighborhoods).
4. The Internet retains almost everything and is thus cumulative.
5. The Internet is likely to have no limits—indefinitely.

Trevor Owens, in an interesting essay, suggests that despite its popularity, the use of terms "crowd" and "sourcing" is problematic as successful projects have little to do with large crowds or the outsourcing of labor.[5]

Types of Crowdsourcing

The term "crowdsourcing" has taken on a life of its own and is now used in a wide variety of setting to accomplish a variety of activities. Rose Holley has suggested that it is important to remember the distinction between crowdsourcing and "social engagement."

> Social engagement is about giving the public the ability to communicate with us and each other; to add value to existing library data by tagging, commenting, rating, reviewing, text correcting; and to create and upload content to add to our collections. Individuals usually undertake this type of engagement for themselves and their own purposes . . . Crowdsourcing uses social engagement techniques to help a group of people achieve a shared, usually significant, and large goal by working collaboratively together as a group.[6]

Citizen science projects have been divided into three fields: *collaborative projects,* members of the public can contribute data (they then may also be asked to analyze data and/or disseminate findings); *contributory projects,* in which individuals can contribute along carefully delineated ways that are selected by the researchers; and *cocreated projects,* in which researchers and the public work together through all of the steps of the scientific inquiry method.[7]

Within the Galleries, Libraries, Archives, and Museums or GLAM sectors, Mia Ridge has suggested seven categories of participation: categorizing, creative, debunking (reviewing and correcting content), linking, recording (e.g., a personal story), stating preferences, and tagging.[8] Another GLAM crowdsourcing topology includes these categories:[9]

- Correction and transcription
- Contextualization (adding context to objects)
- Constructing or creating user-generated content
- Complementing collections (adding additional content to a specific collection)
- Classification
- Co-curation (using nonprofessionals to create/curate web exhibits)
- Crowd funding (pool money and other resources to support the efforts of others).

Combining several typologies, I would suggest that crowdsourcing projects or activities can be categorized based on the type of activity:

- Knowledge discovery
- Implicit crowdsourcing
- Question answering
- Problem solving
- Citizen science
- Crowd voting
- Crowd funding.

Knowledge Discovery. People have been involved in a wide range of interesting crowdsourcing projects. When members of the British Parliament were discovered to be taking numerous dubious claims for reimbursement, the British newspaper *The Guardian* quickly set up a website and encouraged people to review each claim—eventually some 20,000 people reviewed a total 700,000 claims found on some two million pages of expense reports. Readers were asked to read each report and then alert others of possible fraud. The resulting public outcry and outrage over this scandal resulted in a number of resignations, sacking, and in some cases the prosecution and sentencing of members of Parliament to jail terms.

Netflix had a fairly good recommendation algorithm (if you liked this movie, then you will probably like these), yet in 2006, the company offered a $1 million prize to an individual or group for the best improvement in a recommendation algorithm. In the end, Netflix received some 13,000 solutions from 2,000 teams, and the winning team developed an algorithm that delivered a 10.05 percent improvement. Yet, Netflix decided not to implement the new algorithm as people started streaming more videos than renting DVDs—and, it turns out, a recommendation algorithm for streaming videos is significantly different from that for renting DVDs.[10]

Wikipedia is a multilingual free Internet encyclopedia that is collaboratively edited by millions of people. All of its articles can be edited by anyone, and it is in the top 10 of the most frequently visited websites in the world. Despite its popularity, the open nature of Wikipedia has led to several concerns including the quality of writing, the quality of information, and the occurrence of vandalism. A 2005 article in *Nature* that compared the accuracy of scientific articles in *Encyclopedia Britannica* and *Wikipedia* found that overall the two sources were roughly comparable.[11] Interestingly, *Encyclopedia Britannica* has changed its business model and now encourages the "crowd" to contribute content to its encyclopedia.

One of the interesting aspects of Wikipedia is that those who create and edit articles, called Wikipedians, strive for neutrality and verifiability.[12] The goal is to identify and discuss major points of view hopefully in a balanced and impartial manner. In addition, Wikipedians are encouraged to use and add third-party published references.[13] In many ways, Wikipedia ends up acting as a curated collection of the best journalism on any given subject (or so say some people but that claim, is of course, under dispute).[14]

Another powerful example of how crowdsourcing can make a huge impact is that of Linux—an open-source computer operating system. Starting with very humble origins and aspirations, Linus Torvalds, a computer science student in Helsinki, released the source code of the first version of Linux in 1991. Torvalds's decision to release the software as open-source meant that people could examine it, suggest improvements, and make improvements to it. The geeks of the world immediately started tinkering with the software with the result that today we now have a robust, complex, and widely used operating system. Over the last 20 years, a worldwide community has embraced Linux, and its share of the market is quite large—some estimates are as high as 90 percent or more (every Google server runs on Linux).

To give you some idea of the magnitude of the effort that underlies Linux, the software has more than 200 million lines of source code. Linux has been distributed—both commercially and noncommercially—and many companies such as IBM and HP have many programmers working full time to enhance and support Linux. A core group of trusted programmers work with Torvalds to ensure the reliability and stability of the software and its future direction. An individual can become a part of this group only after demonstrating that he or she produces quality code and is consistently willing to share ideas through bulletin boards and conferences.

A similar group of dedicated individuals support *Apache*, the open-source server that drives much of the Internet.

Every day, thousands of individuals around the world assist one another in their genealogical research using Ancestry.com. The site provides access to more than 160,000 message boards (and more than 17 million message posts) where participants discuss local names and surnames from a specific place. People are also cooperating by bringing and transcribing local historical records collections to the Internet. More than 2 million paying subscribers have created more than 60 million family trees.

Metadata Games is a digital gaming platform that encourages people to add information to photos, audio files, and video files, and more importantly the software is a free open-source software. Several games have been developed and these include:

- *Zen Tag*—It provides a player with a single photographic image and asks them to input as many tags as he or she would like—points are awarded for each tag submitted (and higher points if the tag has been previously submitted). A "version" of this game called "Alum Tag" has been used by libraries asking players to identify the names of people found in alumni photos.
- *Nextag*—Players can earn points to tag audio and video clips as they "play" clips.
- *Guess What!*—Two players work together to identify images and earn points. One player sees the image and provides hints to the image by describing it (using tags). The other player seeing 12 images and must guess the correct image based on the clues from the first player.
- *One Up*—Allows you to challenge a friend to see whether you can come up with the best descriptions.
- *Pyramid Tag*—This is a one-player game that asks the player to match one-word descriptors that other people have used when they saw the image.
- *Stupid Robot*—Asks a player to teach a robot about an image, and as it learns, you are asked to use longer and longer words.[15]

The British Library is using Metadata Games in three games: *Ships Tag* (tag naval images), *Book Tag* (tag archived book covers), and *Portrait Tag* (identify the names of 16th- through 18th-century portraits of celebrities). Fun stuff.

Implicit Crowdsourcing. Implicit crowdsourcing is an indirect way for users to contribute without knowing that they are doing so. A classic example is the use of reCAPTCHA (an acronym for Completely Automated Public Turing Test to Tell Computers and Humans Apart) on a website that asks a user to decipher some text that is displayed by entering the text in a response box as shown in Figure 8-1. The use of

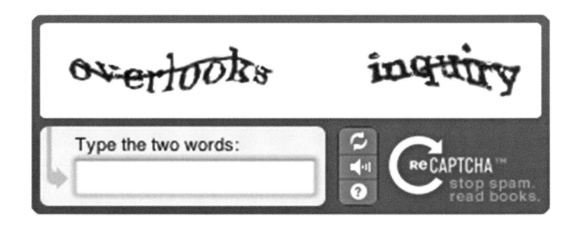

Figure 8-1 A Sample reCAPTCHA.

reCAPTCHA is designed to reduce spam, and the positive by-product is that it helps to digitize books, newspapers, and old-time radio shows. Words that can't be read by computers (actually by optical character recognition or OCR software) are sent in the form of CAPTCHAs for humans to decode. Depending upon the age of the material being digitized and the type font and many other characteristics, in some cases, 20 percent or more of the digitized text cannot be read. After several people enter the same text for the bad word, the system assumes that the word has been correctly converted.

Question Answering. Given the richness and vastness of the web along with the many links connecting one page to another, makes the accumulation of content even more usable and valuable. Some collections of content are carefully selected, such as medical sites assembled by knowledgeable professionals, and provide high-quality content that is able to respond to a great variety of questions (within the domain of the website). Other sites invite people to contribute what they know and to critique what others have contributed.

A question-answering service such as AllExperts.com allows someone to ask a specific question of a specific person (expert) that you select, and answers are generally provided within a short period of time. While such an approach is popular, a much more interesting tactic that has arisen in the last few years is to simply broadcast your question using Twitter and wait for those following you to respond.

Problem Solving. Prizes have long been used as a way to create a much larger and more diverse pool of minds working on a problem. In the early 1700s, the British parliament announced a prize of £20,000 (adjusting for inflation, the prize would amount to about $4 million today) for accurately determining the East–West position of longitude of a ship at sea. Establishing an accurate longitude would make long-distant sea travel much safer. As recounted by Dava Sobel in his wonderful book *Longitude*, John Harrison, the son of a carpenter and a self-taught watchmaker, took up the challenge and tinkered with the problem of longitude for almost 50 years as he developed a series of chronometers.[16] His final chronometer, completed in 1759 and nicknamed H4, represents a mastery of design and materials that is truly amazing.[17] Harrison ultimately needed to petition parliament and the king before the Board of Longitude awarded only a portion of the total prize (since he wasn't educated in an elite school and didn't socialize in the right circles of friends, his efforts couldn't possibly lead to a solution to the problem).

More recently, the X Prize Foundation is offering more than $100 million in prizes that will reward creativity and innovation in such fields as automobile energy efficiency, oil cleanup, and using genetic information to predict diseases. The stated goal of X Prize is "to bring radical breakthroughs for the benefits of humanity, thereby inspiring the formation of new industries and the revitalization markets." The first X Prize was awarded to SpaceShipOne when they took three men to the edge of the atmosphere (about 62 miles above the surface of the earth).

And on the Internet, Mechanical Turk (MTurk), launched by Amazon in 2005, facilitates people working on small distributed tasks for a set amount of money (often a penny or two and sometimes more per task). Each task is fairly simple to accomplish—for instance, identifying the color of a piece of clothing—which a computer has difficulty completing accurately and consistently. Work that may be found on MTurk includes verifying that a photo of a business is really a business, answers trivia questions, rating and image tagging, and transcribing podcasts. Not surprisingly, those involved with MTurk call themselves "turksters," and the jobs are called HITs—human intelligence tasks. The site has become so popular that dubious HITs are posted quite frequently that, in reality, are spamming social media metrics—requests to "Like my YouTube video," "follow me on Twitter," "test the ads on my website," and so forth.

Citizen Science. Many people get involved in some way with a crowdsource project with a scientific focus. Among these scientific projects are:

- *Old Weather*—This project is simply attempting to gather more information about historical weather variability, to improve our understanding of all forms of weather variability in the past and so improve our ability to predict weather and climate in the future. The more people that take part in Old Weather, the more accurate the extracted data will be. Each logbook will be looked at by more than one person allowing mistakes and errors to be identified and corrected. The logbooks of sailing ships in the 1700s and 1800s are digitized, and then people are asked to transcribe the contents of each logbook (one famous logbook is from the *Beagle*, which Charles Darwin was a passenger on his voyage of discovery). Many archives and libraries from the United States and England are collaborating on this wonderful project. As can be seen in Figure 8-2, there is plenty of work to do (only 18% of the logs have been completed), and there are several ways for people to be involved and recognized.

- *Galaxy Zoo*—This project started in 2007 and asked volunteers to classify galaxies, and provide more detailed information about specific galaxies. The response has been truly amazing. In its first year, 150,000 people classified more than 50 million galaxies. The Zooniverse website illustrates the many ways people can get involved—see Figure 8-3. Note the almost 900,000 people who were involved at the time when I grabbed this screen shot.

- *CamClickr*—This project, hosted by the Cornell Lab of Ornithology, asked volunteers to catalog nesting behavior of birds. This completed project tagged more than 622,000 images with almost 2-1/2 million tags. Volunteers can now participate in other crowdsourced science projects: Great Backyard Bird Count, Celebrate Urban Birds, eBird, NestWatch, and others.

- *Be a Martian*—NASA has a project enlisting volunteers to help them map the planet of Mars. Several NASA missions have sent back vast amounts of data that are yet to be explored. Mars has been divided up into 32 areas to help people navigate and pick an area to learn about and work in. Volunteers work to earn points as they map the Martian landscape. Visit http://beamartian.jpl.nasa.gov/welcome

Crowd Voting. Popular filtering sites such as Reddit and Digg filter, organize, and rank stories, music, and movies based on the votes of millions of members each day, eliminating the need for editors—the most popular are displayed first. Reality TV shows use crowd voting to determine the "most talented, the best singer, the best singing group," and so forth.

Figure 8-2 Old Weather Home Page. OldWeather.org

Threadless.com is a site that supports artists and designers by having people vote on the design of T-shirts and sweatshirts. More than $8 million has been paid to artists worldwide as people not only vote but also purchase their favorite T-shirts.

Crowd Funding. People now have an increasing number of ways to raise money directly from other people using a variety of tools. These funding options allow folks to bypass the traditional route of approaching banks for a loan or as angel investors or venture capitalists for an investment. Perhaps the most well-known crowd-funding site is Kickstarter. Kickstarter is an Internet site for soliciting small contributions from a number of people such that the total amount raised can be significant—especially to the individual or group receiving the money. Artists, inventors, designers, filmmakers, and others have used Kickstarter to fund creative ideas and projects. There are no experts, and no extensive proposals need to be submitted for review, but rather everyone has the option to determine what should be funded and what should not. Kickstarter is

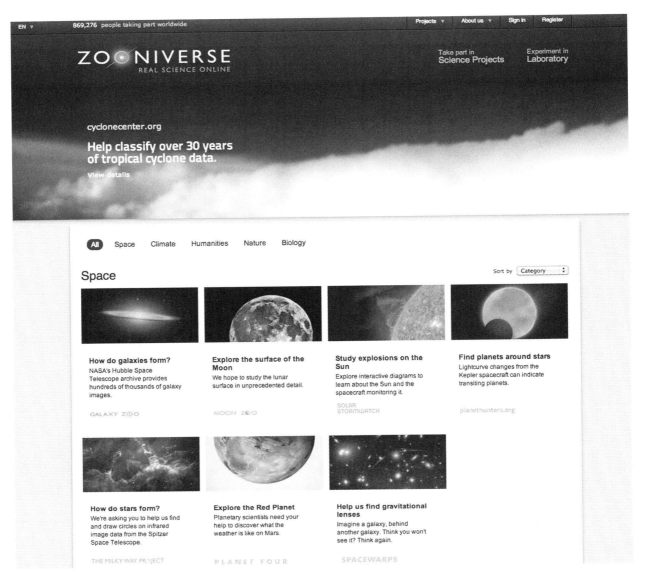

Figure 8-3 Zooniverse Website. Zooniverse.org

not about traditional investing as the project creators maintain 100 percent control over their intellectual content. The writer Kevin Kelly calls this kind of activity the web's "gift economy."

To kick things off, a creator sets a funding goal along with a deadline and puts together a compelling project description and, in some cases, offers a reward to funders (rewards range from a simple pen to T-shirts, options to receive a limited edition of a product, and other creative prizes—tickets to a performance, or a signed copy of a CD). Individuals who contribute some amount receive email updates on the status of the project—some projects are funded in days and others take weeks. If the funding goal is not achieved, all pledges are cancelled, and no monies actually change hands (slightly less than half of all projects fail to reach their goals). Kickstarter receives a 5 percent commission of all funds raised and raises more than $200 million in a single year.[18]

Prosper

www.prosper.com

Prosper offers a handy and transparent way to obtain a personal loan or invest in loans on terms more favorable than from a local bank. Members can request a loan or bid on providing some portion of a loan using an online auction process. The Securities and Exchange Commission has ruled that Prosper is a peer-to-peer marketplace and not a bank (and thus need not comply with banking regulations).

Prospective borrowers describe how they will use the money and identify the highest interest rate they are willing to pay. Lenders have the opportunity to review multiple loan requests and can then bid on them in increments that range from $25 up to $25,000. Prosper informs the winning bidders and combines the bids with the lowest rates into a single loan for the borrower. Prosper has almost 2 million members and has facilitated $626 million in loans.

Other peer-to-peer organizations include Zopa, Lending Club, BigCarrot, GreenNote, Kisskissbankbank, SmartyPig, auxmoney, and smava.

Kiva

www.kiva.org

Kiva is a nonprofit organization with the goal of connecting people through lending to alleviate poverty. Kiva uses the Internet and a worldwide network of microfinance institutions to create opportunities around the world. Individuals receive a loan for a very specific purpose—purchase a cow, goat, bull, sheep; buy a sewing machine; purchase a refrigerator; and so forth—which they then work to pay back. With about 1 million lenders, Kiva has loaned some $475 million to individuals in 72 different countries. Kiva does not take a commission but rather relies on optional donations from lenders to pay for the operation of Kiva. Thus, 100 percent of all funds go directly to a network of microfinance institutions that administer the loans.

The goal is to provide access to safe, affordable capital to those in need, which helps them create better lives for themselves and their families. The great thing about microloans and Kiva is that the repayment rate is over 99%—a great track record.

Other sites such as *Causes.com* allow people to support a specific nonprofit charity or a similar site *DonorsChoose.com*, which connects people wanting to contribute to teachers to support innovative projects.

However, one study found that crowdsourcing activities and crowd funding may not appeal to the motivational factors that contribute to people being involved with a crowdsourcing project (intellectual challenge, interest in the material, and enjoyment of the task.[19]

Reasons for Collaboration

Collaboration is really about working together, either physically or virtually, to create value. So if we are not creating value, then perhaps we might be engaged in building a personal network, socializing, sharing our interests and activities, but we are clearly not collaborating.

Individuals that get involved in a crowdsourcing activity seem to do it for a variety of reasons: seeking a challenge, earning status and recognition within a community, intellectual enrichment, satisfying curiosity, working for the public good, or simply having fun. Perhaps a majority of really active crowdsourcing individuals do it for both personal and extrinsic motivations for themselves and for others! Often, the subject matter of a project must be of interest to the individual, and the opportunity to engage with others with a similar passion can be important. In some cases, the social rewards are explicit—the most active individuals are acknowledged and, in some cases, are recognized in an academic publication.

The collaborative and cocreative organization is not about the Field of Dreams approach to engaging others—"Build it and they will come." Rather, it is about providing a virtual place where a community can come, and we will build it together (and the people are already there and engaged). They are interested, they are committed, and they want to contribute. If cultural organizations engage individuals as active cocreators, then they will help define and deliver value (to themselves and, as a by-product, to the organization also).

Many individuals contribute to empower other creative people to realize their dreams or the social reward of knowing that your money is going to an individual that will help them "learn how to fish" rather than receiving a one-time gift of fish. Many crowdsourcing projects are on the receiving end of more than one million hours of volunteer effort each year! Consider the contributions of people to *Wikipedia, OpenStreetMaps, Ancestry, Freebase, Galaxy Zoo, I-spot, Old Weather, Milky Way Project, reCaptcha, CamClicker, LibraryThing, Trove, DigitalKoot*, and many more sites that I am not aware of (but you probably are). The total amount of voluntary human intellectual effort being given each year to all of the various collaborative sites on the Internet has got to be more than hundreds of millions of hours annually.

Clay Shirky, in his book *Here Comes Everybody*, suggests that real power is transferred to people when people are given tools to do things better, without the need for traditional organization structures. Clay posits, "The increase in the power of both individual and groups, outside traditional organizational structures, is unprecedented."[20]

And if the tools that people are given for any particular task help them to learn about standards and the practices of professionals, then the end result is not only the successful completion of a project but also that the participants learn something valuable so that in the future they can make suggestions about better ways to accomplish a particular task.[21]

Types of Collaboration

Collaboration or cocreation exists in many different forms. The individual or organization creating the collaboration initiative determines the type of collaboration and the way in which people can join and participate. Thus, a group of people, oftentimes called a crowd, may be participating in one of four types of collaboration:

- *Crowd of people*—Usually called crowdsourcing, a large group of people get involved in a wide variety of activities ranging from solving problems, working on projects (tagging, identifying, commenting, transcribing, and so forth).

- *Club of experts*—Individuals are invited to participate in a group based on their expertise, experience, and associated skills. The group will be asked to work on a particular often complicated or thorny problem, and it is the combination of skills that will often provide a new and creative solution.

- *Coalition of parties*—Often, a variety of groups will be asked to participate and work together to deal with complex situations. A coalition of parties is often formed to deal with challenging technical problems encountered in manufacturing or attempting to implement a specific standard.

- *Community of kindred spirits*—People with similar values and interests will often come together to work on projects for the greater good. Those involved in the *Threadless* community (where people vote on the best T-shirt design each week) are doing it for the cred (where fellow enthusiasts—in this case, designers—acknowledge their contributions in the form of kudos).[22] People who contribute are developing a standing in the emerging reputation economy.

The Center for Advancement of Informal Science explored the ways visitors participate with cultural institutions in a project called the Public Participation of Information Science (PPIS).[23] For more than a century, amateurs have been asked to participate in scientific research projects by measuring soil quality, report nonnative plant species, and counting birds. The PPIS project identified three broad categories of public participation:

- *Contributory projects*—Designed by scientists, members of the public are asked to contribute data in a very controlled process. In a library or museum setting, people might be asked to leave comments in response to a specific question or to contribute a story in response to a display or exhibit.

- *Collaborative projects*—While under the direction of scientists, people might become involved with the project design, contribute and analyze data, and disseminate project findings.

- *Cocreated projects*—Members of the public and scientists work together in most or all steps of the project. In cultural organization settings, users have been asked to help plan space in a remodeling project. But much more is possible in asking users of a cultural organization to become a partner in re-imagining all of its services.

Successful Collaboration

More than 10 years ago, Tim O'Reilly suggested the term "the architecture of participation" to describe the nature of systems designed for people to contribute and collaborate. The resulting system needs to be *modular* (so people can participate in several different ways and select the one that appeals to them), *scalable* (so that all of the people who wish to contribute can do so), and should facilitate *community building* (let people chat and share with one another).

It is also important to note that volunteers are people who lead busy lives and thus might not volunteer regularly but still offer the potential of volunteering on an ad hoc basis. Encouraging participation, especially in an online environment, will bring new people interested in furthering your goals and mission, tackle organizational challenges with new thinking, accomplish projects that cannot be completed by staff (due in part to their size or complexity), and building a community of people who are interested in your library, archive, gallery, or museum.

Charles Leadbeater, in his interesting and very readable book *We-Think*, suggested that there are five key principles that are present in successful collaboration projects:[24]

- *Core*. Any project must start somewhere, and the somewhere typically is the creation of someone who devotes an inordinate amount of time and effort to get a project off the ground. Linus Torvalds contributed the original nucleus of the Linux software (and continues to provide guidance to the ongoing development and maintenance of the world's most used software). A good core tends to get a conversation going and invites people to contribute through their participation.

- *Contribute*. A successful collaboration recognizes that strength comes from people with different talents, different perspectives, and different ideas. The goal is to build a community of people who are willing to devote the time and energy to get things going and to sustain the effort. Beyond the core group, a project will attract some individuals who are willing to contribute a moderate amount, while the largest group of people will only devote an occasional hour or two each month to address a specific concern. Collaboration that involves thousands in the testing of software, for example, will find many more errors than a single programmer running a thousand tests.

- *Connect*. Due to a wide range of Internet offerings, it is fairly easy to create a community of people with similar and often esoteric interests. These Internet services through the use of application program interface (API) tools allow people to connect in a wide variety of ways. A large group of collaborators, often called a crowd, need neutral meeting spaces to explore ideas and have constructive and creative conversations. All of these services combined with the huge number of people on the Internet mean that there are thousands of experiments occurring each day. Many of these experiments die after a short life, but a few can grow quite quickly. The secret seems to be that some groups seem to learn how to agree to collaborate.

- *Collaborate*. Groups with a sense of purpose seem to do better and live longer than those groups with diverse interests and values. Diverse ways of thinking are essential to fostering and maintaining innovation, but diversity of values often leads to disagreements, sometimes-destructive arguments.

- *Create*. Groups working together collaboratively on a project typically have a clear sense of purpose, and while much of the time each individual may be working independently, the end result is a collective "we." The project grows as content is added, and people have an opportunity to make comments, provide encouragement, and make suggestions. Almost all collaborative projects have a place—whether it may be a website, a forum, a wiki, or a magazine—

where information is shared and discussed. Given that people have a range of skills and interests, it is important for the community to establish norms and bounds for how things are accomplished. Usually, those involved in a group will employ a form of peer review so that quality is maintained.

When all five principles come together collaboration reaches its real potential. Expertise multiplies when an environment is provided in which networked conversations and a pool of diversely talented people can easily get together to share and create together. It would seem that the complexity of a task, the need for specialized knowledge, confusing directions (or a complicated user interface), and a lack of feedback to the participants will lead to low levels of participation. Some crowdsourcing projects start off with fairly simple tasks and progress to more challenging activities as a way to engender immediate participation as well as to encourage a deeper level of engagement.[25]

What we see when an organization uses structured team-based collaboration in an effort to solve a problem or improve productivity is really the tip of the iceberg as seen in Figure 8-4. However, we rarely acknowledge all of the activities that happen below the waterline—the social interactions that are involved in sharing information, seeking more knowledgeable people to become involved, and the community building that occurs to build trust so that people become committed to a shared purpose. The goal of all these most hidden activities is to create value for the customers of the organization.

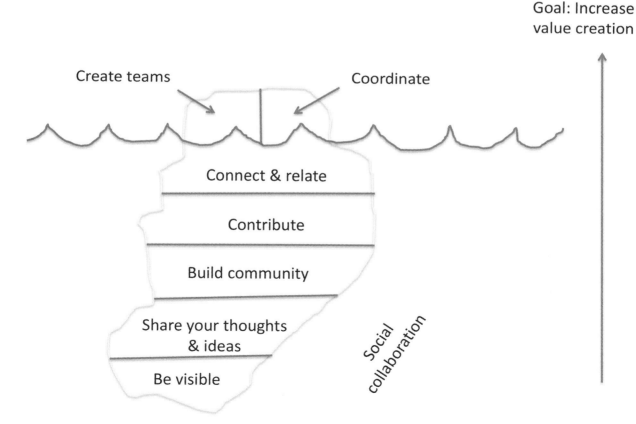

Figure 8-4 The Collaboration Iceberg.

Some have called for librarians to become more involved in open-source projects as it affords the opportunity to learn firsthand about the governance and reward structure of a group. How does someone become an "expert," and who decides what an "expert" is? What skills are needed, and how does someone learn to develop the support and trust of others in the group? How does the group disperse the responsibilities of a portion of the project to others? How are newbies encouraged to participate yet learn that their initial efforts might not be good enough? Clearly, all of these issues are transferable to libraries as we learn to collaborate in developing collections and deliver services across the web.

One interesting experiment, conducted by the Brooklyn Museum, wanted to determine whether crowds could "wisely" judge something subjective as art. *Click! A Crowd-Curated Exhibition* was conducted in three phases: people could submit photos on the theme "the changing face of Brooklyn," people could vote, and finally people could see the results of the voting either in person or online (you can still see the result of the voting and the photos at http://www.brooklynmuseum.org/exhibitions/click/). What was interesting about *Click!* was that people could not see the scores of other people who were also voting. This was done since James Surowiecki argues in his book *The Wisdom of Crowds* that crowds are "wise" only if they are not influenced by others. People who were voting were asked to indicate their self-reported art knowledge. Interestingly, of the top 10 photos selected by the "official" experts, 8 were also selected by the "crowd." Also, of note, the photos were displayed in size relative to their rank.[26] The museum has continued to experiment with *Split Second*, an online experiment viewing paintings, and *Go*, a community-curated open studios project.

For-profit companies are also starting to realize that their future success lies in creating shared value, which creates economic value for the firm at the same time creating value for society by addressing its needs and challenges.[27] The principles of creating shared value work well in both for-profit companies and government agencies. What matters is that society benefits regardless of who creates the value. Companies can create shared value in three ways:

- *Redefining value in the value chain (or supplier chain)*—Improving the quality, cost, and reliability of supplies and resources while acknowledging that they have a role to play as stewards of natural resources is one proven method for creating shared value.
- *Reinventing products, services, and markets*—Improving quality while reducing costs allows a company to better serve its existing customers while offering the opportunity to access new markets.
- *Enabling local economic development*—Companies do not exist in isolation from their surroundings and rely on local suppliers, an infrastructure of roads and telecommunications, and access to skilled and talented workers in order to sustain their business.

A review of the literature pertaining to customer participation and value creation in the service/product development life cycle found several benefits for both the company and the customer as seen in Table 8-1.[28]

Table 8-1
Outcomes of Customer Participation

Value for the Company	Value for the Customer
Economic value	*Economic value*
Increased productivity	Cost reductions, discounts
Greater customer loyalty	
Better brand image	
Relationship value	*Better fit*
Improved customer satisfaction	Increased control and empowerment
Enriched two-way communication	Improved perception of service quality and value
Positive evaluations	
Innovation value	*Knowledge enhancement*
Improved service/product development and innovation	Better understanding of service/product offerings
Increased customization	

Why Engage Our Communities?

Professionals in cultural organizations should become more engaged with their communities for any one (or more) of several reasons:

- Achieve goals the cultural organization would never have the time, money, or staff resources to complete on its own.
- Achieve goals in a much faster time frame than if it worked on its own.
- Tap into the knowledge, expertise, and interest of the community.
- Add value to existing content through the addition of comments, tags, reviews, and ratings.
- Improve the quality of existing content by correcting text or transcribing content that can't be converted to digital format using OCR software—with the result that more content is correctly indexed (or indexed for the first time) and thus more content becomes accessible.
- Making cultural organization resources discoverable in new and different ways.
- Gaining insights about what is valuable from the customer's perspective.
- The high level of community involvement is another way to demonstrate the value of the cultural organization.
- Participants become personally invested and are much more vocal about the value of the cultural organization in their lives.
- But perhaps the most important reason for engagement is that the community that is involved with the cultural organization becomes much larger and is a more active participant.

But important as all of these objectives are, libraries, museums, and other cultural institutions need to take a step back and ask a real fundamental question: Why are we putting these important collections online in the first place? Trevor Owens in an interesting and timely blog posting suggested that:[29]

> The general idea of crowdsourcing is described as an instrument for getting data that we can use to make collections more accessible. Don't get me wrong, crowdsourcing does this. With that said it does so much more than this. In the process of developing these crowdsourcing projects we have stumbled into something far more exciting than speeding up or lowering the costs of document transcription. Far better than being an instrument for generating data that we can use to get our collections more used it is actually the single greatest advancement in getting people using and interacting with our collections.

Another perspective on this important phenomenon is that of Paul Ford, who asks the question: "Why Wasn't I Consulted?"[30] Paul suggests that the reason for the success of so many websites is that they tap into the need for people to be consulted. Consider the success of *Wikipedia, Stack Overflow, Reddit, MetaFilter, YouTube, About, Yelp, Flickr, Craigslist, GitHub, flickr, Ebay, Amazon*, and many others (including the open-source movement). Their success is directly tied to the engagement of so many people who both post content and comment, rate, review, and are otherwise engaged with a whole community of other interested individuals.

Many projects that have embraced crowdsourcing have found that use of their digital collections increases significantly, new donors are attracted, but perhaps most importantly is that people from far-flung places around the globe become engaged with these collections. The individuals who become involved with a crowdsourced project become so enthusiastic that they invite others to become involved and they develop meaningful online relationships with others who are like-minded. As Owens further noted: "At its best, crowdsourcing is not about getting someone to do work for you, it is about offering your users the opportunity to participate in public memory." Crowdsourcing offers the opportunity to participate in something bigger. This also demonstrates that there are other systems of value than money that are important to people.

Summary

One of the real challenges for any cultural organization in considering ways to engage with a larger group of people, especially if the goal is to engage people who may be unaware of the institution, is how can the unique capabilities of people be leveraged in exceptional ways for the creation of public good? Really successful projects not only ask people to collaborate with the content but to also communicate with other collaborators and with the staff of the cultural organization.

Given the many reasons why people are willing to share their time and expertise in order to participate in a shared online project, it is crucial that the cultural organization reach out in ways that will be meaningful for those who might want to participate. The challenge is to provide an engaging and meaningful experience that will draw people back time after time, and to share their enthusiasm with others who might be interested in a project. People like to believe that they are making a contribution that expands our understanding and knowledge about science, history, and culture. And while many people are likely to be involved at a low level, a few will become engaged and make a significant investment in time and energy (another example of the 80/20 rule). The goal is not to complete a transcription project but to reach the many (perhaps thousands or tens of thousands) from around the world who are interested in a particular topic or event. Reaching that larger audience, especially if the cultural organization can engage with them over a long period of time is something that all participants will find of value.

Checklist for Adding Value Using Collaboration

	Yes	No
Has your cultural organization identified ways in which it might engage with a larger online audience?	☐	☐
Has your cultural organization sought donors to contribute to the digitization of most, if not all, of your special collections?	☐	☐
Have you identified different market segments who would be interested in your collections?	☐	☐
Has your cultural organization discussed partnering with the local historical society, library and/or museums to provide access to a broader range of materials and collections?	☐	☐
Has your cultural organization created a Wikipedia page for the Library?	☐	☐

If you answered "no" to one or more of the questions in the checklist, then your library is not doing all it could to add value using collaboration.

Main idea:	Collaborating with customers creates value in the life of the customer and for the cultural organization
Opposing view:	Cultural organization professionals as experts
Key concepts:	Collaboration, cocreation, innovation, experimentation, embracing change
What has changed?:	Everything
Catalyst:	The Internet
Open debate:	How much control should librarians relinquish? What kind of tools should be used? Should librarians moderate content added by users?

Notes

1. Rick Levine, Christopher Locke, Doc Searls, and David Weinberger. *The Cluetrain Manifesto: The End of Business as Usual*. New York: Basic Books, 2001, 199.

2. Simon Winchester. *The Meaning of Everything: The Story of the Oxford English Dictionary*. Oxford, England: Oxford University Press, 2004.

3. Jeff Howe. "The Rise of Crowdsourcing." *Wired*, June 14, 2006. Available at http://www .wired.com/wired/archive/14.06/crowds.html

4. David Weinberger. *Too Big to Know: Rethinking Knowledge Now That Facts Aren't the Facts, Experts Are Everywhere, and the Smartest Person in the Room Is the Room*. New York: Basic Books, 2011.

5. Trevor Owen. "The Crowd and the Library." *Trevor Owens* blog. May 20, 2012. Available at http://www.trevorowens.org/2012/05/the-crowd-and-the-library/

6. Rose Holley. "Crowdsourcing: How and Why Should Libraries Do It?" *D-Lib Magazine*, 16 (3/4), March/April 2010. Available at http://www.dlib.org/dlib/march10/ holley/03holley.html

7. Rick Bonney, Heidi Ballard, Rebecca Jordan, Ellen McCallie, Tina Phillips, Jennifer Shirk, and Candie Wilderman. *Public Participation in Scientific Research: Defining the Field and Assessing Its Potential for Informal Science Education*. Washington, DC: Center for Advancement of Informal Science Education, 2009. Available at http://www.birds.cornell.edu/citscitool kit/publications/CAISE-PPSR-report-2009.pdf

8. Mia Ridge. "Frequently Asked Questions about Crowdsourcing in Cultural Heritage." *Open Objects* blog. June 3, 2012. Available at http://openobjects.blogspot.co.uk/2012/06/ frequently-asked-questions-about.html

9. Johan Oomen and Lora Aroyo. "Crowdsourcing in the Cultural Heritage Domain: Opportunities and Challenges." *Proceedings of the 5th International Conference on Communities and Technologies*, 2011, 138–149. Available at http://www.iisi.de/fileadmin/IISI/upload/2011/ p138_oomen.pdf

10. Mike Masnick. "Why Netflix Never Implemented the Algorithm That Won the Netflix $1 Million Challenge. *Innovation* blog, April 13, 2012. Available at http://www.techdirt .com/blog/innovation/articles/20120409/03412518422/why-netflix-never-implemented-algorithm-that-won-netflix-1-million-challenge.shtml

11. Jim Giles. "Internet Encyclopedias Go Head to Head." *Nature*, 438, December 15, 2005, 900–901.

12. See http://en.wikipedia.org/wiki/Wikipedia:Five_pillars

13. Interestingly, a lengthy article, *Reliability of Wikipedia*, appearing in Wikipedia explores the whole topic of reliability of content and includes some 230 citations providing fodder for the strengths and weakness of Wikipedia versus an encyclopedia.

14. Nicco Mele. *The End of Big: How the Internet Makes David the New Goliath*. New York: St. Martin's Press, 2013.

15. More information about Metadata Games may be found at http://www.metadatagames .org/about/

16. Dava Sobel. *Longitude: The True Story of a Lone Genius Who Solved the Greatest Scientific Problem of His Time*. New York: Penguin, 1995.

17. Visit http://collections.rmg.co.uk/collections/objects/79142.html for photos and more information about Harrison's longitude watch.

18. Steven Johnson. *Future Perfect: The Case for Progress in a Networked Age*. New York: Riverhead Books, 2012.

19. Julia Noordegraaf, Angela Bartholomew, and Alexandra Eveleigh. *Modeling Crowdsourcing for Cultural Heritage*. Presentation at the Annual Conference of Museums and the Web, April 2–5, 2014, Baltimore, Maryland. Available at http://mw2014.museumsandtheweb.com/paper/modeling-crowdsourcing-for-cultural-heritage/

20. Clay Shirky. *Here Comes Everybody: The Power of Organizing without Organizations*. New York: Penguin Press, 2008, 107.

21. Ben Brumfield. "The Collaborative Future of Amateur Editions." *Collaborative Manuscript Transcription* blog. July 13, 2013. Available at http://manuscripttranscription.blogspot.com/2013/07/the-collaborative-future-of-amateur.html

22. Jeff Howe. *Crowdsourcing: Why the Power of the Crowd Is Driving the Future of Business*. New York: Three Rivers Press, 2008.

23. Rick Bonney, Heidi Ballard, Rebecca Jordan, Ellen McCallie, Tina Phillips, Jennifer Shirk, and Candie Wilderman. *Public Participation in Scientific Research: Defining the Field and Assessing Its Potential for Informal Science Education*. A CAISE Inquiry Group Report. Washington, DC: Center for Advancement of Informal Science Education (CAISE), 2009.

24. Charles Leadbeater. *We-Think*. London: Profile Books, 2008.

25. Julia Noordegraaf. *Modeling Crowdsourcing for Cultural Heritage*. Presentation at MW2014: Museums and the Web 2014, April 2–5, 2014, Baltimore, MD. Available at http://mw2014.museumsandtheweb.com/paper/modeling-crowdsourcing-for-cultural-heritage/

26. Joyce Shelby. "Brooklyn Museum Set to Open Exhibit Picked by Internet Vote." *New York Daily News*, June 23, 2008. Available at http://www.nydailynews.com/new-york/brooklyn/brooklyn-museum-set-open-exhibit-picked-internet-vote-article-1.293447

27. Michael Porter and Mark Kramer. "Creating Shared Value: How to Reinvent Capitalism—and Unleash a Wave of Innovation and Growth." *Harvard Business Review*, 89 (1/2), January/February 2011, 62–77.

28. Adapted from Mekhail Mustak, Elina Jaakkola, and Aino Halinen. "Customer Participation and Value Creation: A Systematic Review and Research Implications." *Managing Service Quality*, 23 (4), 2013, 341–359.

29. "Crowdsourcing Cultural Heritage: The Objectives Are Upside Down." March 10, 2012. *Trevor Owens* blog. Available at http://www.trevorowens.org/2012/03/crowdsourcing-cultural-heritage-the-objectives-are-upside-down/

30. Paul Ford. "The Web Is a Customer Service Medium." *Ftrain.com* blog. January 6, 2011. Available at http://www.ftrain.com/wwic.html

9

Collaboration in Libraries, Museums, and Archives

The leading edge is where absolutely all the action is.
The leading edge contains all the infinite possibilities of the future.

Robert Pirsig[1]

I believe that we are at the threshold.
But just at the very threshold—the very beginning.
The incunabula period of the digital age.

T. Scott Plutchak[2]

The National Library of the Netherlands, the National Library of Finland, the National Library of Australia, the University of Iowa, and others provide collaboration opportunities for people to transcribe newspapers, restaurant menus, manuscripts, oral histories, or other digital materials. The New York Public Library (NYPL) and the British Library (BL), have used the assistance of volunteers to "anchor" historical maps using a process called Georeferencing. Georeferencer software has also been used in the Moravian Library (Czech Republic), the National Archief (The Hague), the National Library of Scotland, and the Institut Cartografic de Catalunya (Barcelona).[3] Other libraries and museums use volunteers to create or correct descriptive metadata using social tagging or folksonomies. Some of the more noteworthy library and museum projects will be discussed in some detail in this chapter.

Many libraries have large collections of ephemera since it is a record of life and social customs, popular culture, and issues of national concern. When ephemera are digitized, the result is an image file that usually is not indexed, and thus any text in the image is not searchable (or only accessible in the most rudimentary of ways). The only way to make the contents of the image searchable, and thus discoverable, is to manually transcribe it or describe it. Clearly, library, museum, gallery, or archive staff does not have time to complete such a massive project presenting the need to involve an interested public.

The New York Public Library

The NYPL is at once a sprawling branch public library system with 88 facilities spread across three of the city's five boroughs as well as an internationally well-known research institution with collections that rival large academic and national libraries. The library serves a diverse array of researchers, students, writers, artists, entrepreneurs, and others who make extensive use of its physical (more than 4.5 million books) and electronic resources (approximately 800,000 digital images).

The NYPL Labs, responsible for facilitating access to its extensive digitized content, has an eclectic staff of hackers, artists, and librarians. Charged with generating some interest and excitement with the library's archive and audiovisual collections, the NYPL Labs has come out of the starting blocks with a rush as it has embarked on some projects that are designed to engage a whole new audience for the library.

One interesting project, called **What's on the Menu?,** uses the digitized images of more than 45,000 restaurant menus dating back to the 1840s. And while some access was provided to a portion of the collection using the online catalog, searches of the OPAC did not retrieve actual food items presented on the menus. There simply was no way to learn how the popularity of pasta changed over time, or how many different ways oysters were prepared, or uncover when pizza first appeared on a menu. Given a variety of objectives, it was decided that manual transcription of each menu including identifying the name, description, and price for each item was the best way to end up with high-quality data.[4]

Transcription volunteers (who for the most part are foodies, chefs, want-to-be-chefs, and New York history buffs) are welcomed to the site, and menus go through a basic workflow—New (yet to be transcribed), to Under Review, to Done. After the initial transcription has been completed, a volunteer can review and make corrections to a menu if needed—as seen in Figure 9-1. Since April 2011, some 1,331,936 dishes have been transcribed from 17,545 menus (as of November 2015). Volunteers can also geographically locate each menu using a Geotagger tool. People participating in this project find that it is fun and very interesting to learn about food dishes in a bygone era. And scholars find it to be a priceless source of historical data. Visit www.menus.nypl.org.

Another popular project at NYPL is called the **Map Wrapper**, a digital map interface that uses high-resolution digital images of historical maps that align one or more points on an old map to a precise latitude/longitude on a contemporary virtual map. Map Wrapper was created using an open-source web alternative to commercial geographic information system (GIS) software. Volunteers must log in and have received some training before they are able to "georectify" or locate and anchor an old map. The result is that the user can "go back in time" and see how the landscape has changed as the old map is synced to today's geography—see Figure 9-2.

And this map wrapping opens up a wide range of possibilities as it will be possible to include other portions of the library's collection that have a geographical dimension—residential and business directories, literary archives, corporate records, photographs, church registries, among a host of other possibilities. It will be possible to build a real complicated network of links from one resource to another with the end result that the user will experience something completely new.[5] Visit www.maps.nypl .org/wrapper/.

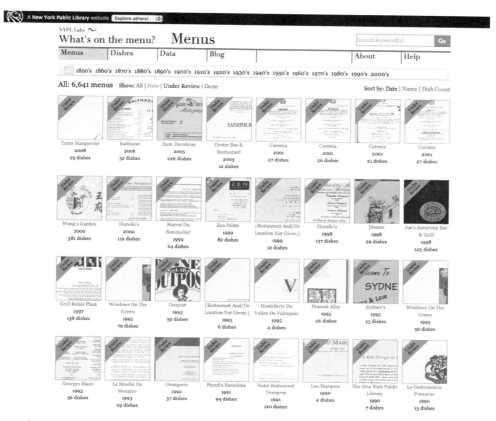

Figure 9-1 The NYPL What's on the Menu Help Review Page. Courtesy of the New York
Public Library. www.nypl.org

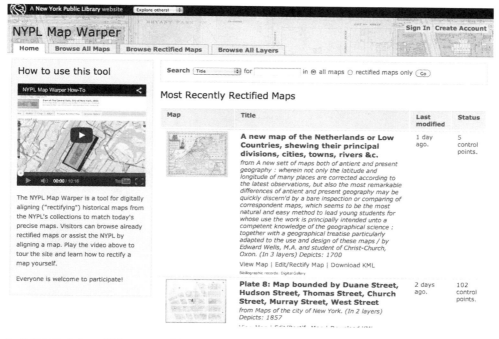

Figure 9-2 NYPL Map Wrapper Page. Courtesy of the New York Public Library. www.nypl.org

Map Wrapper also enables the volunteers to capture a tremendous amount of information contained in the map via the color-coding, written text, codes, and other markings that must be transcribed by hand. These map "features" may include landmarks, points of interest, political boundaries, municipal or state boundaries, building footprints, and elevations.

A recently introduced variation of Map Wrapper, called **Building Inspector,** encourages people to improve the accuracy of digitized fire insurance maps from the 1850s and 1860s (maps are not always drawn to a consistent scale). Building Inspector is a website developed to work on smartphones in the expectation that people will fix some maps while waiting in line or on the subway. This is an example of using a crowd of people, doing a little bit at a time, to improve the quality of the maps.

The third innovative project, called the **Stereogranimator,** animates more than 40,000 historical stereographs in the NYPL digital collections. Stereographs are a pair of images taken from slightly different perspectives, and when viewed with a hand-held stereoscope device, they produce a 3D effect. This is inspired by artist Joshua Heineman, who created *Reaching for the Out of Reach* on his website, CursiveBuildings. com using stereograph images from the NYPL Digital Gallery. Heineman used animated gifs—a sequence of two or more images that when run as an infinite loop produce twitchy cinematic effects. It is even possible to create red-cyan anaglyphs for the dedicated 3D fans (glasses are required). Volunteers can create a gif for a stereography or view collection stereographs that have already been converted—see Figure 9-3. Visit www.stereo.nypl.org.

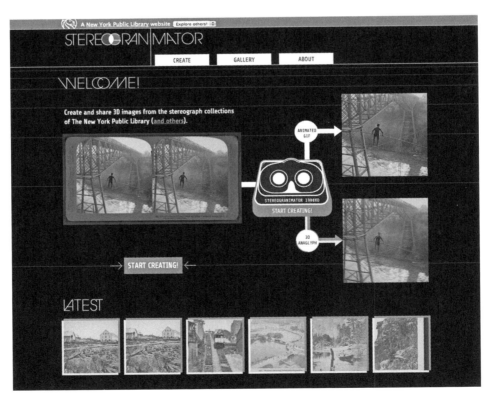

Figure 9-3 NYPL Stereogranmator Page. Courtesy of the New York Public Library. www.nypl.org

DirectMe NYC: 1940 is a mashup of the 1940 U.S. Federal Census data combined with old maps, genealogical tools, and *NY Times* headlines. In addition to being able to search, people are encouraged to share stories about names and addresses to create a cultural memory bank. Visit www.directme.nypl.org.

Biblion, an app for the tablet that can be downloaded from the NYPL website, presents some of the library's content preserved from the 1939 World's Fair. The app, developed at the request of the NYPL, encourages exploration of the World Fair content in interesting and intuitive ways that goes way beyond the traditional library online catalog or museum catalog. Check it out!

The NYPL Labs have also introduced the *New York City Chronology of Place,* which allows the online visitor to select an address or the name of a building and transcend time by viewing historic photos, restaurant menus, phonebook entries, census records, building permits, and other resources from the library's collections. This is really cool stuff.

One NYPL librarian, Jessica Pigza, started a blog related to handicraft-related materials in the library's collections.[6] Encouraged by the level of participation and comments to her blog, Pigza started offering *Handmade*, a class designed to appeal to crafters who would learn about library materials that could inform and inspire their creative DIY projects. The success of these programs led to the development of *Handmade Crafternoons*, a monthly program that brings crafters together to learn about how other artists have used the NYPL collections for inspiration. In addition, a series of videos called "Design by the Book" are available on *YouTube* and the library's website that document how local artists draw inspiration from materials in the library. Jessica has written a really interesting book sharing her experiences.[7]

NYPL Labs has a number of other ongoing projects that can be discovered by visiting their website—visit www.nypl.org/collections/labs/. The NYPL Labs is also actively involved in developing and promoting a set of application programming interfaces or APIs that other sites can use to discover and use NYPL collection resources. Clearly, this is one library that has found reaching out to people in new and engaging ways and creates collaborators rather than the usual library patron.[8]

The National Library of Australia

Trove, as in treasure trove, is the National Library of Australia's discovery service that aggregates resources from the cultural heritage sector and provides access to more than 459 million Australian and online resources including images, historic newspapers (more than 130 million articles), maps, music, archives, and of course books (as of November 2015). Trove is designed to not just "find" something but to be able to "get" the item in a way that is easy, quick, and seamless.[9] Trove is a collaboration of several major libraries in Australia and is designed to locate resources about Australia and Australians (http://trove.nla.gov.au/).

Trove's purpose is to encourage the active participation among visitors such that they can transcribe historical newspapers, tag items, and add comments for items in the collections and even submit images to the library as seen in Figure 9-4. The guiding design principle is that Trove is intended to evolve with people's feedback rather than remaining fixed over time. The idea was to provide a tool that would allow the library's

Figure 9-4 National Library of Australia's Trove Home Page. Trove, National Library of Australia http://trove.nla.gov.au

users to interact with the National Library staff and among themselves. And interact they do. Trove has more than 138,000 active volunteers who transcribe newspaper articles, and once transcribed, then the total content of the article is re-indexed and thus the full contents become accessible to all (by January 2016, more than 181 million lines of newspaper text have been corrected). Note in Figure 9-4 that in the left-hand column, almost 50,000 corrections were made on the day the screen shot was captured.

Once a user gets down to the individual document level, several social bookmarking and social networking tools become accessible. And a user can add one or more tags to an item—to the more than three million tags that already exist. Tags are searchable, and you can restrict your tag search using several criteria.

Clearly, one of the more important goals of Trove is to engage the community so that people are encouraged to collaborate and build on the Trove platform and share with others. The TroveNewsBot tweets newspaper articles from Trove using other tweets as inspiration.[10]

The National Library of the Netherlands

The Dutch National Library is planning on digitizing all printed publications since 1470 (estimated to be some 730 million pages) over the coming 20 years.[11] Some of the digitization efforts to date include the *Dutch Parliamentary Papers* (2.3 million pages), the *Historical Newspapers Project* (more than 8 million pages), the *Early Dutch Books Online Project* (2.1 million pages), *Illustrated Manuscripts*, and *Memory of the Netherlands*.

The library is moving from having separate data silos for each project with their own websites and branding to a single front-end website that will provide access to all of the library's digital assets—full text, images, photographs, audio and video files. The goal is to provide a system that is easy to use while allowing the user to filter the content by time, geographic location, object type, theme, and so forth in order to best meet the needs of the user.

The library engaged in a strategic planning process in 2009 and developed the Business Model Innovation Cultural Heritage or BMICE Ring Model that recognized the different ways institutions make their collections accessible in order to generate added value (Figure 9-5). The four ways collections can be accessed include the following:

- *Analog in-house*—The materials are displayed or made physically accessible in an archive, reading room, collection, or exhibition.
- *Digital in-house*—Digitized resources are made available within the walls of the institution using a computer or computer network provided by the institution.
- *Online*—All or part of the digital collection of the institution is offered online though a website, without explicit rights of use or reuse explained.
- *Online in the network*—All or part of the digital collection of the institution is offered online. Rights of use are explicitly granted to third parties (the public, students, scholars, other institutions) for use or reuse.[12]

Figure 9-5 BMICE Ring Model.

Libraries and other cultural institutions have historically focused on analog materials but, over the course of the past 10 years or so, have been moving toward providing online access. The goal should be to offer the same level of access to digital (and analog) content wherever and whenever the customer wants it.

The Library of Congress

The Library of Congress (LC) embarked on an interesting project with Flickr in January 2008 when it uploaded about 3,000 photos. Today, there are slightly more than 12,000 LC images available on Flickr. The intent of the project was to determine to what extent the Flickr community would engage with the content that LC made available. Within 24 hours, it was evident that there was a lot of interest with a total of 1.1 million views; a week later, the total reached 3.6 million views. Conversations between LC and Flickr lead to the creation of the Flickr Commons—see Figure 9-6.

The Flickr community can add information in several ways: tags, free-form comments, and appending a note directly to the photo. The comments allowed people to

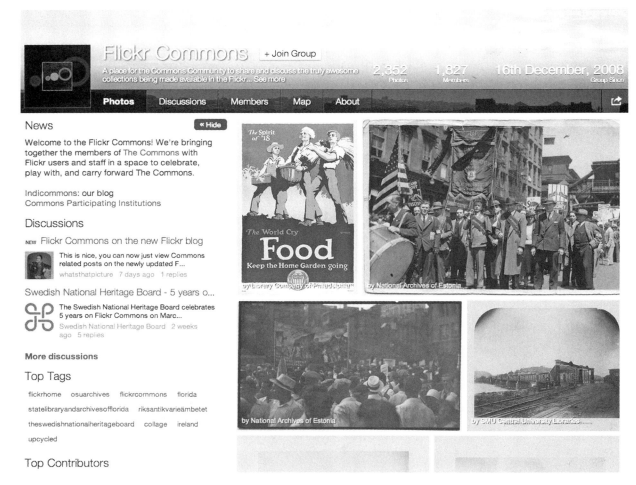

Figure 9-6 Flickr Commons.

share their memories and often identified precise locations of photos. In addition, corrections and additions were also provided—often with accompanying links to published articles and subject-specialized websites. LC updated its catalog records (giving credit to the Flickr Commons project). The tags people added often included place names, personal commentary, and tags in multiple languages. And the annotations left on the photos often identified specific individuals in the photo or deciphering the words on a placard or sign.

A report released in October 2008 demonstrated that the LC Flickr community had:[13]

- Left more than 7,000 comments on 2,873 photos
- Made 79 percent of the photos a "favorite"
- Added 67,176 tags
- Contributed at least one tag to 98.5 percent of the available photos

In addition to raising the visibility of the library and its collections (as evidenced by the increasing traffic on the library's online catalog), the Flickr project provided valuable experience to some of the library's staff in the realm of social networking. Continued heavy traffic both on the LC website and on Flickr for the LC posted content attests to the high interest and the desire to interact with photographic materials.[14]

Among the other LC collections of significance are *American Memory*, *Historic Newspapers*, *Prints & Photographs*, *Performing Arts*, *Sound Recordings*, *Film*, *Maps*, *Manuscripts*, and *Veterans History*.

The National Library of Finland

The National Library of Finland has taken a different approach to the transcription of its digitized content. That is, it is using gaming as a way to engage the crowd and get transcription completed. Starting in March 2011, the library released its Digitalkoot (Digital volunteers) program, which uses volunteers from around the world to complete small tasks or microtasks, to assist in correcting digitized content. Two online games were available (Mole Hunt and Mole Bridge), and more than 110,000 participants completed fixing eight million words (one volunteer M. Petri completed 348,422 microtasks while online for some 395 hours).[15] The end result of all this work by the crowd is that the digitized content has been corrected, and thus the indexes to the content are also accurate so that scholars and interested citizens can gain access in a timely manner.[16]

The library launched a project, called Kuvatalkoot at the end of 2013, which allows volunteers to annotate newspaper articles.

The British Library

The BL has engaged in several crowdsourcing projects since 2010. The first project invited people in the United Kingdom to record sounds (UK Soundmap) from their environment (work, home, and leisure activities, using an app on their mobile phones). Over 2,000 recordings were uploaded over the course of the yearlong project.

Another interesting project asked people to identify a piece of writing that represents a place they know—Pin-A-Tale (visit http://writingbritain.bl.uk/). People were asked to tell how the chosen item (novel, poem, play, or song lyric) captures the essence of the place and what it means to them. This is a really interesting project and presents a clear way in which collaboration and adding context add real value for current and future visitors.

In 2011, the library released several thousand historical maps and asked people to "georeference" them to a current map location. These historical maps included fire insurance maps; plans covering cities, towns, and ports; and maps from around the world—some dating as far back as the 16th and 17th centuries.[17] The results allow anyone to search and see a variety of maps online representing a specific location—see Figure 9-7.

It is clear that georeferencing is almost addictive as many people spend a lot of time "pinning" maps when they explore the past (I think maps are really fascinating)[18] while improving the quality of information so that others can more easily find and explore these maps.

More recently, the BL has uploaded more than a million images onto Flickr Commons for anyone to repurpose, remix, and use as they see fit (the images come from

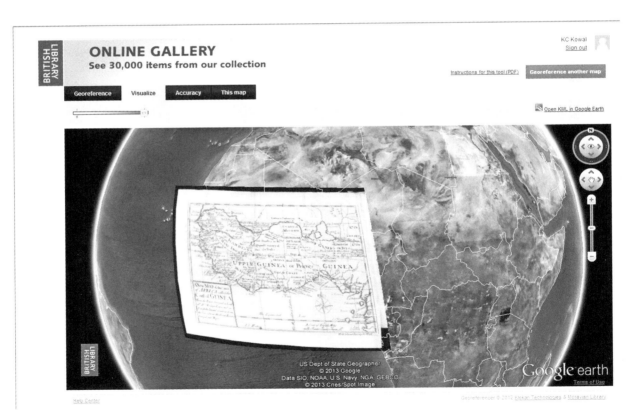

Figure 9-7 Georeferenced Historical Map from the British Library. British Library. © The British Library Board.

midt i Centrum at den mylrende, brogede
ar Sommerferietiden kommer, tyer det udenfor
række frisk Luft, og det er der, han skal følge
op-
oen
han
· at
lses
Pa-
ivre
For
aris'
har
ade-
Den
· af
ied,
:ttet
ide-
der
over
ikke
Den
af
ble-
:rog

I Acclimatationshaven. Ridetour paa Kamelen.

tore Verdensstads Midtpunkt.   Pariserne og Alt,
rakteristisk ved Paris, er nu paa helt andre Steder,

Figure 9-8 Sample Illustration from the British Library on Flickr Commons.

pages of the 17th-, 18th-, and 19th-century books digitized by Microsoft, which subsequently released these images into the public domain). These images are totally awesome and include beautiful illustrations, satire, illuminated and decorative letters, colorful illustrations, paintings, and landscapes—see Figure 9-8 for a sample illustration. The Flickr community has already demonstrated great interest in this content by adding tags and comments.

And while these images are linked to the specific book they were drawn from, the BL is looking for new and creative ways to find, navigate, and display these "unseen" illustrations. In fact, the BL has announced that it will pay 25,000 pounds to create a feedback loop for tracking and measuring the use and impact of this public domain content. Currently, the BL is trying to capture innovative reuse of digital content as best they can manually, primarily by scouring social media channels for mentions, but this is hardly sustainable nor scalable, and the library acknowledges that there is much inspired activity the library is missing.

The British Library created a "Off the Map" competition to encourage use of digital resources in new and creative ways. Some of the winners include:

- In 2013, a group of 7 students from De Montfort University created a wonderful video of 17th-century London (http://youtu.be/SPY-hr-8-MO).
- In 2014, the winning team was from the University of South Wales in Australia who created a Fonthill Abbey inspired game called Nix using Oculus Rift (http://youtu.be/8ESieZO4VHw).
- In 2015, folks have the opportunity of using Alice in wonderland materials. One team, "Off our rockers," has created a great video (https://youtu.be/ uuG5sAtEZzs).

David Normal, a California-based artist, used 19th-century images from the BL to create the *Burning Man 2014 "Crossroads of Curiosity" Light Boxes*. Now, that is an out-of-the-box use of retrieved images by any measure!

In addition, the BL has encouraged people to take its images and other digital content and to populate this content into Wikipedia. The library has also created the British Library Labs to encourage scholars to experiment at scale with BL collections and data. Competitions are held each year to engage scholars and build new services. In 2013, Pieter Francois used statistical tools to support text analysis; in 2014, Desmond Schmidt and Anna Gerber created a text to image linking tool, and Bob Nicholson created a Victorian Meme Machine.

The National Library of Wales

The **Welsh Newspapers Online** project at the National Library of Wales has put slightly more than one million pages of Welsh history online—up to 1910—free of charge. Users can both browse digital copies of the original newspapers and also search for names, words, and dates.

Rijks Museum in Amsterdam

The Rijks Museum (https://www.rijksmuseum.nl/) provides access to some 150,000 digital high-quality images of works of art in its collections—see Figure 9-9.

The Rijks Museum provides an inventive tool called the Rijksstudio, which allows you to select a portion of a work of art (or the complete work) and add it to an existing

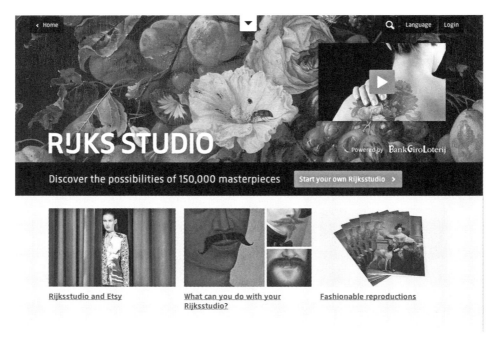

Figure 9-9　Rijks Museum Studio. Rijks Museum. https://www.rijksmuseum.nl/en/rijksstudio? ii=0&p=0

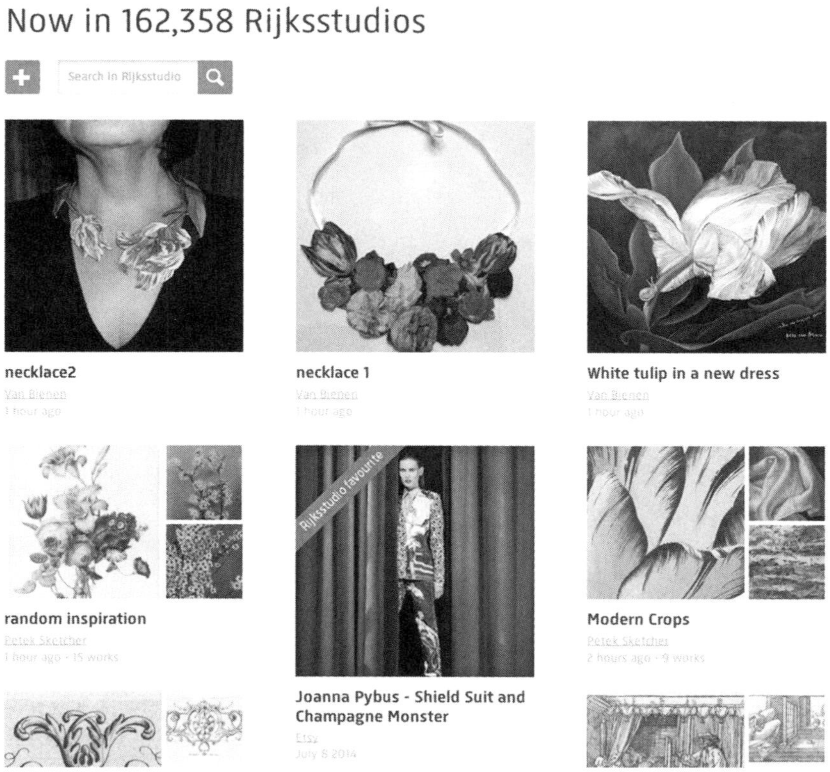

Figure 9-10 Sample of Rijksstudios. Rijks Museum. https://www.rijksmuseum.nl/en/rijks studio/42425—geri-meftah/collections/kat?ii=0&p=0

set or create your own set that will be saved in Rijksstudio. As of January 2016, more than 233,000 sets had been created by people from around the world as unique sets as seen in Figures 9-10 and 9-11.

The University of Iowa Libraries

The University of Iowa Libraries launched its crowdsourcing initiative, The **Civil War Diaries & Letters Transcription Project** (now re-branded as **DIY History**), as an experiment in the spring of 2011. The library selected Scripto, an open-source software for documentary transcription, as the tool to engage its crowdsourcing activities (http:// scripto.org). The goal is to engage a large crowd with each individual contributing a little bit with the result that a lot of work gets done. Interest in the project really took off once it had been mentioned on Reddit, in which users vote on interesting Internet websites. The library had to allocate more bandwidth to the project's servers to cope with the huge influx of users wanting to participate.

One of the by-products of the publicity about the Civil War diary transcription project encouraged a number of individuals to donate period diaries and letters to the archive. But perhaps more importantly, some of those who began the project with the desire to assist in the transcription process became emotionally involved with

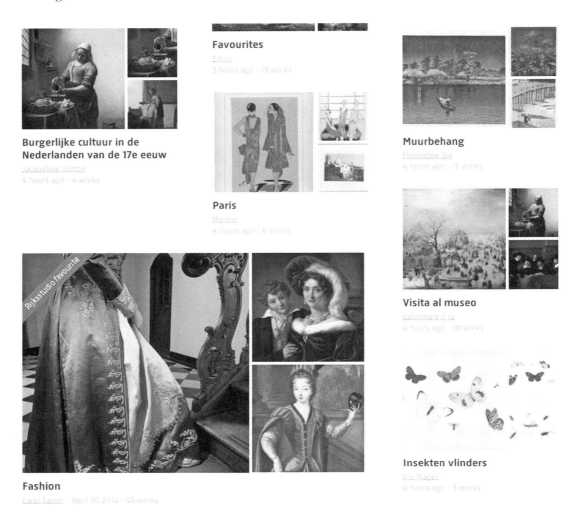

Figure 9-11 More Samples of Rijksstudios. Rijks Museum. https://www.rijksmuseum.nl/ en/my/collections/42425—geri-meftah/kat/objecten#/RP-T-1892-A-2661,1

the people in the diaries to such an extent that they view these historical individuals almost as part of an extended family. The end result is that library staff and project participants have developed a deeper appreciation for their involvement and complementary skills.[19]

Today, the DIY History website allows people to transcribe a wide variety of handwritten resources including the Szathmary Culinary Manuscripts and Cookbooks— more than 20,000 cookbooks, Pioneer Lives, Iowa Women Lives: Letter and Diaries, Building the Transcontinental Railroad, Civil War Diaries and Letters, and the Nile Kinnick Collection (correspondence to his family and friends during World War II). Aside from the obvious benefit of providing access for full-text searching, crowdsourcing projects open the door to reach new audiences who enjoy engaging with the resources of the library.

The University of Oklahoma

The University of Oklahoma has launched a site that encourages people to transcribe civil war materials as shown in Figure 9-12. The project is called *Transcribing the Past: Civil War Manuscripts* and features handwritten letters (1862–1863) exchanged between Lt. Lyle Garrett of the 23rd Iowa Infantry and his wife, Mary; and a diary (1861–1865) kept by Charles Kroff, who was a soldier in the 11th Indiana Volunteer Infantry (https://transcribe.ou.edu/).

The University of Oxford

The Oxford Digital Library (www.odl.ox.ac.uk) provides access to a large number of online collections including the Early English Books Online, Images of Medieval Manuscripts, Bodleian Broadside Ballads Project, Oxford Portraits Project, Celtic and

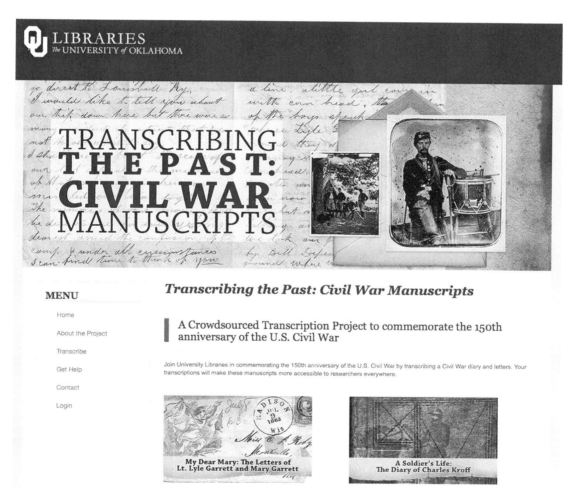

Figure 9-12 University of Oklahoma's *Transcribing the Past: Civil War Manuscripts*.
University of Oklahoma's Transcribing the Past. http://transcribe.ou.edu

Medieval Manuscripts, the Tradescant Collection, and a database of Athenian Pottery. Two projects have received a fair amount of attention:

> **The Great War Archive** was established to collect digital versions of memorabilia originating from the First World War and includes service records, war diaries, correspondence, poetry manuscripts and stories passed down from one generation to another—visit www.aucs.ox.ac.uk/ww1Lit/gwa. The result is a rich resource for students, teachers and researchers wishing to learn more about the war's impact in the lives of soldiers and their families back home.
>
> The **Ancient Lives Project** presents volunteers with fragments of 1,000-year-old papyri to decode. A majority of 700 boxes of papyri discovered by researchers from Oxford, potentially carrying about 500,000 fragments, have yet to be decoded. Volunteers who match the unknown characters on the fragment to known characters from a grid can decode the papyrus. Volunteers also add measurements of the fragments and the columns within them. A very difficult task, historically completed by scholars, has been effectively simplified, whilst retaining the challenge that is found in crosswords or code-breaking.

University College London

Volunteers to the **Transcribe Bentham** have transcribed an average of 44 manuscripts per week. The University College London Library holds 60,000 papers written by Jeremy Bentham that is of immense historical and philosophical importance. Visitors transcribing this material for the first time discover that they will be "making Bentham's thought accessible to the world at large, which will be of value to students, teachers and researchers around the world."

Those who are involved in the Transcribe Bentham project become amateur paleographers—the practice of deciphering and reading historical manuscripts. And attempting to decipher the handwriting of Bentham's manuscripts is a clear challenge. A quick start guide and detailed guidelines are provided to assist those in learning how to transcribe these manuscripts.

Yet, the project had to scale back in part due to the processes used to ensure the quality of the transcription. That is, a significant portion of the original grant for this project was to pay staff who were double-checking the quality of the transcriptions made by the crowd (rather than allowing the crowd to double-check the work of other volunteers). It should be noted that the university expects to use these transcripts as the basis for printing additional volumes of Jeremy Bentham.[20]

This raises a really important point of whether the professionals or experts will ever really trust the work of amateurs. In addition, the technology supporting the efforts of the crowd in the transcription process must be designed to enable the full participation of amateurs.

The U.S. National Archives

The U.S. National Archives encourages "citizen archivists" to enhance the content in the archives by adding tags, transcribing content (handwritten diaries, letters, and so forth), editing articles, uploading and sharing content, as well as transcribing Artic ship logs (dementing the weather each day) in a project called "Old Weather"—see Figure 9-13. The great thing about the National Archives is that it provides a wide variety of content that citizen archivists can choose to become involved in. In addition, members of the Flickr community can add tags to National Archives images.

The U.S. National Archives provides a tool called *Digital Vaults*, which offers students a great way to discover and work with primary source materials. Digital Vaults contains some 1,200 items plus a set of tools to assist students (and parents)

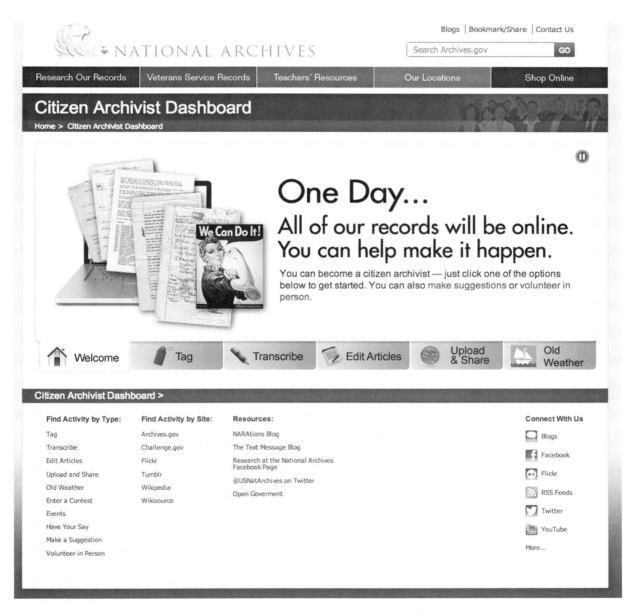

Figure 9-13 National Archives Citizen Archivist Dashboard. National Archives and Records Administration.

discover connections between primary sources. Quizzes are provided that ask the student to analyze a specific resource and then find a related document within the vault. A companion website, *Docs Teach*, offers access to seven tools to create interactive learning activities: Finding a Sequence, Making Connections, Focusing on Details, Interpreting Data, Mapping History, Seeing the Big Picture, and Weighing the Evidence.

Other Projects

Cornell University and the **University of Warwick** (UK) are partnering in a joint project that asks Yiddish speakers from around the world to translate some 1,500 pages of journals and newspapers written in London and New York in the late 19th century for working-class Jewish immigrants.[21] The project was completed in June 2014.

The **Albert Einstein Archives** located at the Hebrew University of Jerusalem contains more than 100,000 documents. These documents were digitized and made accessible on March 19, 2012. In the first few days, the site received more than 21 million hits from some 650,000 unique visitors.[22]

The **Metropolitan Museum of Art** in New York is providing access to 400,000 digital images of public domain works of art that can be downloaded from the Museum's website for noncommercial use.

The **Kansas City Public Library** has developed a wonderful website pertaining to the U.S. Civil War—The Missouri–Kansas Conflict: Civil War on the Western Border. The site encourages you to explore by providing navigation tools that allow you to view of map with links to documents, see a timeline, explore relationships as well as browsing the collection—see Figure 9-14. A related site may be found at the University of Oklahoma's *Transcribing the Past: Civil War Manuscripts*—see Figure 9-12.

The **Scottsdale (AZ) Public Library** partnered with the local historical society to digitize historical photos and provide access to audio files describing the history of many buildings using posted QR codes.

OpenGLAM, an initiative run by the Open Knowledge Foundation, promotes free and open access to digital cultural heritage materials held by galleries, libraries, archives, and museums (visit www.openglam.org). OpenGLAM provides a series of tools that organizations can use to broaden their appeal to a larger audience. For example, *Muse Open Source* is available for rapid publication of native apps in iOS and Android for tablets and smartphones. The *Muse Open Source* has been used to provide access to Europeana collections, the Inventing Europe website, and the Rijksmuseum digital collections.

The Rijksmuseum allows online visitors to create their own studio by selecting and organizing images from the museum's collection, and these studios can then be shared and viewed by others—see Figures 9-9–9-11.

The **9/11 Memorial Museum** has reached out and asked for videos, photographs, and narratives of this historical event in its Make History Project. In addition to creating a much richer and deeper collection, the project is helping the museum create a shared narrative so that visitors can experience the event from a number of unique and quite personal perspectives.[23]

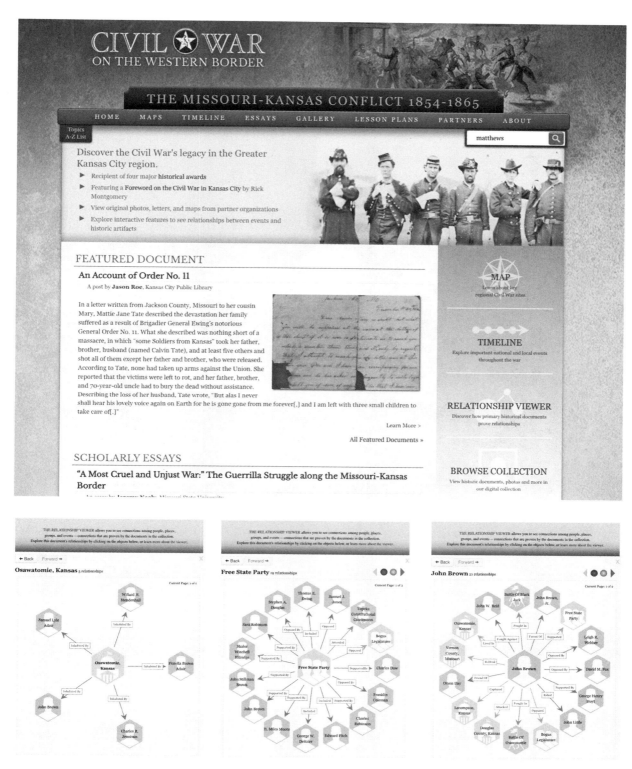

Figure 9-14 Kansas City Public Library website pertaining to the U.S. Civil War.

The Smithsonian is recruiting Digital Volunteers to help transcribe field notes, diaries, ledgers, logbooks, currency proof sheets, photo albums, manuscripts, biodiversity specimen labels, and more. (visit https://transcription.si.edu/).

Tips for Crowdsourcing

Rose Holley has managed a number of collaborative digitization projects in New Zealand, Australia, and England. Based on her experience, she has developed a series of tips for success.[24] These tips include:

Tip 1:   Develop a clear and transparent goal (the goal MUST be a BIG challenge).
Tip 2:   Provide a chart that tracks the progress toward your goal.
Tip 3:   Make the total environment one that is easy to use and intuitive.
Tip 4:   Make the activity easy and fun.
Tip 5:   The project must be interesting.
Tip 6:   Use topical events to encourage participation.
Tip 7:   Add new content/work to keep the site fresh.
Tip 8:   Provide options and choices.
Tip 9:   Ensure that the results/outcomes are visible.
Tip 10: Provide visibility to volunteers (if they opt in).
Tip 11: Encourage competition through the use of volunteer ranking tables.
Tip 12: Facilitate communication among volunteers to build team spirit.
Tip 13: Treat your volunteers with respect.
Tip 14: Assume volunteers will do it right.

Summary

The value of all of this digitized content is considerable and can be demonstrated from several perspectives. The benefits to the research community—both those in the academic arena and the more knowledgeable expert from the general public—all are benefiting from gaining access to this immense digital content. People are able to engage with this digitized content in new and interesting ways without having to travel—in some cases, considerable distances.

Many of these library and museum websites encourage the development and nurturing of a sense of community, as people are able to openly discuss a variety of issues ranging from the content itself to becoming active co-participants in the improvement of the content when people transcribe and/or translate content. Even the smaller and more specialized collections of digital content will find an audience far larger, and more engaged, than most librarians can even imagine.

As librarians, archivists, and museum professionals move to embrace creating value through the engagement of community using collaboration and crowdsourcing activities, they will realize that while they are giving up some control, they are unleashing a tremendous driving force of worldwide community members who wish to actively participate and contribute.

Main idea:	Cultural organizations can use collaborative projects as a means of engaging a larger audience
Opposing view:	Cultural organizations should not relinquish control over content and the quality of that content
Key concepts:	Participation, collaboration, quality of data
What has changed?:	The Internet
Catalyst:	Some projects are so large that the cultural organizations will never have sufficient resources to complete
Open debate:	Quality of the data, how to control participation

Notes

1. Robert Pirsig. *Zen and the Art of Motorcycle Maintenance*. New York: Bantam, 1974, 47.
2. T. Scott Plutchak. "Breaking the Barriers of Time and Space." *Journal of the Medical Library Association*, 100 (1), January 2012, 10–19.
3. Christopher Fleet, Kimberly Kowal, and Petr Pridal. "Georeferencer: Crowdsourced Georeferencing for Map Library Collections." *D-Lib Magazine*, 18 (11/12), December 2012, np.
4. Michael Lascarides and Ben Vershbow. "What's on the Menu?: Crowdsourcing at the New York Public Library," in *Crowdsourcing Our Cultural Heritage*, edited by Mia Ridge. London: Ashgate, 2014, 113–137.
5. Ben Vershbow. "NYPL Labs: Hacking the Library." *Journal of Library Administration*, 53, 2013, 79–96.
6. You can visit Jessica's blog at http://www.nypl.org/voices/blogs/blog-channels/hand-made
7. Jessica Pigza. *Bibliocraft: A Modern Crafter's Guide to Using Library Resources to Jumpstart Creative Projects*. New York: Abrams, 2014.
8. Alexis Madrigal. "What Big Media Can Learn from the New York Public Library." *The Atlantic*, June 21, 2011. Available at http://www.theatlantic.com/technology/archive/2011/06/what-big-media-can-learn-from-the-new-york-public-library/240565/
9. Rose Holley. "Resource Sharing in Australia: Find and Get It in Trove—Making 'Getting' Better." *D-Lib Magazine*, 17 (3/4), March/April 2011. Available at http://www.dlib.org/dlib/march11/holley/03holley.html
10. Tim Sherratt. "Life on the Outside: Collections, Contexts, and the Wild, Wild Web." *Discontents* blog. September 20, 2014. Available at http://discontents.com.au/life-on-the-outside/
11. Olaf Janssen. "Digitizing All Dutch Books, Newspapers and Magazines—730 Million Pages in 20 Years—Storing It, and Getting It Out There." *Research and Advanced Technology for Digital Libraries. Lecture Notes in Computer Science*, 6966, 2011, 473–476.
12. *Business Model Innovation Cultural Heritage*. Amsterdam: The DEN Foundation and Knowledgeland, 2010. Available at http://www.den.nl/art/uploads/files/Publicaties/BusModIn_eng_final.pdf
13. Michelle Springer, Beth Dulabahn, Phil Michel, Barbara Natanson, David Reser, David Woodward, and Helena Zinkham. "For the Common Good: The Library of Congress Flickr Pilot Project." Report Summary. Washington, DC: Library of Congress, October 30, 2008. Available at http://www.loc.gov/rr/print/flickr_report_final_summary.pdf

14. Bray, P. et al. "Rethinking Evaluation Metrics in Light of Flickr Commons," in *Museums and the Web 2011 Proceedings*, edited by J. Trant and D. Bearman. Toronto: Archives & Museum Informatics. Published March 31, 2011. Available at http://conference.archimuse.com/mw2011/papers/rethinking_evaluation_metrics

15. See the Digitalkoot website for more information about the project. Available at http://www.digitalkoot.fi/index_en.html

16. Bruce Sterling. "Digitalkoot, a Game-ified Social Finnish Cultural Endeavor." *Wired*, March 17, 2011. Available at http://www.wired.com/beyond_the_beyond/2011/03/digitalkoot-a-game-ified-crowdsourced-finnish-cultural-endeavor/

17. Kimberly Kowal and Petr Pridal. "Online Georeferencing for Libraries: The British Library Implementation of Georeferencer for Spatial Metadata Enhancement and Public Engagement." *Journal of Map & Geography Libraries: Advances in Geospatial Information, Collections & Archives*, 8:3, 2012, 276–289.

18. For more of the wonderful world of maps, see Simon Garfield's *On the Map: A Mind-Expanding Exploration of the Way the World Looks*. New York: Gotham Books, 2013.

19. Trevor Owens. "Crowdsourcing the Civil War: Insights Interview with Nicole Saylor." *The Signal Digital Preservation* blog. December 6, 2011. Available at http://blogs.loc.gov/digital preservation/2011/12/crowdsourcing-the-civil-war-insights-interview-with-nicole-saylor/

20. Patricia Cohen. "Scholars Recruit Public for Project." *New York Times*, December 17, 2010.

21. For more information, visit transcribe.lib.warwick.ac.uk

22. Dalia Mendelsson and Edith Falk. "The Albert Einstein Archives Digitization Project: Opening Hidden Treasures." *Library Hi Tech*, 32 (2), 2014, 318–335.

23. Sally Ellis. "A History of Collaboration, a Future in Crowdsourcing: Positive Impacts of Cooperation on British Librarianship." *Libri*, 64 (1), 2014, 1–10.

24. Rose Holley. "Crowdsourcing: How and Why Should Libraries Do It?" *D-Lib Magazine*, 16 (4/4), March/April 2010. Available at http://dlib.org/dlib/march10/holley/03holley.html

10

Community

Unrestricted by physical distance, they collaborate with each other
without the direct mediation of money or politics.
Unconcerned about copyright, they give and receive
information without thought of payment.
In the absence of states or markets to mediate social bonds,
network communities are instead formed through
the mutual obligations created by gifts of time and ideas.

Richard Barbrook[1]

The success of the *social media sites such as* Facebook, Twitter, Flickr, Pinterest, YouTube, and a host of other sites is due, in large part, because they really encourage the development and nurturing of a sense of community. And even some of the more popular commercial sites such as *Amazon*, *Apple*, and *Google* have also focused on developing and maintaining a sense of community. And community can be defined in any number of ways aside from the obvious physical and/or virtual/online.

- Communities in the physical sense of the term are residents of a city, municipality, or other unit with some physical limits as to how far people are willing to travel to be a part of a community.

- An online or virtual community develops over time using one of many online tools or platforms. Participation within an online community might be restricted in some way or may be open to everyone. In this arena, geographic limits on users are eliminated, and the cultural organization can welcome an expanded set of supports, contributors, and collaborators. And reaching a larger worldwide community raises interesting questions about financial support and the role of dispersed professionals serving scattered customers.

Academics and other observers have been attempting to understand what people do in an online setting, what motivates people's participation, what the rules of engagement are (they might be explicitly stated, or the participants themselves might develop a set of criteria for acceptable conduct), and why some people actively participate and others simply lurk in the background.

The notion of a platform, especially an open platform, is important in that it allows people to participate in a community in a wide variety of new and interesting ways. Cultural organization's have historically been a place where informational resources and social infrastructures interact under the umbrella of a physical infrastructure.

Platforms have been around for some time. We can consider various technologies (such as landline telephones, fax machines, cell phones, and now the Internet) as providing a platform that allows people to communicate. We can also look at media (e.g., newspapers, radio, and television) as a platform that allows people to consume content—the one-to-many model. And with the Internet, businesses are able to connect with a broader array of consumers, consumers can purchase things and share experiences, and governments can (in theory) connect in new and innovative ways with their citizenry.

Every successful technology platform
has had a thick application catalog around it . . .
Compared to thirty years ago, the difference today is twofold.
First, AppStores and ecosystems are being fueled by entire communities
of hundreds of thousands of mom and pop stores and entrepreneurs.
Second apps today are priced to sell billions of copies
via high-speed downloads. The sheer scale is unprecedented.

Vincent Mirchandani[2]

The Concept of Platform

The whole notion of a platform, especially a platform in the sense of information technology, is that a core infrastructure is developed upon which others can then build, expanding the size and scope of the reach of the original platform. Enlisting others to use their creativity opens the door to a much larger market than if the platform was closed.

When IBM introduced the personal computer, it used off-the-shelf parts and an operating system from Microsoft. And not only did IBM wind up selling millions of PCs, but also a number of other manufacturers' built PC "clones" using those same off-the-shelf parts. This was possible due to the creation of a platform using standardized parts and an operating system that ran on every PC (because Bill Gates insisted on a nonexclusive agreement with IBM). And Microsoft introduced the use of standardized application programming interface or API that allowed other software developers to build on the PC platform and add value for their customers. As the PC platform matured and was beginning to run out of gas, along came a new disruptive innovation that became a new platform—the Internet.

A whole new platform was created when the Internet and the World Wide Web, both of which came with a simple set of rules that allowed programs and websites to cooperate and communicate, with the result that hundreds of thousands of companies were able to grow and prosper. And the Internet platform continues to provide a basis for innovators and inventors to find success.

And when Apple published specifications for its iPhone, it opened up a flood of creative and wonderful apps—from games, stargazing, banking, and so much more—to an even larger group of software developers and ultimately to us. And we are seeing similar innovation with the use of Google's Android operating system (and its family of APIs) that has become a dominant force in the cell phone industry.

The power of the platform and how it can leverage additional, and often exponential, growth can be illustrated by looking at the success of such companies as *Google*, *Amazon*, *Apple*, *Facebook*, *GoodReads*, and *Twitter*. The platform is, in essence, a set of services, tools (often called APIs), and in some cases data that enable independent software developers to create new applications—thus extending the original platform into something bigger and better.

Examining the success of these platforms, it is possible to suggest that there are some lessons for us to learn.

Lesson 1—Start with a simple system and let it grow and evolve. It was, and is, the profoundly simple TCP/IP protocol that has allowed the Internet to grow richer and more complex. Amazon uses a shared services platform that allows its development teams to focus on the user experience and not the underlying infrastructure.

Lesson 2—Openness promotes innovation and growth. When the barriers to entry are low, innovators and inventors are free to create a new future. Designing the underlying infrastructure of any platform is key so that others can build upon it. Rather than a grand scheme, it is better to start with a minimal set of features and functions that are accessible and extensible by others.

Lesson 3—Encourage hackers to play and explore. Eliminate any barriers to experimentation. *Google Maps* has become so popular because an independent programmer found a way to "mashup" street address information with Google Maps and post the resulting new map to a third website. Google subsequently published a Google Maps API to make it easier for others to easily accomplish the same thing, and as a result, almost everyone sees a Google mashup map.

Lesson 4—The goal for any platform is participation. And for people to want to participate, the user experience has to be simple to grasp and it must be effortless to contribute. The more successful websites are those that have embraced the "open by default" option. That is, if you contribute your photos to Flickr, they are accessible to everyone. Post a video to YouTube, and everyone can see it. And once the content has been posted, then anyone can have at it—make comments, add tags, rate it, and so forth.

The popularity of any platform begets even more popularity—which in turn brings about more value and power to the platform. This is a wonderful example of the *network effect*—sometimes known as Metcalfe's law, the value of a network grows exponentially rather than linearly as more people join the network (or platform).

And when something becomes popular on another platform, follow the advice of Charles Colton "Imitation is the sincerest form of flattery."

Lesson 5—Harness the data to make the experience even better; improvement should never stop. Companies such as Google, Amazon, eBay, and many, many more all conduct little experiments several times a day. A small change is made to the system, and data are collected for 5, 10, or 15 minutes, and then the system is returned to its original state. The resulting data are examined to determine whether the user of the site had a better experience (stayed at the site longer, bought more merchandise, explored other options, and so forth). The idea is to embrace experimentation and rapid iteration (or fail fast). Governments, nonprofits, museums, galleries, archives, and libraries could, and in my view, should make their data open and provide an accompanying set of APIs to allow people to explore, create, and share their results. One of the obvious implications of the concept of platform is that libraries will need both hardware (servers) and software programmers (geeks) to innovate and evolve the platforms so that they stay relevant for those living in the community.

Any computer-based platform is obviously going to be composed of both hardware and software. And if libraries are going to extend the concept of platform to those they serve, and libraries will, then it is important for some lateral thinking about hardware and software.

Marcus Westbury wrote an interesting article about urban renewal in which he suggested that the stagnating city of Newcastle, Australia, was the result of both hardware—the buildings, streets, and parks—and software—the planning rules, regulations, real estate systems, traditions, and cultural norms then in place. The solution to promote urban renewal was to "hack" the rules and to find creative solutions that would encourage artists, entrepreneurs, and others to take a chance in the decaying downtown area as a means to revitalize and transform the physicality of the city.[3]

Library as Platform

David Weinberger, a senior researcher at the Harvard Berkman Center for Internet & Society, introduced the notion of the library as platform at a recent ALA Conference and in a *Library Journal* article.[4] David suggests that an open library platform, unlike a portal (the library's website that you pass through to gain access to electronic resources), would be about developing community and knowledge. The platform would:

- Primarily serve a geographically bounded community
- Be open and serve all
- Provide access to a wide variety of content—regardless of format
- Provide links to other valuable resources
- Knowledge is no longer found only in books and other containers but rather is readily accessible via the Internet
- Provide tools that would encourage people to contribute in a wide variety of ways
- Provide resources that encourage others to create and flourish
- Encourage the generation of a knowledge network not simply access to information and knowledge resources
- Enable new products and services to be built

According to Weinberger, the idea of library as platform is to focus more attention on what library resources do in the lives of our users and less on the provisioning of those resources. The value of the platform and of the library will only increase as users contribute their insights, their experiences, their knowledge, and their history to the larger community. And while the existing library data in its integrated library system and other licensed information resources would be a part of the platform, the goal of the platform is to engage a community that is larger than the library currently serves.

And while the library as platform would encourage the same behaviors people currently exhibit while using social networking sites—provide reviews and ratings, add comments, tag items, add content, create and publish lists, and share their expertise—it is also hoped that people will find value being engaged with others about what they are reading, what they are viewing, what blog postings raised an issue or concern, and so forth.

David has suggested that the platform model "focuses our attention away from the provisioning of resources to the foment (the messy, rich networks of people and ideas). We need to focus on how our libraries function as, and as part of, an interconnected set of spatial, intellectual, technological, and social infrastructures."[5]

As an illustration of the power of a community in a networked environment, David cited sites such as *Stack Overflow* that serve software developers. Programmers are willing to share their knowledge with others who are struggling with a specific problem in exchange for the opportunity to learn from others. The learning and sharing of best practices happens in the public eye so that everyone in the community benefits from the sharing of knowledge. Often, the solutions and suggestions of one programmer will lead to a wide-ranging discussion of the many different approaches that can be taken identifying in the process the comparative strengths and weaknesses of each approach. This type of shared knowledge and learning could be happening in libraries—only if we could provide a platform.

Lee Rainie, director of the Pew Research Center Internet Project, asserts that,

> The grand theme is that ubiquitous education and learning rises with ubiquitous computing. Persistent education and learning are the reality as people march through their days with their smartphones and, soon, the Internet of Things embedded everywhere. The library as people, place and platform is the new knowledge institution that can serve all those needs.[6]

Another interesting online community is *Wikipedia*, which simply gets better and bigger over time as people actively involved in the community both improve articles by their iterative editing and add notices that the reader should use caution as a particular page might "need additional citations" or "neutrality is disputed." These quality notices are a red flag that the page needs improvement (which anyone can do) as well as alerting the reader to use caution when considering the content. And the Wiki community has developed a set of both explicit and implicit rules, and as problems have arisen, the community has acted to solve them in a very transparent way so that the best interests of the community are served.

And knowledge arises within a community such as *Wikipedia* because not everyone agrees. As additional perspectives get added, with appropriate citations and indicators of evidence, everyone has the opportunity to learn something and gain additional insights. Libraries have always attempted to have at least two differing perspectives on a particular topic, but in a large online community, there can be tens or hundreds of perspectives and opinions.

One possible unifying concept for a library platform is to create a Library Graph similar to Google's Knowledge Graph or Facebook's Social Graph. The building blocks for these graphs are the sets of quality metadata that are being created as libraries, archives, museums, and galleries are moving to embrace a Resources Description and Access framework that relies on the linked data model. More recently, the Library of Congress has been moving to a new model called BIBFRAME—Bibliographic framework. BIBFRAME differentiates between conceptual content and its physical manifestations, focuses on identifying information entities, and works to expose relationships among and between entities.[7]

A platform provides efficient and effective connectivity so that others can easily create, add, remix, distribute and contribute value to the library platform and ultimately to the community served by the library. The library platform must provide a set of tools (a set of published application programming interface or APIs) so that people will be encouraged to come and contribute. The more people the library is able to attract (by providing access to content and context) the greater the probability that the library platform will serve as a self-fulfilling virtuous circle of adding value. People self organize around platforms that provide value creation with a purpose. The sole purpose of the library platform is the ongoing exchange and cocreation of value.

Facebook is another classic example of a platform where each individual who decides to share content with others adds value. As your circle of friends is recommending a particular book, or movie, or entertainer, or . . ., it is this cumulative action of all these individuals that brings this information to your attention in a proactive manner rather than you asking about X.

A community that develops around a platform also becomes an arena in which serendipity is more likely to occur. Serendipity—the discovery of something we did not know we were looking for—happens in libraries on a regular basis due to the arrangement of materials (items pertaining to a particular topic are located near one another due to the classification system). But serendipity can also occur with people and the knowledge that they have developed over time. And serendipity can be encouraged through the use of amplifiers that help us reach and connect to a larger community.[8] An amplifier relates to the places we visit online (the virtual communities that we are a member of), what conferences and gathering we attend, where we live, and what we do in the social media environment to be an active member of a community (do we blog, use Twitter, have a Facebook page, and so forth). Obviously, any library platform should have a set of tools that encourages developing connections between objects such as books and other materials in a library's collection but also among and between people interested in a particular topic.

Building on the concept of library as platform, Carl Grant has suggested creating a "Knowledge Creation Platform" in an academic library environment. Such a platform will lead to the development of new ideas through the realization of connections between explicit and tacit knowledge in the individual's mind. Carl posits that a "knowledge creation platform would be a place where users could apprehend truth or fact and determine how to solve created or defined problems and then openly communicate those ideas to others."[9] Carl identifies and explores a number of components that might become a part of a Knowledge Creation Platform: discovery; social networking;

librarianship; predictive, proactive library services; tools for creating new knowledge; serendipity and contextual support.

Shana Ratner has suggested that we are moving to a new learning system that radically changes the way in which people learn.[10]

- With the old education system, learning is transactional in nature. Since knowledge is objective and certain, learners receive knowledge. Stable, hierarchical structures are used to organize knowledge. And our "intelligence" is based on our individual abilities.
- In the new education environment, learning is a process. Learners create knowledge that is subjective and provisional. Rather than using a hierarchical system, knowledge is organized "ecologically" (i.e., disciplines are integrative and interactive). And our "intelligence" is based on our learning communities.

David Weinberger goes on to suggest that a platform designed to serve a defined community is best for two reasons. First, most libraries serve a geographically defined community, and thus the library is better able to serve the community it is funded to serve. And, second, the best user networks depend upon local interests, norms, and knowledge.

Some have suggested that a library platform could evolve out of a library's online catalog (OPAC) or a discovery system. However, in my view, a library platform will need to be created with a fresh and broader perspective using current technology tools so that the result will be a platform that will have legs—that is, the resulting platform will be at the start of its life cycle rather than at its end (as is the OPAC). An open platform built for flexibility and with a published set of APIs will, in the long run, perform better for any library compared with a library's OPAC—which is becoming the "court of last resort" when it comes to looking for information.

The University of Utrecht has embarked on a radical departure from the trend of implementing discovery services by consciously deciding to basically ignore discovery and focus on delivery.[11] The implications of this focus on delivery are interesting. The library has acknowledged that users will continue to use Google and has decided not to attempt to compete (a Red Ocean strategy) but rather to adopt a Blue Ocean strategy—don't compete in the area of discovery but rather focus on ways to deliver real value to the library's customers.

Conceiving of the library as platform opens up a world of possibilities (and concerns) as seen in Figure 10-1. Services and tools are provided as a part of the underlying infrastructure. Data and metadata plus links, profiles of community members identifying their interests and expertise, along with a host of other resources provide the content and the context that will be one of the major drivers of the library as platform. A wide range of applications or apps, some developed by the library, but a majority developed by community members are available to all. These apps enable people to develop and maintain links with others who have similar interests or wish to communicate in some manner. And of course all of the activities that a community member might be interested in doing may be found at the top of the figure.

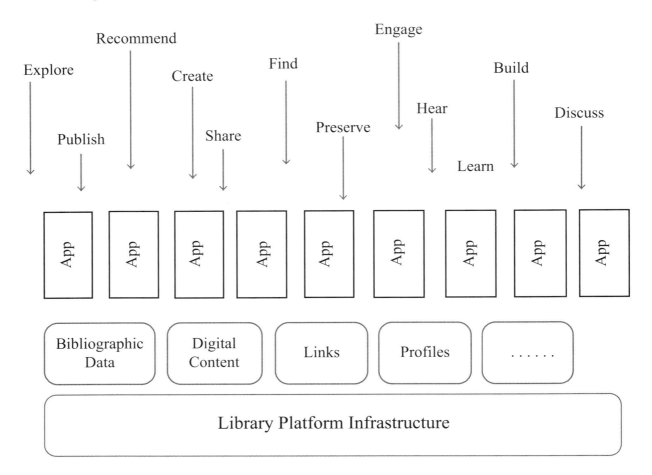

Figure 10-1 Library as Platform.

In an interesting report, the Aspen Institute asserts, "The emerging value proposition of the public library is built around three assets—people, place and platform:"

- *People*—As the hub of civic engagement, the public library fosters new relationships and strengthens the human capital of the community. Librarians facilitate learning and knowledge creation for children and adults alike.
- *Place*—The library is a welcoming space for many purposes—learning, reading, playing, meeting and getting business accomplished. Its physicality provides an anchor for economic development and neighborhood revitalization, and helps reinforce social bonds and community identity.
- *Platform*—The library provides occasions for individuals and the community to gain access to a variety of tools and resources with which to discover and create new knowledge.[12]

The value of the platform will increase as more people are drawn to it and participate in some way. As more people use the platform, the more attractive it will be for software developers to develop new apps. This circle of increasing participation that makes any platform more attractive for software developers has been called a *virtuous circle*. And as the platform grows, its value to the community will also grow in like manner. And it should not be surprising that people will contribute to the library platform in different ways depending upon their interests and talents.

Wikipedia is not an encyclopedia. It is a virtual city,
a city whose main export to the world is its encyclopedia articles,
but with an internal life all of its own.

Michael Nielsen[13]

If the library is providing a community-based platform, then its vision for content must be significantly expanded, and it must embrace and trust the community. If the library places digital content of the history of the community on the platform, then it must provide a set of tools that will allow the community to respond in creative and complimentary ways. Some may want to post digital images of their family's old photos and home movies that relate in some way to the history of the community. Others may want to add comments, tags, ratings, links to related materials, and so forth. The library as platform has the opportunity to become the place that facilitates intergenerational knowledge transfer of family, community, and cultural history. The idea is to facilitate a community's communication and to design a platform that makes interaction with one another in meaningful ways a lot of fun—so much fun that we want to spend hours on the library platform every day.

A library platform will allow people to be:

- *Creators*—Publish their own work as eBooks (and pBooks) whether it is a novel, a work of nonfiction, to a memoir. The work might be text but could also include photos, video, and audio tracks. Authors, artists, and other creative individuals would find a local audience.

- *Activist*—Some people will want to write reviews, comment on other reviews, rate the work of others, add tags, publish list, pin items of interest, write a blog, post pictures on Flickr, and so forth. The library platform could have links to all of the creative output of a community so that it would be visible to all. I am sure that people would be surprised and amazed at the creative knowledge and contributions to social media that are made daily by the nearly "invisible" members of a specific community.

- *Conversationalist*—Many members of a community would be thrilled to share their thoughts and observations with others about what they are reading, seeing, and hearing on the library platform. These conversations historically have taken place within the context of a Book Discussion Club, but many more conversations could be happening if the infrastructure of the library platform was in place.

- *Geeks*—Some software developers would be thrilled to develop local apps using the tools, the infrastructure, and the data made accessible using APIs provided by the library platform. Eli Neiburger at the Ann Arbor District Library, Michigan, has argued that libraries should be hiring geeks to help take care of the large servers and other IT hardware and software that will be needed to control the library's digital distribution infrastructure.[14]

The other interesting aspect of the library as platform is that it changes the criteria for success. Rather than focusing on the traditional library output measures (keeping track of how busy the library is), the library can actually use the community itself to help identify and articulate the value of the library as platform. In the end, what matters is what impact do library resources and services have in the lives of their customers. Once the library as platform becomes operational, the platform ceases to "belong" to the library, and the new owners are the community members themselves. In a sense, they become the library since the library is theirs.

Thomas Frey has spoken recently about the future of the library and suggested that libraries should become "liquid networks—a breeding ground for future ideas." Frey suggested that ideas, similar to a parasite, need a host that will extend their shelf life. If libraries can provide a platform for people to share and shape ideas, they will evolve and grow and somehow reach a critical mass. Libraries can play a critical role by building and sustaining liquid networks of ideas that will spark the creativity in others.[15]

In an interesting blog post, Hugh Rundle suggests that libraries should be a "platform for enabling innovation, learning and cultural development to occur in our communities without the need for capital."[16] So rather than focusing on the stuff found in libraries, the engaged community is focused on ideas and learning through conversation that is started and nurtured as people share, discuss, remix, rewrite, and reinvent concepts and physical objects. Craig Watkins has argued that:

> To a significant degree, the knowledge economy gives birth to the creation economy, a free-agent economy in which opportunities for lifelong learning must be abundant and people need skills as knowledge creators, not simply information consumers. Importantly, these learning opportunities must be present throughout the community and persistent throughout a lifetime.[17]

Several years ago, the Hartford (CT) Public Library recognized that citizens and decision makers often did not have access to information that would be relevant to a variety of topics that were important to the community. Typically, the data needed to be accessed and limited to specific neighborhoods, zip codes, block or street level. As a result, the library created HartfordInfo.Org, and this website allowed individuals to select specific data set, specific areas of the city, or a particular topic.[18] The site was heavily used, and it was fairly easy to navigate and to view (and download) the available data in a variety of ways. Data Driven Detroit is another great example of one component of what a library platform could be (visit http://datadrivendetroit.org/).

In many ways, we have come full circle with the notion of the library as platform if the concept of knowledge creation is important. David Lankes has suggested for several years that

The mission of librarians is to improve society through facilitating knowledge creation in their communities.

So, if you embrace the mission of librarians as espoused by Lankes (as I do), then this would suggest that librarians need to be doing radically different things in a library than what they have been doing for the last few years (few decades). The time to embrace change is now to reposition the library as a platform for the community. Librarians can help build the new library (as a platform) if we are willing to let go and to let our users be cocreators, coinventors, and collaborators in this new big thing!

In the olden days, libraries owned "things," and these things were shared as a mechanism for economic efficiency—save the money of the user. Now in the digital world, collaboration is central, contributions are encouraged (blogs, tweets, share photos and videos, post content to Facebook, and so forth), and people recognize that sharing adds value for everyone.

Gobinda Chowdhury, Alan Poulter, and David McMenemy have suggested that libraries should embrace Ranganathan's famous five principles (with a slight twist). The twist is that libraries should become actively involved with their communities so that all "community knowledge" is accessible and that libraries provide tools for creating, finding, storing, making available, and preserving "community knowledge."[19] This means moving from a model of classification, organization, and curation to the cocreating, cosharing, and cocuration model of knowledge.

———————

*A library in the middle of a community is a cross
between an emergency exit, a life raft, and a festival.
They are cathedrals of the mind; hospitals of the soul;
theme parks of the imagination.
On a cold, rainy island, they are the only sheltered public spaces
where you are not a consumer, but a citizen, instead . . .
A mall—the shops—are places where your money
makes the wealthy wealthier.
But a library is where the wealthy's taxes pay for you
to become a little more extraordinary, instead.*

Caitlin Moran[20]

———————

The Physical Library Platform

Historically, libraries have embraced the concept of programs as a means of growing and nurturing a sense of community. Imagine a group of people gathered together linked by a common bond—the focus of today's program. The program might be aimed at very young children, teens, adults, seniors, and so forth who are interested in a story time puppet show, learning to use the latest social media website, attending an author's talk, discussing a best seller at a monthly meeting of a book club, hearing several political candidates discuss their positions, learning about investments, and so many more topics. The end result is that these people have the opportunity to interact with one another and, over time, develop relationships.

Any library, but especially public libraries, has the opportunity to use the "library as place" as a way to help engender the library as a community asset. And it is important to focus on the fact that libraries offer knowledge, information, and learning to a community, often using innovative methods. In this way, libraries serve as the center of a community, which is much more than being a "community center." Public libraries are viewed as trusted and safe spaces for people of all ages. Libraries serve as a neutral space allowing diverse points of view to be shared and discussed. And importantly libraries have the opportunity to be advocates for intellectual freedom values day in and day out.

One library repurposed space with the intent that the design would encourage collaboration and open sharing. The space, called "The Edge," provided collaborative lounge space, computer, and audio recording studios.[21] People used the space in three different ways:

- *To access technology resources* for free that otherwise is too expensive to buy by one individual.
- *For coworking* with individuals and groups.
- *For the informal learning environment* as a result of library-organized workshops, presentations, hackathons, exhibits, and similar events. And it was primarily through library-organized events that collaboration and sharing really occurred.

Other libraries have used outdoor space to create community gardens with the library providing space, water, and plot sign-ups. Those who are participating then organize themselves into teams, create schedules, and establish policies. Other libraries partner with other community organizations such as CompuGirls—a program that teaches girls about technology, software, and social justice. The library provides space and technology, and the partner provides the instructors and encouragement to the participating girls.

Embracing community also means recognizing that buildings can be thoughtfully designed so that tranquility, clamor, and noise levels in-between can peacefully coexist. Some libraries have decided to group noisy activities on the bottom levels, while the quieter areas are located near the top of the building.[22] For any library to embrace community, it needs to recognize that it will need to organize its staff and budget in new ways so that the library can respond to opportunities as they arise.

Value Creation

The value created in communities and networks is associated with the learning enabled by community networking and the networks people inhabit. We can focus on the value created when community members are sharing information, best practices (sometimes called tips for success), documents, assisting each other with challenges, learning from the experiences of one another, creating knowledge, stimulating conversations and change, and offering new opportunities for learning.

One interesting suggestion for articulating this value is to consider cycles of value creation:

- *Cycle 1. Immediate Value: Activities and Interactions*
    The activities and interactions of participants *provide* value in and of themselves. Someone might assist with a challenge, answer a question, or provoke

a discussion about possible solutions to a problem. Collaboration among participants leads to insights and can be fun and inspiring.

- *Cycle 2. Potential Value: Knowledge Capital*

    Not all of the value in a networked community is immediately realized. The resulting knowledge capital can take different forms:

    - Human capital—personal assets
    - Social capital—relationships and connections
    - Tangible capital—resources
    - Reputational capital—collective intangible assets
    - Learning capital—transformed ability to learn.

- *Cycle 3. Applied Value: Changes in Practice*

    Since knowledge capital is a potential value it must be adapted and applied in a specific situation at some future moment in time. Applying knowledge capital can lead to innovations as well as changes in practice, approaches and systems.

- *Cycle 4. Realized Value: Performance Improvement*

    While it is possible to assume that the application of new ideas have lead to improvements in performance it is important to determine how performance has actually changed.

- *Cycle 5. Reframing Value: Redefining Success*

    And a final cycle of value creation can be achieved when people reconsider the criteria by which success is defined.[23]

Summary

Cultural organizations matter in different ways in each community they serve. The key is identifying the range of services that will appeal to different market segments of the community and to provide excellent customer service to each segment. Each library must engage in an ongoing process to re-imagine itself as a community organization with a unique and essential role.

The Netherlands Institute for Public Libraries has recently published a report about the future of the public library that stressed less collection and more connection.[24] The report suggested more connection in four important ways:

- *Connecting people and information*—the library as a portal to knowledge
- *Connecting people to other people*—library as platform
- *Connecting the community to itself*—library as societal heart
- *Connecting information sources*—information in context.

The *Communities-Led Libraries Toolkit* provides a host of suggestions for staff members to reach out and engage various segments of a community that will result in developing more inclusive public libraries.[25]

Back in 2010, when a little more than 2 billion people were connected to the Internet, Clay Shirky in *Cognitive Surplus* suggested that about a trillion hours of free time were being used for civic engagement, learning, and community action. By the time we reach 2020, perhaps as many as 5 billion people will be online with the result that some 4 to 5 trillion hours of free time will be available each year to accomplish a wide variety of tasks and activities. This represents a HUGE opportunity for libraries, archives, museums, and galleries to engage this online community in ways that will benefit the cultural institutions directly, but more importantly, it offers us the chance to engage with a much larger worldwide community of people who are longing for opportunities to both make contributions of value and benefit from their engagement.

Remember that the organizations that are able to craft and deliver a "unique value proposition" are organizations that are going to thrive and provide real value in the lives of their customers. Value is both immediate and long term. A customer-focused sustaining organization works to deliver value that provides immediate benefits as well as long-term cumulative impacts. Continually investing in platforms that deliver real value is going to be critical to long-term success.

Checklist for Adding Value Using Community

	Yes	No
Has your cultural organization identified segments of the community in which it might engage with a larger online audience?	☐	☐
Has your cultural organization considered the concept of "institution as platform"?	☐	☐
Has your cultural organization explored ways in which it might leverage its physical space to become the "physical platform" in your community?	☐	☐
Has your cultural organization identified ways to deliver value to different market segments that are both immediate and long term?	☐	☐

If you answered "no" to one or more of the questions in the checklist, then your library is not doing all it could to add value using community.

Main idea:	Engaging with the community is essential for cultural organizations to thrive
Opposing view:	Professionals should continue to "hang out" in the cultural organization
Key concepts:	Conversations, connecting, communicating, listening, engaging, changing
What has changed?:	The people we serve (or should be serving)
Catalyst:	The Internet
Open debate:	To what degree should professionals "leave" the cultural organization in order to engage with the community?

Notes

1. Richard Barbrook. "The Hi-Tech Gift Economy." *First Monday*, December 2005. Available at http://firstmonday.org/ojs/index.php/fm/article/view/1517/1432
2. Vincent Mirchandani. Quoted in Phil Simon. *The Age of the Platform: How Amazon, Apple, Facebook, and Google Have Redefined Business.* New York: Motion publishing, 2011, 212.
3. Marcus Westbury. "Cities as Software." *Volume*, May 23, 2011. Available at http://www.marcuswestbury.net/2011/05/23/cities-as-software/
4. David Weinberger. "Library as Platform: Creating an Infrastructure for the Circulation of Ideas and Passions." *Library Journal*, 137 (18), November 1, 2012, 34–36.
5. Shannon Mattern. *Library as Infrastructure. Places*, June 2014. Available at https://placesjournal.org/article/library-as-infrastructure/
6. Lee Rainie. Quoted in Amy Garmer. *Rising to the Challenge: Re-Envisioning Public Libraries.* Washington, DC: The Aspen Institute, October 2014, 9.
7. Library of Congress. *Bibliographic Framework as a Web of Data: Linked Data Model and Supporting Services.* Washington, DC: Library of Congress, November 21, 2012. Available at http://www.loc.gov/bibframe/pdf/marcld-report-11-21-2012.pdf
8. John Hagel, John Brown, and Lang Davison. *The Power of Pull: How Small Moves, Smartly Made, Can Set Big Things in Motion.* New York: Basic Books, 2010.
9. Carl Grant. *Knowledge Creation Platforms: The Next Step after Web-Scale Discovery.* 1 (2), 2013, *027.7* blog. Available at http://www.0277.ch/ojs/index.php/cdrs_0277/article/view/32/78
10. Shana Ratner. *Emerging Issues in Learning Communities.* St. Albans, VT: Yellow Wood Associates, 1997.
11. Simone Kortekass. *Thinking the Unthinkable: A Library without a Catalogue—Reconsidering the Future of Discovery Tools for Utrecht University Library.* Presentation at the LIBER Conference 2012. Available at http://www.uksg.org/librarycatalogue
12. Aspen Institute Dialogue on Public Libraries. *Rising to the Challenge: Re-Envisioning Public Libraries.* Washington, DC: The Aspen Institute, October 2014.
13. Michael Nielsen. *Reinventing Discovery: The New Era of Networked Science.* Princeton: Princeton University Press, 2011, 54.
14. Michael Kelley. "Geeks Are the Future: A Program in Ann Arbor, MI Argues for a Resource Shift Toward IT." *Library Journal*, April 26, 2011. Available at http://lj.libraryjournal.com/2011/04/technology/geeks-are-the-future-a-program-in-ann-arbor-mi-argues-for-a-resource-shift-toward-it/#_
15. Thomas Frey. "The Future Library—A Liquid Network for Ideas." August 12, 2014. *FuturistSpeaker.com* blog. Available at http://www.futuristspeaker.com/2014/08/the-future-library-a-liquid-network-for-ideas/
16. Hugh Rundle. "Libraries as Software—Dematerializing, Platforms and Returning to First Principles." *Information Flaneur* blog. April 4, 2012. Available at http://www.hughrundle.net/2012/04/04/libraries-as-software-dematerialising-platforms-and-returning-to-first-principles/
17. S. Craig Watkins. *The Young and the Digital: What the Migration to Social Network Sites, Games, and Anytime, Anywhere Media Means for Our Future.* New York: Beacon Press, 2010, 74.
18. Matt Poland. "Hartford Public Library's Innovation: HartfordInfo.Org." *Huff Post Tech*, May 1, 2104. Available at http://www.huffingtonpost.com/matt-poland/hartford-public-library-_b_775441.html

19. Gobinda Chowdhury, Alan Poulter and David McMenemy. Public Library 2.0: Towards a New Mission for Public Libraries as a "Network of Community Knowledge." *Online Information Review*, 30 (4), 2006, 454-460.
20. Caitlin Moran. "Libraries: Cathedrals of Our Souls." *The Huffington Post*, November 14, 2012. Available at http://www.huffingtonpost.com/caitlin-moran/libraries-cathedrals-of-o_b_2103362.html
21. Mark Bilandzic and Marcus Foth. "Libraries as Coworking Spaces: Understanding User Motivations and Perceived Barriers to Social Learning." *Library Hi Tech*, 31 (2), 2013, 254–273.
22. Shannon Mattern. "Resonant Texts: Sounds of the American Public Library." *Senses & Society*, 2 (3), 2007, 277–302.
23. Etienne Wenger, Beverly Trayner, and Maarten de Last. *Promoting and Assessing Value Creation in Communities and Networks: A Conceptual Framework*. Rapport 18. Amsterdam: Ruud de Moor Centrum, Open University, 2011. Available at https://www.ou.nl/documents/14300/23cd8044-ce98-48d3-8733-8fa0404380ab
24. The Netherlands Institute for Public Libraries. *The Library of the Future: Hub for Knowledge, Contact and Culture*. The Hague: The Netherlands Institute for Public Libraries, 2014.
25. Sandra Singh. *Community-Led Libraries Toolkit*. Vancouver, BC: Working Together Project, Vancouver Public Library, 2008.

11

Stepping Up—To Lead

. . . why are libraries struggling so hard today?
My feeling is that as librarians, we've lost our focus.
We've let the technology, the collections accessed,
and even our buildings define us.
And that has been very, very unfortunate for our profession.

Carl Grant[1]

Having explored the five ways (the 5Cs) libraries, museums, galleries, and archives can create increasing value in the preceding chapters, it is time to note that we have come full circle. If GLAM institutions really want to add value and retain relevance in the life of their customers, then these organizations will need to embrace change. And the change that is needed is not the incremental or evolutionary change that is occurring around the edges of our profession but rather something that more closely resembles revolutionary change.

Yet, cultural organizational professionals as leaders face a real dilemma confronting change. As Clayton Christensen has explained so well, established organizations are almost always unable to confront disruptive change since their more important customers are not interested in change. And cultural organizations of all types have a long history of serving their most important customers well and thus have difficulty even in recognizing that disruptive change is all about us.

Assisting in the process of creating transformational libraries are leaders who:

- Inspire all members of an organization to achieve more than they thought possible.
- Empower staff members to embrace change and translate intention into action (empowerment leads to more empowerment).
- Communicate a clear vision so that staff willingly embrace change that leads to achieving the organizational mission.
- Are passionate about their responsibilities and obligations to staff. In short, the transformational leader exhibits these characteristics in a natural and compelling manner.[2]

The challenge cultural organization leaders face is how do we move from a conventional mind-set of what an organization is and does toward a institution that is willing to embrace innovation and experimentation in order that it might have a more significant role in the life of its customers. In many ways, the challenges cultural organizations face are not any more difficult than that traditional businesses are facing from start-ups that are willing to leverage all of the advantages that the Internet has to offer. These new start-ups focus on the unique and distinctive ways that they can add value in the life of their customers and not to feel constrained by the traditions of either an industry or the existing cost structures found in the older and more traditional firms.

Philip Kotler has urged not-for-profit and government organizations to engage in a three-step value creation and delivery sequence:[3]

- *Choose the value*—Understanding the market through segmentation, selecting market targets (who the cultural organization wishes to focus on), and developing a unique value proposition for each target market segment.[4]
- *Provide the value*—deliver the services that have real value for each of the targeted market segments.
- *Communicate the value*—the value proposition must be communicated to the targeted market segments in ways that will resonate with each market segment.

Cultural organization leaders, board members, community and campus stakeholders, and customers must recognize that while we are involved in planning the future of the organization, we must address a number of important topics along the way. Using a business model (discussed in Chapter 1) can assist a cultural organization in better understanding the likely impacts of a proposed new business model.

If we are busy considering and adopting new ways of adding value, one obvious question arises, "What is the value we think we are creating in the lives of our users?"

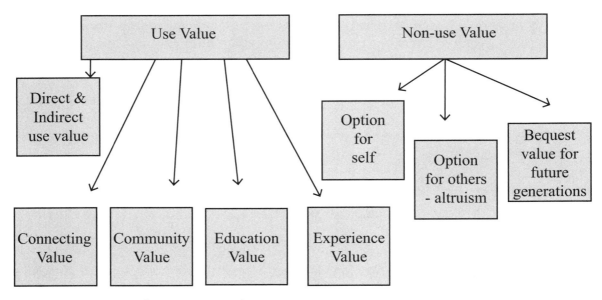

Figure 11-1 Use and Non-Use Values.

Using categories based on a number of articles plus my own experience, I would suggest that it is possible to identify six different perspectives for considering value as shown in Figure 11-1:[5]

- *Use or utility value*—Accessing physical and/or digital resources can add real value in someone's life.
- *Community value*—Providing access to collections for customers of GLAM institutions is an important value that provides a bridge between the past, present, and future. People value being a part of a community that is afforded the opportunity to interact with online and physical resources.
- *Education value*—GLAM institutions also serve as learning environments, especially when they explain and interpret the present and the future by means of materials gathered from the past.
- *Connecting value*—People benefit from knowing that they have the opportunity to connect with others, whether they live in or outside a specific community, using the resources available within an institution (the collections) as well as communicating about their experiences with others.
- *Experience value*—People value the option of sharing family resources, passed from one generation to another, to a broader audience by donating resources to libraries, museums, galleries, and archives.
- *Non-use value*—This can be considered as an option value (the option for you or others to use at some point in the future) as well as a possible bequest value.

Communicating Value

Developing an ongoing relationship with stakeholders is crucial to the long-term success of the library. A stakeholder can provide support or drive a stake through the heart of the library (especially at budget time).

Telling a story, in particular telling an effective story, about the value of the cultural organization is an important tool for any professional to develop. One great resource is the toolkit developed by Michael Margolis that can be downloaded for free (visit GetStored.com).[7]

Professionals can improve on the way in which they communicate the value of the cultural organization to their stakeholders. More often than not, a cultural organization will attempt to communicate value using cultural organization and/or information technology jargon that is simply meaningless to the stakeholder.

Often, the message being communicated focuses on an aspect of the collection or service (oftentimes called a feature). A feature can be thought of as something that is provided by the cultural organization, while a benefit is what the customer gets as a result of using the product or service (with its many features). And people (and organizations) buy benefits—not features.

One helpful exercise is to examine the cultural organization's marketing materials, and for each sentence or bullet point, ask yourself, "Is this a feature or a benefit?" If the sentence does not describe a benefit from the user's perspective, then it likely is a feature. Rewrite the sentence until it describes a benefit. This will do much in helping the cultural organization communicate its value.

Carol Scott has suggested that it is important to identify and discuss three types of value. A cultural organization's collections and services have a range of intrinsic value (the set of values that relate to the subjective experience of use intellectually, emotionally, and spiritually) for both an individual and the community; instrumental value (the value achieved through use of collections and services) for the individual and the community; and institutional value for the community—especially creating public value.[6]

Respond to Customer Needs

Knowing your customers is key since the customer's definition of "value" is going to change over time. And to better understand how customers interact with information and make decisions about whether to use (or not use) cultural organization services means that professionals must get out of the cultural organization's and observe and interact with customers where (and when) they are working.

Understanding your customers means recognizing that each cultural organization's has many different types of users. Dividing the cultural organization's customers up into different categories, called market or customer segmentation within the marketing arena, is one very effective way of better understanding your customers. Assuming the cultural organization obtains the name, snail mail address, and email address for each individual, the cultural organization can use these data, in combination with other data sources, to construct differentiating and interesting market segments.

The cultural organization needs to be able to answer some very specific questions about their customers and noncustomers for each market segment. Among the more important questions are:

- Who is visiting the physical space?
- Who is using the cultural organization's website?
- Who is logging in to use eResources?
- How frequently does each customer visit the physical and virtual organization?
- Where in the physical space do they visit (and ignore)?
- What type of materials does each customer borrow (and disregard)?
- What type of customer attends cultural organization programs?
- Which materials are most frequently used (high turnover rates)?
- Which materials are never used?
- What is each market segment hoping to accomplish when they visit the cultural organization's?

Gina Millsap, CEO of the Topeka and Shawnee County (KS) Public Library, recognized that it was possible to group customers into market segments. Armed with this information, she felt that it would be possible to learn in greater detail about the characteristics of each segment and how each group used the library. Partnering with *CIVICTechnologies* who correlated anonymized library usage data with marketing segmentation data, the library learned that many of the assumptions that they made about different market segments were not aligned with reality.[8] For example, the assumption had been made that rural customers were more interested in DVD movies than books, while the data revealed the reverse is true.[9]

The library's integrated library system (ILS) can be set to capture a copy of each transaction (stripping out the unique identifying information), which can then be analyzed. The library's circulation transaction data become the foundation for the *collectionHQ* service that analyzes these data and then makes recommendations about what specific titles and types of materials to order (and discard) for each branch location. The *collectionHQ* materials purchasing recommendations, when tracked over time, will reveal that the library collection-related resources are being used in the wisest possible manner (more time in the hands of customers and less time on shelves).

The library's ILS system can generate a set of reports that identify who is using the library as well as what portion of the collection is being used and what is not. A librarian needs to spend time to learn how to print/view the reports and then to use them

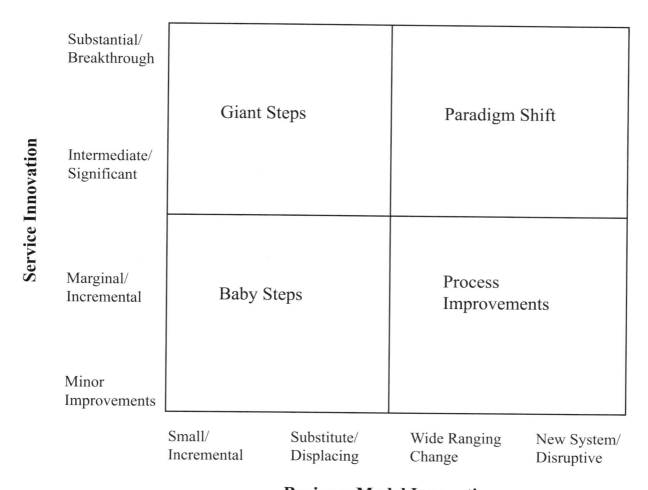

Business Model Innovation

Figure 11-2 Service and Business Model Innovation.

in a consistent manner, and they will be able to achieve results that are similar to what *collectionHQ* provides.

Remember that the goal of all the data gathering and analysis is *insight* into what market segments are using the library and why they are doing so. It is also important to recognize that the amount of service innovation can range from quite small to substantial, while at the same time, the amount of business model innovation an organization is willing to consider will span a considerable distance as seen in Figure 11-2.

Rethink

When Pam Sandlian-Smith was being interviewed for the library director's position at the Rangeview Library District in Adams County, Colorado (now the Anythink Libraries), she informed the interview team that she was passionate about libraries as she had a "shoot for the moon" attitude and would welcome the opportunity to design, implement, and operate a thriving world-class public library.[10]

Pam was fortunate in that she inherited a progressive management team that welcomed the opportunity to embrace innovation. The result is an award-winning series of libraries and their associated services that are focused on the customer—the Anythink Libraries received the 2010 National Medal from the Institute of Museum and Library Service. The goal for all Anythink Libraries staff members is to make the user experience delightful, intuitive, and comfortable.

To say that Anythink is willing to "rethink" just about everything would be a mild understatement. Consider

- *Library shelving*—Given that a majority of people entering the library would prefer to browse the collection (they typically do not have a specific title in mind), the libraries have embraced merchandising with bookstore-style shelving—titles are placed face out. Display furniture and merchandising spaces provide thematic zones to develop high-profile displays that appeal to customer interests. The collections of circulating books and other materials are the most visible attribute of a rewarding experience to library visitors. The merchandising of library materials is achieved through:

  o *Consistency*—All the branches follow the same merchandising practices so that visitors will have a similar experience regardless of the location they visit.
  o *Flexibility*—Displays that work (materials are borrowed) are retained while those that don't are quickly changed.
  o *Timeliness*—The time of year is an important factor in determining what displays to use—holidays, elections, planting of a garden, outdoor cooking, and so forth.
  o *Positioning*—The use of display shelves, display tables, shelf ends, end caps, and so forth helps create a themed neighborhood.

- *Dewey or don't we*—Rather than continuing to use the traditional Dewey classification system, Anythink made a major shift by using bookstore words as a foundation and has created a word-based classification system—WordThink (a guide that maps Dewey to WordThink can be downloaded from the Anythink website). Large colorful signs help wayfinding and assist in creating topical "neighborhoods."

- *Job titles*—Rather than continuing to use standard and staid job position titles, Anythink invented some interesting new job titles.

    o *Wranglers*—Called shelving assistants, pages or material handlers in many libraries, help keep the shelves neatly arranged, facing out titles where appropriate, and fill in gaps to keep the shelves looking fresh.

    o *Concierges*—Welcome people as they enter the library, ensure that display signage is in place, and assist in keeping the shelves "fluffed" (looking neat).

    o *Guides*—Typically but not always librarians, have a variety of responsibilities including reaching out to the community, coordinating system-wide merchandising displays, connecting customers to the information they seek, a trainer and program coordinator at the branch, and a natural born leader.

The Anythink staff manifesto, as seen in Figure 11-3, acknowledges that staff is part wizard, part genius, and part explorer. Anythink staff is hired primarily for their smile (take delight in providing caring and helpful assistance to visitors) rather than their existing job skills. And a staff member is easy to identify as they all wear a bright orange lanyard and name tag.

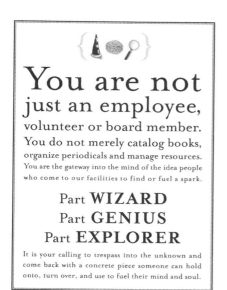

Figure 11-3 Anything Staff Manifesto. Courtesy of Anythink Libraries.

- *What? No fines.* Rather than employing fines, Anythink uses a series of friendly worded reminders to get people to return materials to the library. Fees are charged for lost items.
- *SHHH is a four-letter word.* Each Anythink library is designed to accommodate people with various tolerances for noise. There are quiet zones and spaces for conversation, story times, technology labs, and so forth.
- *Anythink brand.* The libraries created a vibrant and nontraditional name for themselves—Anythink—along with a logo that some think is a doodle, some a pile of spaghetti, or the logo can be anything you want it to be. Fun! The intent is to create a cohesive brand with a consistent look, style, and presentation (no hand-lettered signs!). Libraries need to do something dramatic. And while marketing usually focuses on features and benefits, creating an emotional connection between your brand and your customers is ultimately what marketing is all about.
- *Play inspires creativity and lifelong learning.* Anythink believes that play is the spirit that drives a curious mind. The library has developed a culture where everyone chips in and "barn raising" teams are used to accomplish some of the bigger tasks among all the libraries. More importantly, a team called the Yellow Geckos works to sustain a culture of optimism by organizing hikes, snowshoeing outings, wellness programs, karaoke night, and the annual bowling tournament (complete with silly team names and costumes).
- *Customer service.* Hospitality is the library's hallmark inspired by putting customers first. Anythinkers (staff) provide high-quality customer service to ensure that their needs are met.
- *Designing spaces for people* rather than focusing on space planning (allocating space for books, tables, chairs, and so forth) is what keeps people coming back time after time. Bookshelves are organized in small clusters rather than straight rows, and overall, the focus is on flexibility and openness.

Well, we could go on and on by examining all of the assumptions librarians make about what a library is, or could be, or should be. Libraries must begin to rethink the future of the library by releasing the shackles of focusing on the internal workings of the library and embracing some out-of-the-box customer-focused thinking.

The **Howard County Library System** in Maryland asserts, "we deliver high-quality education for all ages." Under the leadership of Valerie Gross, the library has partnered with local schools and the community colleges under the banner of "A+ Partners in Education" and delivers education under a curriculum that consists of three pillars:[11]

- Self-directed education
- Research assistance and instruction
- Instructive and enlightening experience

To assist in conveying the message of the value of the library, Gross has traded library jargon for words that everyone can understand.

Instead of	*the Library uses*
Library director	President and CEO
Librarian/Library associate	Instructor/Research specialist
Circulation clerk	Customer service specialist
Programs	Curriculum
Story time	Children's class
Emergent Literacy	Childhood Education
Register	Enroll
Help/Serve/Reach	Enhance/Advance/Teach

Clearly, this approach is resonating with the community. Borrowing of materials has doubled, research interactions are greater, physical visits increased to three million while virtual visits jumped to six million, and attendance at classes also increased.[12] Using education as the linchpin for all that it does has proven to work in the Howard County Library System and in other public libraries across the United States and in Canada.

The **Richland Library** in Columbia, South Carolina, is working to remake its space into a "studio," in which the focus is on a community that is engaged in making, consuming, practicing talents, uncovering passions, exploring ideas, and being innovative. The goal is to remodel the central library and a number of branches so that spaces designed to facilitate content creation also provide space for content presentation.[13]

As a group, libraries are terribly inefficient. Libraries replicate so many services, as a sector, all in the name of being responsive to our unique communities and their needs. In reality, libraries are much more alike than they are dissimilar. Libraries can gain efficiencies by identifying activities that add little or no value and either eliminate them or pay another organization to perform them. Consortia (or outsourcing options) exist because they can perform an activity faster, better, or cheaper than a library can do so on its own. Lorcan Dempsey, vice-president of research at OCLC, has called for libraries to consider moving some services that libraries currently do on their own to a consortium. Many libraries are placing some portions (often significant portions) of their collections in a shared book storage facility. Others are moving to share ILSs—often cloud-based—that involve a large number of libraries.

Transaction costs are those costs associated with arranging for another organization to do something you would rather not do (e.g., you might contract with a firm to clean your organization nightly). The Internet and its many services have allowed organizations to significantly reduce transaction costs—consider the success of Netflix and the demise of Blockbuster. This reality of lower transaction costs on the net raises some important questions:

- What traditional services can we externalize (shift to another organization)? Typically, any service that is externalized provides little value to the customer.
- What type of organization should a cultural organization consider when shifting a service to an external provider—for-profit, consortium, a specialized organization (delivery service provider), and so forth?

In my view, there is a huge disconnect between what institutions *could do* online and what they *do* online that in many ways is reflected by the clothesline paradox, a term coined by Steve Baer to describe how activities that can be easily measured (drying your clothes in a dryer) are valued over something that is difficult to measure (drying your clothes outside on a line—the energy saved disappears from our accounting).[14] In the same way, cultural institutions typically measure and report door counts, journal articles published by our faculty, and number of downloads over the perhaps more meaningful (but certainly more difficult to measure) activities such as the sharing of institutional content on social media sites.

Recently, Steve Denning suggested that organizations need to ask five important questions:[15]

1. How can we delight our users and customers? Continuing to operate as vertical bureaucracies will ensure libraries won't have the institutional smarts to determine what users really want.
2. How can we manage the library to enable continuous innovation? This will require managers to become enablers using horizontal conversations.
3. What will make things better, faster, cheaper, more mobile, more convenient, or more personalized for our users? The key is to focus on how to make things better for the user.
4. What needs could cultural organizations meet that users haven't even thought of? Organizations need to explore new ways of delivering services where the user is (and users are spending an increasing amount of time online).
5. What are the things that cultural organizations are currently doing that users already love? Whatever users love, cultural organizations need to figure out how to do them better, more conveniently by providing more personalization.

An even more important question might be

If we were asked to invent a cultural organization today, would it look anything like the cultural organizations that are around us?

And while I would hope for a dramatic departure from what we typically find in a library, museum, or archive today in this newly "invented cultural organization," many (and perhaps most) professionals would likely "invent" something that they are familiar and comfortable with. When any cultural organization begins the journey of rethinking what the organization could be, the real focus needs to be on answering the question: "How does the cultural organization add value in the life of each customer?"

Funding Perspective

Stakeholders in the public arena responsible for allocating funds raised from tax payers typically want to ensure that the taxpayer receives value for the monies any public agency is allocated. The funding stakeholders must budget competing requests for funds from a variety of departments that typically provide a broad range of services—

police, fire, parks, libraries, water and sewer, streets and so on. More often than not these funding stakeholders are concerned about transparency to ensure that public funds are not misused.

A different funding perspective has been adopted by a large number of philanthropists and corporations who provide funds to not-for-profit community organizations over the last two decades. These individuals are much like people who invest in a organization and are interested in knowing their likely return on investment or ROI. Note that the return on an investment does not necessarily mean some kind of financial consideration. In short, these individuals are interested in learning about the likely outcomes for their investment—learning new job skills, improved literacy, or getting a job. Most investors ask:

- What changes or outcomes are expected for what segments of the population?
- How does your organization propose to achieve these outcomes?
- Has your organization developed a logic model for the planned outcomes?
- How does your proposed service add long-term value in the life of those who receive the service?
- What changes are needed in terms of organizational capacity to achieve the goal?
- Will your organization need to partner with one or more other community organizations to achieve the goal?
- How will success be measured?

Thus, a change in perspective can make a significant difference in how cultural organizations engage in strategic planning.

Culture

Organizational culture is a blend of attitudes, beliefs, and actions that create either sustainable momentum or miserable stagnation. A strong culture embraces a clear set of values and norms that guide the way an organization and its employees operate. Employees of organizations with a strong culture are passionately engaged and operate with a sense of empowerment and purpose. Performance-oriented organizations do not put up with mind-numbing bureaucracies and extensive procedures. As Peter Drucker once observed, "Culture eats strategy for lunch."

Vibrant and alive organizational cultures are characterized by being:

- *Aligned*—The entire organization is aligned toward achieving its vision, mission, and goals.
- *Connected*—Everyone works to ensure that department boundaries (silo mentality) are minimized.
- *Motivated*—Staff members are excited to come to work and enjoy working with one another.
- *Fun*—The organization works to build team spirit and engaging in activities inside and outside of work that foster fun and enjoying life. Celebrate success (and failure too).

Culture is what determines whether your library's strategy and brand thrives or dies a slow and painful death. Can you sense the culture of your library? At the end of his tenure as CEO, Lou Gerstner observed, "I came to see in my time at IBM that culture isn't just one aspect of the game—it is the game. In the end an organization is nothing more than the collective capacity of its people to create value."[16]

An analysis of several collaborative projects was conducted in libraries, archives, and museums to determine why some projects failed to get started or to be completed successfully was due, in part, to professionals being threatened or becoming uncomfortable with the projects.[17] Michael Edson has remarked that most organizations have very slow metabolisms and hyperactive immune systems when it comes to change.

Nina Simon has suggested that there are five issues that may arise when planning a participatory project:[18]

- Some cultural professionals perceive participatory experiences as a fad to be avoided.
- Participatory projects are threatening to institutions because they involve a partial ceding of control.
- Participatory projects fundamentally change the relationships between the institution and visitors.
- Participatory projects introduce new visitor experiences that can't be evaluated using traditional assessment techniques alone.
- Participatory projects require more staff time and budget allocated for operation than for development.

Continuous Innovation

A startup mentality enables us to navigate through the uncertainty of disruption. It frees us to think differently instead of towing tradition along begrudgingly. In this sense, we're not upgrading the library but rewriting the source code.

Brian Mathews[19]

The majority of library strategic planning could more accurately be called "incremental planning." That is, libraries start off assuming that they will retain all existing services and will make small incremental improvements over the coming three to five years as illustrated in Figure 11-4. Real strategic planning involves establishing a clear destination and then considering a wide range of options for reaching that destination (sometimes called a goal or objective). Strategic planning also calls into question whether it is worthwhile in continuing to provide an existing service or product. Very few cultural organizations actually stop providing an existing service—no matter how few people use the service or how little value a service may provide.

Innovation may focus on improving existing services by reducing the costs to provide each service or to improve the quality of the service (such as reducing the time

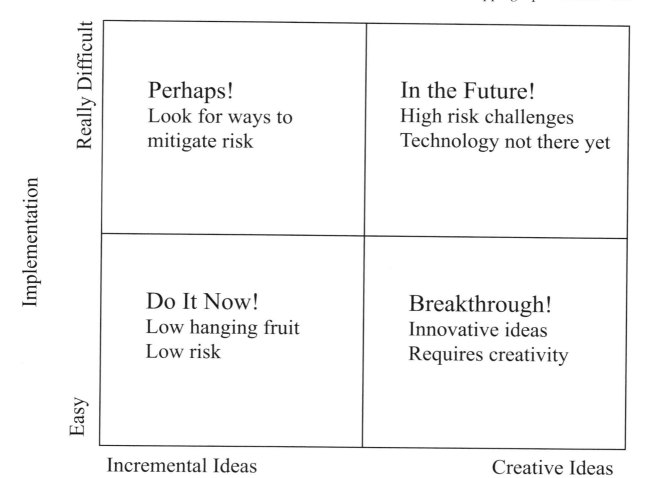

Figure 11-4 Innovation Categories.

it takes to provide a service). John Huber in a wonderful book *Lean Library Management* presents 11 strategies that can be used to cut waste and costs significantly while at the same time improving customer service.[20] John presents ways to transform your holds/reserve service, the delivery of new books, and the selection of overall library service performance metrics. Like all "lean" advice books, John recommends identifying activities that are duplicated, identifying activities that can be eliminated, reducing the number of activities in a process, reducing the number of times an item is handled, and so forth. In short, libraries should be determining for each activity whether it can be eliminated, simplified, or automated.

One significant aspect of reducing costs with internal library operations is to ask what value is being added by each activity. As noted earlier, many of the activities that libraries have historically done to add value such as cataloging and technical services are declining in value in the mind of our customers. Thus, many libraries have outsourced these activities to either the suppliers of library materials or organizations that are focused solely on providing these services for a low fee.

Innovation may also involve the introduction of new services or experimenting with different ways of providing services. For example, some cultural organizations are providing a very narrow range of services (for children or young adults) in smaller outlets. Focusing on customers and their needs may mean providing a materials dispensing machine (library in a box) on the platform of subway/train stations, in shopping malls, and so forth.[21]

Give customers an experience that they will want to brag about as many customers who use Zappos do with their friends and family. Bring your services to where your customers happen to be (physically and virtually), and it's likely that they will begin to incorporate services into their flow of activities. Provide a real focused experience that will WOW your customers, and they will return again and again. And remember that as people adopt innovation, they alter them, and they adapt them and are changed by them in ways we can't even imagine.

Consider the amazing experiences when someone visits Disneyland, a Build-a-Bear, or an American Girl store. The American Girl stores are designed to promote healthy imaginations and encourage the whole family to have a great deal of fun. The focus is on providing a unique experience that is primarily driven by the customer making choices and becoming engaged in various activities so that they co-construct their experiences (and the value they receive).

While process excellence demands precision, consistency, and repetition, innovation calls for variation, failure, and serendipity.

Brian Hindo[22]

When it comes to innovation, there are a number of approaches and techniques that can be used depending on the needs of the library and the number of people participating. Brian Mathews has suggested that innovation is rooted in ideation—"the formation, incubation, and advancement of ideas into specific outcomes."[23] Several authors and organizations have developed specific approaches to innovation:

Customer Development Focusing on customers allows a team to prove value using feedback, evaluation, and usage.	**Agile Teams** Agile promotes breaking a project down into smaller parts in which the work is incremental and iterative. Adaptation is the key.
Lean Start-Up This approach builds prototypes quickly in order to judge customer reactions (measure), and the lessons learned are included in the next iteration of the prototype.	**Positive Deviance Approach** Five steps are involved in this approach: define, determine, discover, design, and monitor. Participants are those who are extremely successful within a community.
Design Thinking Developed by IDEO, this approach suggests observe, visualize, evaluate, and refine.	**Challenge-Driven Innovation** This approach has seven steps: idea gathering, filtering, dissection, channel distribution, evaluation and confirmation, assembly and integration, and launch.
Percent Time Popularized by 3M, Hewlett-Packard, and Google, this approach gives employees some amount of time each week to explore new ideas.	**Hack-a-thons** Intense late night events encourage people to explore ideas, create code, and brainstorm. The results of each team's efforts are evaluated the following morning.

Recently IDEO, a design and innovation consulting firm, developed a toolkit for patron-centered design that libraries can download (thanks to the Bill and Melinda Gates Foundation for making this great resource possible). The toolkit has three documents that can be downloaded at www.designthinkingforlibraries.com:

- *Design Thinking for Libraries*
- *Design Thinking for Libraries: Activities Workbook*
- *Design Thinking in a Day*

Shape a Digital Identity

Libraries, museums, galleries, and archives need to have a much more effective presence in the online arena. This is not to say that a cultural organization will ever have the financial resources that the really effective Internet companies have to be able to invest significant sums into building a truly awesome website. But there is much that organizations can do without expending a great deal of cash.

It is clear that libraries cannot compete with search engines (read Google) in terms of speed, relevance of search results, and retrieval results—people have already voted with their fingers, and those fingers are not clicking on a cultural organizations website. And while libraries provide access to quality online resources (by licensing online eResources annually), only a small proportion of a community is actually using these resources.

Libraries, especially public libraries, are often constrained by a city or county information technology department that insists that the library website must have the same look and feel as the rest of the government's website—even in the face of a lot of evidence that library users interact in fundamentally different ways than when using the rest of the government's website. And while there is no easy cure, some libraries have been successful in creating websites that library customers come back on a frequent basis given their ease of use.

Some of the tools that a cultural organization might wish to employ to improve their website include: using search engine optimization (SEO) techniques to improve the visibility of a website when people use a search engine; use of a software analytics tool (such as Google Analytics) that provides detailed information about what is and is not being used on the library's website; and observation of five to six users attempting to complete one or two tasks while using a website. The goal is to improve the user experience as evidenced by fewer people leaving the website quickly or not returning at all. Aaron Schmidt and Maanda Etches have produced a new book that provides lots of practical tips for improving the user experience, both online and in the physical library. *Useful, Usable, Desirable* is well worth reading carefully.[24]

As noted in Chapter 9, there are any number of museums and libraries that have developed a good website that attracts tens of thousands and hundreds of thousands of individuals to their sites on a monthly basis. Many of the features on these sites could be copied in order to improve a cultural organization's website.

Reconsider Your Metrics

As cultural organizations redefine their mission and vision, they will of necessity also need to change the metrics they use to demonstrate success and value. The traditional (inward-looking) output measures of activity—see how busy we are!—simply do not convey how the library adds value in the life of each customer.

Libraries have historically focused on transactions—materials borrowed, reference queries, item cataloged, programs offered, and so forth. Even the ILS is designed solely to keep track of transactions within the library. And yet, organizations all around us are moving from transactions to identifying ways to engage with their customers. And some organizations are moving from engagement to providing a meaningful experience. So the upshot is that we are moving (or should be moving) from transactions to engagement to experiences. And as we make this journey, the performance measures we use to communicate how the cultural organization adds value must also change—in many cases, change radically. Understanding what success or failure looks like (as evidenced by the performance measures you use) is the key to knowing whether you have achieved either. The focus should be to measure what you value rather than valuing what you currently measure.

In the digital environment, the liberating idea is to recognize that the user interface is not limited by fixed geographical boundaries or space constraints but rather represents a *possibility space* open to a wide range of experimentation. Rather than being confined by the limitations of video, audio or print media, the online environment is much more flexible and allows cultural organizations to define a user interface based on the real needs of the user rather than conforming to traditional assumptions.

John Huber and Steven Potter have suggested in a recent book, *The Purpose-Based Library*, that libraries should develop a dashboard showing a series of performance measures based on Maslow's hierarchy of needs. Such an approach allows each library to select measures that will resonate with its local community.[25]

No organization should ever "set and forget" the performance measures it uses to track its progress in achieving its goals. Your organization needs to:

- Recognize the need to make ongoing changes to performance measures.
- Acknowledge the need to delve deeply into data about the actual use of the cultural organization's physical and virtual space.
- Appreciate that people's loyalties, desires, and behaviors change over time.
- Start the process of trying to measure outcomes and refine the outcome measures you start with so they get better over time.
- Use the language of your key stakeholders to communicate the value of the organization.
- Use storytelling to assist you in communicating the value of the organization as suggested by Stephen Denning.[26]

The library can reach out to people in many more ways than has ever been possible with the more tried-and-true traditional media that libraries have had many decades of experience. This capacity for reinvention means that there are an almost limitless number of doors through which we can chose to travel. We need to open lots of doors and travel down the road awhile to see whether a particular highway is going to lead to an interesting and compelling destination—a destination that the customer wants to reach.

Summary

The end result is that libraries, museums, archives, and galleries need to move to a model that delivers real value to its customers—whether the customer physically visits a facility or is interacting online. As shown in Figure 11-5, we can conceive of a progress of activities that deliver value as well as a progression of performance measures that move from input and output measures to outcome measures.

The future of successful libraries (and other heritage organizations) will be one of constant re-imaging to adapt to, or outsmart, the forces of constant change. And to do this will require that the cultural organization reach out and embrace its community and involve them in new and interesting ways to enlist their aid in helping to reinvent the organization. It is also important for leaders to acknowledge that they have two roles: decision-making (cognitive) and motivational (cathectic) with the

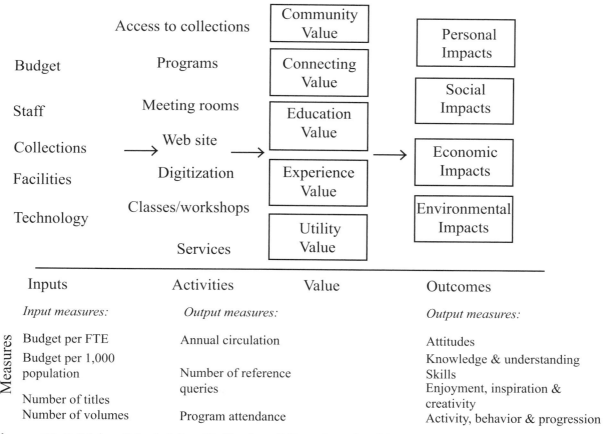

Figure 11-5 Value Model for Galleries, Libraries, Archives, and Museums.

latter role inspiring staff members to fully embrace the values and objectives of the organization.

In an interesting blog post, Nick Poole asks what "if Steve Jobs made a museum?"[27] Nick goes on to suggest that Steve Jobs had three very important qualities that inspired him and drove his passion for excellence that should also resonate for museums (and other cultural institutions):

- Exceptional leadership
- Remarkable design sensibility
- A singular focus on the total user experience

So if Steve Jobs were embarking on a journey to create a new institution, I think he would be quite clear as to its place and purpose—without trying to be all things to all people. In other words, Steve would focus on one or more market segments and deliver a delightful experience that many would appreciate (while at the same time acknowledging that some people simply don't "get the Apple way"). Visitors to the physical and virtual museum, library, archive, or gallery designed by Steve would feel welcome, would intuitively understand how to move about and become engaged, and have such an awesome experience that they would want to return again and again.

So I wonder if Steve Jobs were to visit your organization, would he be delighted or would he be frustrated with the total user experience and not want to return? You have the power to change your organization so that it adds value each and every time a customer interacts with you.

Checklist for Adding Value

	Yes	No
Does your cultural organization identify a specific market segment(s) for each service it provides?	☐	☐
Has your cultural organization engaged in strategic planning in such a way that it considers discontinuing an existing service?	☐	☐
Have you explored ways to make something easier? Simpler? Greener? Faster? Smarter?	☐	☐
Can you make a service more convenient? More connected? More enjoyable?	☐	☐
Have you looked at the services your cultural organization provides in order to identify the value a customer receives?	☐	☐
Have you considered outsourcing one or more activities currently performed in the organization (that may be providing little value)?	☐	☐
Have you imagined what customers might love if anything was possible?	☐	☐
Does the organizational culture in your heritage organization inspire you?	☐	☐

Have you encountered a great idea and "stolen it" so you
  can implement in your cultural organization in the last year?   ☐   ☐
Have you reached out using an innovative project to embrace
  a much larger (worldwide) community?   ☐   ☐

If you answered "no" to one or more of the questions in the checklist, then your library is not doing all it could to add value.

Main idea:	Leadership counts
Opposing view:	Bottom-up approach to making change
Key concepts:	Change, innovation, market segments, adding value, leadership
What has changed?:	Speed of change, change management
Catalyst:	Empowering everyone
Open debate:	How fast to go

Notes

1. Carl Grant. "Value Added Librarianship: Creating It in Our Services and in the Infrastructure upon Which We Rely." *Public Library Quarterly*, 32, 2013, 27.
2. Peter Hernon and Nancy Rossiter. "Emotional Intelligence: Which Traits Are Most Prized?" *College & Research Libraries* 67 (3), 2006, 260–275.
3. Philip Kotler. *Marketing Management*, 14th ed. Upper Saddle River, NJ: Prentice-Hall, 2011.
4. Christie Koontz and Lorri Mon. *Marketing and Social Media: A Guide for Libraries, Archives, and Museums*. New York: Rowman & Littlefield, 2014.
5. DSP-group. *More Than Worth It: The Social Significance of Museums*. April 2012. Available at http://www.museumvereniging.nl/Portals/0/NMV%20'More%20than%20worth%20it'.pdf
   Simon Tanner. *Measuring the Impact of Digital Resources: The Balanced Value Impact Model*. 2012. Available at http://www.kdcs.kcl.ac.uk/fileadmin/documents/pubs/BalancedValueImpactModel_SimonTanner_October2012.pdf
6. Carol Scott (Editor). "Museums and Public Value: Creating Sustainable Futures." Surrey, England: Ashgate, 2013.
7. Michael Margolis. *The Library Story: A Strategic Toolkit for Public Libraries*. Get Storied, 2014. Available at http://www.getstoried.com/librarystory/
   See also, Michael Margolis. *The Emerging Story of California Public Libraries*. Get Storied, 2013. Available at http://www.getstoried.com/librarystory/
8. Ian Chant and Matt Enis. "The Numbers Game." *Library Journal*, May 1, 2014, 28–30.
9. Other vendors offering a similar service include Gale (Analytics on Demand) and Orange Boy (Cluster Development).
10. For more about the Anythink Libraries, see Pam Sandlian-Smith. "The Anythink Revolution," in *Reflecting on the Future of Academic and Public Libraries*. Chicago: American Library Association, 2013, 211–223.

11. Valerie Gross. *Transforming Our Image, Building Our Brand: The Education Advantage*. Santa Barbara: Libraries Unlimited, 2013.
12. John Berry. "Pillar of Community Education." *Library Journal*, 138 (11), June 15, 2013, 30–32.
13. Meredith Schwartz and Rebecca Miller. "Design4Impact: Starting from Scratch." *Library Journal*, March 15, 2014, 80.
14. Steve Baer. "The Clothesline Paradox." *The Co-Evolution Quarterly*, Winter 1975.
15. Steve Denning. "Do We Need Libraries?" *Forbes online*, April 28, 2015. Available at http://www.forbes.com/sites/stevedenning/2015/04/28/do-we-need-libraries/
16. Lou Gerstner. *Who Says Elephants Can't Dance*. New York: HarperBusiness, 2003, 71.
17. Diane Zorich, Gunter Waibel, and Ricky Erway. *Beyond the Silos of the LAMs: Collaboration among Libraries, Archives and Museums*. Dublin, OH: OCLC Research, 2008.
18. Nina Simon. *The Participatory Museum*. Santa Cruz, CA: Museums 2.0, 2010.
19. Brian Mathews. Too Much Assessment Not Enough Innovation: R&D Models and Mindsets for Academic Libraries. A presentation at the Library Assessment Conference in October 2012, Charlottesville, Virginia. Available at http://vtechworks.lib.vt.edu/bitstream/handle/10919/19047/Too_Much_Assessment_R%26D_Paper_Mathews_Enhanced_Version.pdf?sequence=1
20. John Huber. *Lean Library Management: Eleven Strategies for Reducing Costs and Improving Customer Service*. New York: Neal Schuman, 2011.
21. Joseph R. Matthews. *The Customer-Focused Library: Re-Inventing the Public Library from the Outside-In*. Santa Barbara, CA: Libraries Unlimited, 2009.
22. Brian Hindo. "At 3M, a Struggle between Efficiency and Creativity." *Business Week*, June 10, 2007.
23. Brian Mathews. *Too Much Assessment Not Enough Innovation*. Presentation at the Library Assessment Conference October 2012 in Charlottesville, VA. Available at http://vtechworks.lib.vt.edu/bitstream/handle/10919/19047/Too_Much_Assessment_R%26D_Paper_Mathews_Enhanced_Version.pdf
    See also, Brian Mathews. "Flip the Model: Strategies for Creating and Delivering Value." *The Journal of Academic Librarianship*, 40, 2014, 16–24.
24. Aaron Schmidt and Amanda Etches. *Useful, Usable, Desirable: Applying User Experience Design to Your Library*. Chicago: ALA Editions, 2014.
25. John Huber and Steven Potter. *The Purpose-Based Library: Finding Your Path to Survival, Success, and Growth*. Chicago: Neal-Schuman, 2015.
26. Stephen Denning. "The Springboard: How Storytelling Ignites Action in Knowledge-Era Organizations." Boston: Butterworth-Heinemann, 2001.
27. Nick Poole. *If Steve Jobs Made a Museum*. December 4, 2011. *Nick Poole* blog. Available at http://nickpoole.org.uk/if-steve-jobs-made-a-museum/

12

Adding Personal Value

Between stimulus and response there is a space.
In that space is our power to choose our response.
In our response lies our growth and our freedom.

Viktor E. Frankl[1]

In this rich digital milieu that we all interact with on a daily basis, it is important to remember as Robert Darnton, university librarian at Harvard, has noted, this is not *the* "information age," but rather it is *an* age of information, one of many in the continuing evolution of information development.[2] And just as libraries, museums, archives, and other cultural institutions are now learning, we must change and adapt to this constantly changing environment in order to better serve our customers. The job of a librarian is shifting from a focus on physical, location-specific collections to a mix of activities that rely on a larger and more complex set of network relationships. The goal is to work with and interact with people as they live in a networked world.

As our cultural institutors are recognizing the need for change, so too should each individual professional reflect on how he or she adds value in the lives of those they serve, directly and indirectly. And while many would suggest that we have a crisis for traditional cultural institutions (such as libraries), I would suggest that there is no crisis for the professional. Cultural organization professional's have demonstrated a tremendous amount of flexibility and developed a plethora of new skills over the past few decades. Yes, lifetime learning is clearly becoming the norm today.

Many professional librarians refuse to acknowledge that change is a constant in our society. Some librarians seem to act as if the principles that Melville Dewey articulated more than a century ago are still the only principles that should be followed today. We need to understand that looking back (often with longing and nostalgia) can hold us back. Focusing on and providing access to collections using traditional tools and services is a sure recipe for a very harsh future.

We are shifting from stable stocks of knowledge and skills (which for our parents often provided good wages over the course of a lifetime) to the reality of today that suggests that the half-life of our skills have eroded, in many cases, to four or five years. Librarians and other cultural organization professionals, like many other professions, need to continuously adapt their skills to a constantly changing environment. And as

John Palfrey has noted, "Librarians need to reinvent themselves and their professions and align what they do with what their communities need from them."[3]

The knowledge and skills that have served us well up to this point are not the skills and knowledge that are going to propel us forward to better serve our customers of tomorrow. We are going to have to reinvent ourselves several times during the course of our careers. Business model innovation is just as important at the personal level as it is at the organizational level. We must figure out (by embracing experimentation and innovation) new ways to create, deliver, and capture value in order to remain relevant in the lives of our customers.

Yet the question remains, "How many cultural organizational professionals on their way to work each day reflect on the ways they could (or should) be adding more value in the life of their customers?" Probably not too many, but it would be great if it were the majority of professionals. So how can you add more value? What differentiates one professional from another?

We need to ask ourselves, "What assumptions and 'sacred cows' might we challenge to better engage our community?" What can we do that will help us better understand the organization's customers, their needs, and their expectations?

We've shifted from stable stocks of knowledge and an archived world
to a world of information flows, participation and states of confusion.
How we create as fast as we learn. The game is more complicated.

John Seely Brown[4]

Listen, Observe, Read

People interested in learning how to add value are, by nature, curious. They will listen to what their customers are really saying, they will observe people in the environments in which they routinely work and see what tools they are using, they will read what their customers are writing and researching, all in an attempt to better understand their customers. With this deeper understanding of the customer's needs, cultural organization professionals can then begin to explore ways in which they might deliver services customers value in new and compelling ways.

You can combine a wide array of existing services, ideas, and concepts from a range of sources outside your organization into something that is new and will be valued and appreciated by your customers. Professionals must be adding to their skills, knowledge, and abilities every week. Are you improving yourself and the processes of your organization? You should not only be reading the professional literature but also be reading in a wide range of fields in order to be exposed to new ideas and concepts. Do you regularly look at articles in *Wired, Harvard Business Review, Inc., First Monday, Communication Arts, How, I.D., .Net, Layers, Fast Company, Fortune, Nvate, MIT Technology Review,* and oh so many more?

If you want to be a brilliant librarian. If you want to make
a difference in people's lives . . . You must be active.

You must see your community as your collection
and you must be into collection development every day.
Not sitting behind a desk . . . not waiting for someone to come to you
and ask for help, but being out there
and saying, "I'm here. You're important . . ."
You are not in the library business. You are not in the book business.
You are not in the building business. You are not in the website business.
You are in the community business.

Dave Lankes[5]

_____

Link and Connect

If you care passionately about what you do (and thus think about what and how you do your work), then you will focus on connecting with your customers—no matter where they may be located—at a deeper level. Really great cultural organization professionals are good at connecting with their customers—connecting with a deeper level of understanding their needs and rapport, and how the organization and its services are of value to specific individuals. Suggest links to resources that will likely be of value. Ask about the degree to which a prior suggestion proved to be of value (this feedback allows you to develop a more complete and accurate understanding of this particular customer and his or her needs). Add some context to the content suggestions.

Be on the lookout for ways to make something better. Take action, be proactive. Make suggestions. Volunteer to take responsibility for getting things done. Stay alert for ideas to simplify processes. Ideas are the currency of influence. Find new and better ways to getting things done. Harold Jarche has suggested a "Seek, Sense, and Share" framework for adding value by actively engaging in content curation.[6] Jarche suggests taking an hour or two a day seeking high-quality content, adding value by providing context through your annotations and perspective, and finally sharing with others. You can't be a social media introvert—you can't sit on the sidelines. You have to be involved, and involved means visible. You are constantly creating and re-creating your personal brand.

Lee Rainie (of Pew Research fame) and Barry Wellman (a professor at the University of Toronto) offer specific suggestions to those who want to do well in today's world of networked individuals:[7]

- Remember the golden rule so that help will be there when you need it.
- Use information and communication technologies nimbly and enthusiastically.
- Use technologies to develop a wider audience that share your interests.
- Do not count on a single tightly connected group to provide all of the assistance you may need.
- Reach out to new individuals and groups.
- Develop a larger and more diverse group of networked individuals.
- Become an autonomous agent to cultivate personal networks.
- Monitor and manage your personal brand—your image and reputation.

Focus on What Matters

Courtney Greene McDonald put together 30 strategies for transforming library services.[8] This list should be required reading for every librarian. Good stuff. Given the limited amount of time at work each day, it is important to identify those activities and tasks that add the most value in the life of your customer. Given you could be doing several things (often several things that are competing for your time), ask yourself "What task or activity is going to add the most value?"

Upon reflection, you should be able to develop a list of activities that add value that you can put in rank order—from the greatest to the least. With this list in hand, prioritize your daily activity so that you have the greatest impact in the lives of your customers. Remember that your time is quite valuable so use it wisely.

Do you know the cultural organization's and the larger parent organization's goals and objectives? Focus on the activities that use your time, talents, and skills most effectively to connect back to assisting the organization achieve its goals and objectives. Effective cultural organization professionals interact with people directly and assist in making them more productive and helping them solve their problems. Be a part of your cultural organization's "bottom line"—even if there is no "bottom line."

Contribute Your Thinking

As you become more comfortable with the depth of your understanding of your customers and their needs, it is important that you contribute your thinking about what they are doing so that your conversations are more that of collaborators rather than a one-off question-and-answer transaction. You can ask questions of clarification that might expose assumptions that are being made or open up lines of inquiry that might not have been previously considered. In short, you become a valuable asset and ally rather than someone sitting behind a service desk.

Michael Stanier has produced a wonderful little book, *Do More Great Work*, that is all about taking your personal impact and contributions to the next level.[9] Michael has identified six great work paradoxes:

1. You don't need to save the world. You do need to make a difference.
2. Great work is private. Great work can be public.
3. Great work is needed. Great work isn't wanted.
4. Great work is easy. Great work is difficult.
5. Great work is about doing what's meaningful. Great work isn't about doing it well.
6. Great work can take a moment. Great work can take a lifetime.

Slow Down

Take time to reflect on your professional life and the ways in which you add value when your customers interact with you personally or with one of the many services your cultural organization provides. Ask yourself if what is currently being done is the best way to deliver a service (and, by implication, the value associated with the service). Too often, we get caught up in the pressures of our daily professional life that we don't take the time to step back and reflect.

Remember that it is important to remain flexible so that you can embrace opportunities when they come along. The Chinese proverb reminds us "Chance favors the prepared mind."

Have Fun

Think about ways of having fun in your organization and how your institution interacts with its customers. Consider setting up a coffee cart in a heavily trafficked area with a banner above the cart that proclaims, "The Librarian is IN!" Take casual Friday to new levels with silly costumes that revolve around the "stereotypical librarian" theme. Choose ways to have fun that reflect your personality and involve others in having fun too. You can even book an appointment with a bibliotherapist at the London-based School of Life.

Be happy—life is too short to live otherwise. Have a positive attitude and attitude drives success. People want to be around positive people. Care about others and help them to succeed. Celebrate success and failures!

A Business Model For You!

One useful tool that can assist you in assessing the impact and value that you are adding in the lives of your customer is to prepare a business model for you. Using the

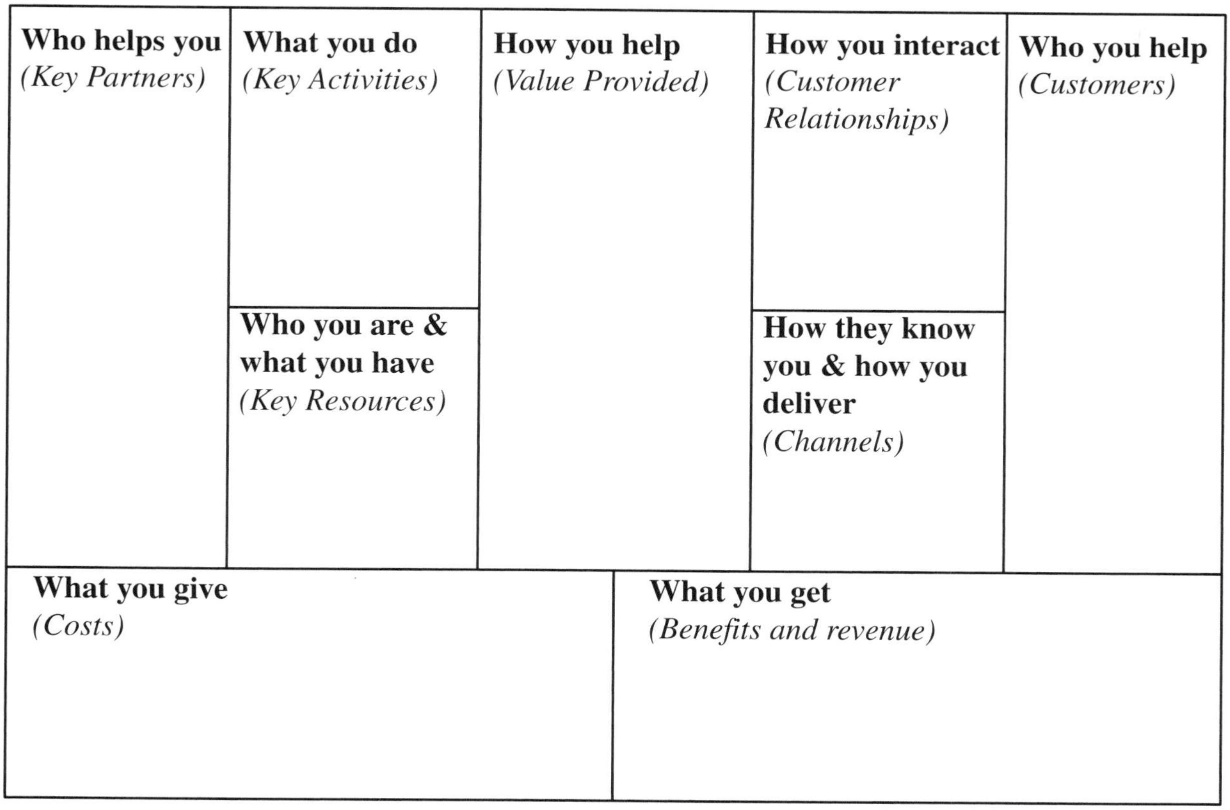

Who helps you (Key Partners)	What you do (Key Activities)	How you help (Value Provided)	How you interact (Customer Relationships)	Who you help (Customers)
	Who you are & what you have (Key Resources)		How they know you & how you deliver (Channels)	
What you give (Costs)			What you get (Benefits and revenue)	

Figure 12-1 The Personal Business Model Canvas. Copyright and Creative Commons License 2012, available at http://businessmodelyou.com/

template provided for you in Figure 12-1, complete each of the boxes recognizing that as a professional you have multiple skills and roles that you play—expert, facilitator, teacher, speaker, connector, and so forth.[10]

As you work to complete a business model for you ask yourself some trigger questions:

- What skills are you not using right now?
- Do you have a network of colleagues that assist you in developing new professional competencies?
- Do you enjoy working with your customers?
- What could you stop doing and nobody (especially your customers) would notice?
- How can you work smarter rather than harder (or longer)?
- Is there some way to free up a big block of time to start work on an important project?
- How can you collaborate with your co-workers to have a bigger impact?
- Do you have a presence in social media?
- Are you sending time online where your customers do their work?
- Can you identify any customer segments you are not reaching now? What should you change to connect with these groups?

Summary

Every individual working in galleries, libraries, archives, and museums should ask themselves:

- Are you aware of the forces outside the control of each of us that is having a significant impact on our professional lives?
- Are you conscious of the ever-shortening shelf life of your professional competencies?
- Can you articulate the ways in which your organization adds value in the life of your customers?
- What new developments and/or technology can you take advantage of in order to provide a more compelling experience for your customers?
- How well do you understand each market segment's end-to-end experience in using your cultural institution (either in person or online)?
- Are you broadening your personal exploration of what is new and innovative in fields outside your professional discipline?
- Are you willing to embrace change and flexibility even if the way forward is not always clear?

Every professional has a personal brand. What is yours? Do people seek you out by name? Do any of your customers recommend you and your services to their colleagues?

What are you known for? Do you focus on having an impact on the lives of your customers rather than on the repeatable tasks you sometimes need to complete? Are you getting better faster? Does your email signature convey a sense of providing services that result in positive benefits?

At the personal level, periodically, it is important to ask yourself these questions:

- What do you want to do?
- What is stopping you from doing it?
- What are you doing about it?

Every day, you can ask yourself, "How am I going to create value for other people?" You must develop a consistent drive to create and deliver value every day. In the end, it is your responsibility to know and understand how you contribute value in the lives of your customers. You then must communicate that value to your customers so that they, in turn, understand the value of the service that you are providing to them. It is not your customer's responsibility to figure it out.

Checklist for Adding Value

	Yes	No
Do I add value to others (customers, other staff members)?	☐	☐
Do I add value to the organization?	☐	☐
Do I delight in acknowledging the contributions of others?	☐	☐
Do I work to involve others in innovative projects?	☐	☐
Do I strive to foster a team culture?	☐	☐
Do we celebrate victories (as well as defeats)?	☐	☐

Notes

1. Viktor E. Frankl. *Man's Search for Meaning.* New York: Beacon Press, 1959, 43.
2. Robert Darnton. "5 Myths about the 'Information Age.'" *The Chronicle of Higher Education,* April 17, 2011. Available at http://chronicle.com/article/5-Myths-About-the-Information/127105/
3. John Palfrey. *Biblio TECH: Why Libraries Matter More Than Ever in the Age of Google.* New York: Basic Books, 2015, 132.
4. John Seely Brown. Quoted in Amy Garmer. *Rising to the Challenge: Re-Envisioning Public Libraries.* Washington, DC: The Aspen Institute, October 2014. Available at http://csreports.aspeninstitute.org/documents/AspenLibrariesReport.pdf
5. David Lankes. *The Atlas of New Librarianship.* Cambridge, MA: The MIT Press, 2011, 67.
6. Harold Jarche. "The Seek > Sense > Share Framework." *Harold Jarche* blog. February 10, 2014. Available at http://jarche.com/2014/02/the-seek-sense-share-framework/
7. Lee Rainie and Barry Wellman. *Networked: The New Social Operating System.* Cambridge, MA: MIT Press, 2012.

8. Courtney Greene McDonald. *Putting the User First: 30 Strategies for Transforming Library Services*. Chicago: Association of College & Research Libraries, 2014.

9. Michael Stanier. *Do More Great Work*. New York: Workman Publishing, 2010.

10. Time Clark, Alexander Osterwalder, and Yves Pigneur. *Business Model You: a One-Page Method for Reinventing Your Career*. New York: Wiley, 2012.

Appendix: Business Model Workbook

Introduction

Organizations that consistently outperform their competitors in both the physical and virtual arena are those that have a clear understanding of how they create value in the lives of their customers. These successful organizations are generally well known, and the management team has either used a formal planning model, such as the business model innovation canvas, or informally worked through a process so that the ways the organization adds value are clearly understood.

The purpose of this workbook is to provide step-by-step instructions on how to use the business model for your particular cultural organization. While anyone can interact with and develop a cultural organization business model, typically it is better to have a group interact with one another and develop the business model collaboratively.

The Business Model

Developed by Alexander Osterwalder and Yves Pigneur, the business model canvas has been successfully applied and used in a variety of organization settings—see Figure A-1.[1] The business model canvas contains nine building blocks. The model can be divided into three areas that answer the how, what, and who questions.

Step 1—**Customer segments** comprise a set of individuals who have common characteristics (demographics, reasons for using the cultural organization, benefits they receive from a service) who will likely respond in a similar manner when they interact with the organization.

But rather than thinking about customer segments from a demographic or frequency of use perspective, it would be better to categorize customers based on the jobs they are trying to get done. A customer job might be the needs they are attempting to satisfy, the

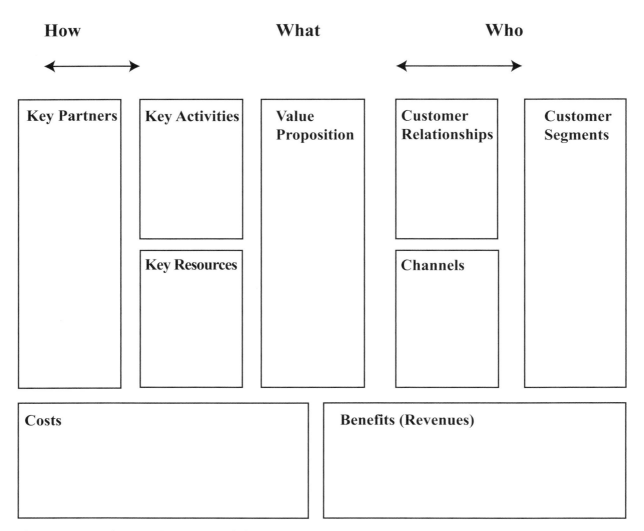

Figure A-1 The Business Model

problems they are endeavoring to solve, or the tasks they are trying to complete. Among the possible customer jobs might be:

- Functional jobs—When your customers are working on a DIY project, write a report, complete a homework assignment, solve a problem, or complete a task.
- Personal jobs—Customers may be seeking a specific emotional state such as feeling good or secure.
- Social jobs—Sometimes customers are interested in power, respect, or status (why else do some people drive BMWs?).
- Supporting jobs—Customers are willing to perform supporting jobs in order to purchase or transfer value.
  - o Buying value—Customers may seek information in order to compare products or services, take time to visit a store to buy a product or service, and so forth.

o Cocreating value—Customers may rate a service offering, write reviews, provide feedback, or actually participate as a partner to design a new product or service.

o Transferring value—Customers may sell a product they own, recycle a product, or dispose of it.

Your Market Segments

Whom do you currently reach? Whom do you want to reach? What are the characteristics of each segment? Where and how do they work? What tools do they use? What does (would) each segment value? What jobs are each segment trying to complete?

_____

_____

_____

_____

_____

_____

Step 2—The **value proposition** is focused on the benefits that each segment receives. How does each cultural organization service translate in benefits and positive outcomes for each segment? What services could be improved (or introduced) to provide more value to a market segment?

It is important to remember the key components of a value proposition:

- *Customer Jobs*—What the customer is trying to accomplish
- *Customer Pains*—The challenges customers face when they work to complete a task or activity
- *Customer Gains*—What are the likely benefits or outcomes for the customer
- *Products and Services*—The products and services offered by your organization
- *Pain Relievers*—How your products and services reduce or eliminate the challenges customers face
- *Gain Creators*—Focuses on how the customer benefits from using your products and/or services.

Describe the cultural organization's value proposition for each customer segment.

Market Segment—
Value Proposition: _____

_____

_____

Market Segment—
Value Proposition: _____

_____

_____

Market Segment—
Value Proposition: _____

_____

_____

Step 3—**Customer relationships** are focused on the types of interactions with customer segments. Will they be self-service? Face-to-face assistance? Chat or email assistance? Cocreation and collaboration opportunities? Group interactions? Presentations? Interacting with the website? What will you do to encourage more engagement with digital resources (assets)? What will you do to encourage more use of physical resources?

_____

_____

_____

_____

_____

Step 4—**Channels** are concerned about how will you reach your customers. How does each customer segment prefer to be reached? How important is mobile access?

Channel	*Priority*	*Activity*
Website	_____	_____
Facebook	_____	_____
Twitter	_____	_____
Pinterest	_____	_____
Flickr	_____	_____
Instagram	_____	_____
YouTube	_____	_____
Blog	_____	_____
One-on-One conversations	_____	_____
Small groups	_____	_____
Classes	_____	_____
Tours	_____	_____
Others	_____	_____

Step 5—**Revenue sources** are concerned with identifying current (and future) revenues. Do the current revenues provide sufficient financial resources for the cultural organization to accomplish its objectives? Are the revenues predictable and sustainable

(when local government revenues go down, are there likely to be large budget cuts for the organization?)? What can the cultural organization do to ensure that its revenues are more sustainable?

_____
_____
_____
_____
_____

Step 6—What **key activities** are needed to deliver on the cultural organization's goals and objectives?

_____
_____
_____
_____
_____

Step 7—What **key resources** are necessary to deliver on the cultural organization's value proposition? Are special skills or resources needed? What physical, human, intellectual, and financial resources are necessary? Is the cultural organization organized to deliver on its value promise?

_____
_____
_____
_____
_____

Step 8—Can the cultural organization develop **key partners** who will team up to assist in delivering the institution's value proposition for one or more customer segments?

_____
_____
_____
_____
_____

Step 9—What costs drive the overall **cost structure** of the cultural organization? What can the institution do to lower its cost of operations?

_____
_____
_____
_____
_____

And please share the business model you develop for your institution so that others can view it, adapt it for use in another institution, and comment on what you like and don't like about using the business model approach. In short, it is my hope that your use of the business model process will assist the staff in your institution to really think about the ways your organization adds value.

Notes

1. Alexander Osterwalder and Yves Pigneur. *Business Model Generation: A Handbook for Visionaries, Game Changers, and Challengers*. New York: John Wiley & Sons, 2010. See also, Alex Osterwalder, Yves Pigneur, Greg Bernarda, and Alan Smith. *Value Proposition Design*. New York: Wiley, 2014.
2. Kathryn Zickuhr, Kristen Purcell, and Lee Rainie. *From Distant Admirers to Library Lovers—and Beyond: A Typology of Public Library Engagement in America*. Washington, DC: Pew Research Center, March 13, 2014. Available at http://www.pewinternet.org/2014/03/13/summary-of-findings-4/

Recommended Readings

Adding Value

Osterwalder, Alex, and Yves Pigneur. *Business Model Generation*. New York: Wiley, 2010.

Osterwalder, Alex, Yves Pigneur, Greg Bernarda, and Alan Smith. *Value Proposition Design*. New York: Wiley, 2014.

Innovation

Chesbrough, Henry. *Open Innovation*. Boston: Harvard Business School Press, 2003.

Christensen, Clayton. *The Innovator's Dilemma*. Boston: Harvard Business School Press, 1997.

Christensen, Clayton, and Michael Raynor. *The Innovator's Solution*. Boston: Harvard Business School Press, 2003.

Godin, Seth. *Tribes: We Need You to Lead Us*. New York: Portfolio, 2008.

Johnson, Steven. *Where Good Ideas Come From*. New York: Riverhead, 2010.

Kawasaki, Guy. *Enchantment: The Art of Changing Hearts, Minds, and Actions*. New York: Portfolio, 2012.

Kuhn, Thomas. *The Structure of Scientific Revolutions*. Chicago: University of Chicago Press, 1962.

Lankes, R. David. *The Atlas of New Librarianship*. Cambridge, MA: MIT Press, 2011.

Martin, Roger. *The Opposable Mind*. Boston: Harvard Business School Press, 2009.

Mauboussin, Michael. *Think Twice*. Boston: Harvard Business School Press, 2009.

Nielsen, Michael. *Reinventing Discovery*. Princeton, NJ: Princeton University Press, 2011.

Pink, Daniel. Drive: *The Surprising Truth about What Motivates Us*. New York: Riverhead Books, 2011.

Rodgers, Everett. *Diffusion of Innovations*. New York: Free Press of Glencoe, 1962.

Marketing

Heath, Chip, and Dan Heath. *Made to Stick*. New York: Random House, 2007.

Moon, Youngme. *Different*. New York: Crown Business, 2010.

Networks

Chesbrough, Henry, Wim Vanhaverbeke, and Joel West. *Open Innovation: Researching a New Paradigm*. Oxford: Oxford University Press, 2006.

Fisher, Len. *The Perfect Swarm*. New York: Basic Books, 2009.

Gray, Dave. *The Connected Company*. Sebastopol, CA: O'Reilly, 2013.
Howe, Jeff. *Crowdsourcing*. New York: Crown Books, 2008.
Kelly, Kevin. *What Technology Wants*. New York: Viking, 2010.
Shirky, Clay. *Cognitive Surplus*. New York: Basic Books, 2010.
Shirky, Clay. *Here Comes Everybody*. New York: Penguin Books, 2009.
Surowiecki, James. *The Wisdom of Crowds*. New York: Doubleday, 2004.
Weinberger, David. *Too Big to Know*. New York: Basic Books, 2012.

Strategic Planning

Barksdale, Susan. *10 Steps to Successful Strategic Planning*. Alexandria, VA: ASTD, 2006.
Bradford, Robert, and Brian Taroy. *Simplified Strategic Planning: The No-Nonsense Guide for Busy People Who Want Results Fast*. New York: Chandler House Press, 2000.
Kim, Chan, and Renee Mauborgne. *Blue Ocean Strategy: How to Create Uncontested Market Space and Make the Competition Irrelevant*. Boston: Harvard Business Review Press, 2005.

Author Index

Subject Index

About the Author

JOSEPH R. MATTHEWS is a consultant who has provided assistance to numerous academic, public, and special libraries as well as local governments. He was an instructor at the School of Library Information Science (SLIS) at San Jose State University and has taught evaluation of library services, library information systems, strategic planning, management, and research methods. Matthews selected as an SLIS Outstanding Scholar, is active in the American Library Association, and has authored more than 30 books, including *Managing with Data and Metrics, Getting Started with Evaluation, Reflecting on the Future, Listening to the Customer, Library Assessment in Higher Education, The Customer-Focused Library, The Digital Library Survival Guide, The Evaluation and Measurement of Library Services, Scorecards for Results, Strategic Planning and Management for Library Managers*, and *Measuring for Results*.